D1433495

The Countryman
Book

BY THE SAME AUTHOR

FAITH AND WORKS IN FLEET STREET. *Hodder and Stoughton*, 1947

ENGLAND'S GREEN AND PLEASANT LAND. *Cape*, 1925. *Cape*, Travellers' Library, 1931. New edition *Penguin*, 1947

SUGAR BEET: SOME FACTS AND SOME ILLUSIONS; A STUDY IN RURAL THERAPEUTICS. *Field*, now *Countryman*. 1911

THE FOUNDATIONS OF JAPAN: 6,000 MILES IN ITS RURAL DISTRICTS AS A BASIS FOR A SOUNDER KNOWLEDGE OF THE JAPANESE PEOPLE. *Murray*, 1922

THE STORY OF THE WOMEN'S INSTITUTES. *Countryman*, 1925

THE COUNTRY CITIZEN. *Countryman*, 1938

THE FOLLOWING ARE OUT OF PRINT

THE PEOPLE OF CHINA, 1900. THE SMALL FARM, 1904. COUNTRY COTTAGES, 1905. POULTRY FARMING: SOME FACTS AND SOME CONCLUSIONS, 1905. THE TOWNSMAN'S FARM, 1908. THE STRANGE STORY OF THE DUNMOW FLITCH, 1909. A FREE FARMER IN A FREE STATE (HOLLAND), 1912. THE LAND PROBLEM, 1913. HINTS FROM THE NOTEBOOK OF AN OLD FARMER, 1914. A PLEA FOR AN OPEN-AIR MUSEUM, 1914. JAPAN, GREAT BRITAIN AND THE WORLD, 1915. THE IGNOBLE WARRIOR (*In English and Japanese*), 1916. THE DYING PEASANT AND THE FUTURE OF HIS SONS, 1926. THE FARMER'S PROBLEM, 1923.

IN PREPARATION

A FAMOUS EDITOR: THE LIFE, WORK AND TIMES OF FREDERICK GREENWOOD, the first editor of a new kind of daily newspaper, the *Pall Mall Gazette*, who secured the Suez Canal Shares for Great Britain. With several hundred unpublished letters.

The author was for nine years on the editorial staff of the *Pall Mall Gazette*.

J. W. Robertson Scott

The Countryman Book

A SELECTION OF ARTICLES
AND ILLUSTRATIONS FROM

The Countryman

MADE BY

J. W. ROBERTSON SCOTT, C.H.

ITS FOUNDER AND FOR TWENTY YEARS
ITS EDITOR

ODHAMS PRESS LIMITED
LONG ACRE LONDON

*To my Contributors
and the Comrades of my Staff
particularly my wife, Assistant Editor
from the beginning*

PUBLISHED 1948

MADE AND PRINTED IN GREAT BRITAIN BY
C. TINLING & CO., LTD., LONDON, LIVERPOOL AND PRESCOT
T.948.S.

Contents

List of Illustrations

Introductory

FIVE publishers and many home and oversea readers of the *Countryman* have urged me to gather together some of the most interesting things that have appeared in its pages during the past twenty years.

In making a difficult choice I have aimed at meeting, in the main, a holiday mood, making a varied selection, treating as thoroughly as possible the different subjects dealt with, and not entirely overlooking Scotland, Wales and Ireland.

The book endeavours to offer, as the *Countryman* has done, not a pretty-pretty, a trifling or a captious picture of rural people and rural life and industry, past or present, but a representation which is true, informing, blithe, and hopeful. Happily the urban public is less easily taken in than it used to be a short time back, by accounts of good old times that never were; and it turns, year by year, a sharper eye on sentimental and ingenuous writing on contemporary social and economic conditions in the countryside.

It is not in the plan of this volume to provide accounts of cropping and stockkeeping, on a large or small scale. There were never more manuals giving trustworthy instruction on these matters. The following pages are primarily concerned with the people who live in the country, with their reasons for staying there rather than in London or provincial cities and towns, with the kind of work they do, with the occupations and interests of their leisure—except sport—and with their mentalities and their hopes for the future.

And, of course, no party political views are expressed anywhere.

The footnotes to articles are designed to be of service chiefly to American readers.

Although, even with present limitations on the number of copies of the *Countryman* which may be printed, the sale is about 60,000, and few periodicals have as many readers per copy, some buyers of this book may not know and may like to have a little light on the history of the magazine I founded in 1927. It did not conform to some accepted journalistic beliefs and usages. The office was not in Fleet Street, but in the heart of the Cotswolds,[1] where it remains. Against the advice of wholesale newsagents, advertisers, advertising agents and journalists, the magazine was pocket-size—a size which has been widely followed. And it did not seek success by a prudent care for 'popularity'—it did not mind affronting widely held views. Further, it declined thirteen kinds of advertising.

Yet, thanks to half a century's experience of journalism, a lifelong interest in rural life, a considerable knowledge of the country and its problems, sympathetic colleagues, and many friendships among rural experts, the periodical paid its way from the start. We were soon able to say that it reached the remotest parts of the world, and at a few years old, in nine consecutive issues, in the days when any amount of paper could be bought, it actually contained an average of 200 pages of advertisements! *The Times* found our 'thought, variety and humour all good,' H. G. Wells declared that he 'never made a better investment than my life subscription,' and the Poet Laureate wrote 'I prefer it to any other periodical.' It may be added that in England the *Countryman* has been imitated in both national and regional publications. In the United States, where it has many friends, it has been studiously copied even to its types, its mottoes, and the precise tint of its green cover.

In preparing this volume, I took pains to send a copy of the articles and sketches to all surviving contributors whose addresses I could discover, so that any desired corrections might be made before reprinting. If writers whom I have been unable to trace see the book, they will be good enough, I hope, to acquit me of discourtesy.

I am indebted to several artists and photographers. There are four cartoons by Thomas Derrick, two by E. G. Barlow and several by Campbell Keith, all excellent specimens of their humorous work. The following have kindly consented

---

[1] During my editorship at Idbury, mentioned in Domesday Book; now at Burford, five miles away.

to the reproduction of photographs: Robert Atkinson ('Young Bracken Uncurling'), Miss Bamford ('What Can I Get Up to Next?'), Viscount Bledisloe ('800-Year Old New Zealand Tree'), G. D. Bolton ('Journeys End in Lovers Meeting'), Eric D. Cheshire ('The Village that Won Viscount Bledisloe's Prize'), Mrs. Crosby ('The Cottage that Crossed the Atlantic'), Surgeon-Commander Cusson ('Some Milestones'), Dr. Fraser Darling ('Come and Join Us'), E. Deuchars ('Sea Kale'), C. B. Dyer ('Arley Hall'), Thomas Fall (dog in car), G. G. Garland ('Oldsters Watching Village Cricket'), J. Hardman ('Why should I Walk?'), F. N. Hepworth ('Spring Crocuses'), Dorien Leigh ('Old and New' and 'The Spider's Claws'), Mrs. Joan Lyne ('Ducklings'), J. R. Marriott ('Some Milestones'), Mondiale ('Shrike and Squirrel Larders'), W. J. C. Murray ('Buttermere and Crummock Water from Green Gable'), Philip T. Oyler (crows on dog's back), Frank Packer ('Getting the Cottages: Second and Third Stages'), Mrs. N. A. Perkins ('Some Milestones'), O. S. Pettingill ('Woodcock Nesting in the Snow'), *Picture Post* ('Getting the Cottages: First Stage'), F. G. Rippingale ('Bullfinches at Home'), J. D. Robinson ('Some Milestones'), Percy R. Salmon ('Four Generations'), *Scotsman* and G. W. Lennox Paterson, the painter of 'Frank Tweedie and the Birds', U.S. Farm Security Administration ('Fifth Grade Class in an American Rural One-room Schoolhouse'), R. F. Walker ('The Ploughman's Art'), Edgar and Winnifred Ward ('Old Style'), John Warham ('Pigeon's Milk'), Mrs. West ('How Farm Animals Get Up' and 'Spring is Here'), Miss M. Wight ('The Comical Arisarum'), Reece Winstone ('Some Milestones' and 'Faked Castles').

IDBURY MANOR
WHERE *The Countryman* CAME FROM

*There is a view into Oxfordshire, Gloucestershire and
Warwickshire, and, up the road, into Berkshire. The offices
occupied the top floor, back and front, and two other rooms.
Most of the house dates back to the fifteen hundreds. The
hamlet of Idbury is described in Domesday Book. The
sketch is by A. van Anrooy, R.I.*

'When He Suddenly Met—'

'ABOUT six one foggy morning,' writes Mr. J. E. Newman, 'I was walking along a footpath at Wantage
when there suddenly loomed up an elephant, also
walking along the footpath. I got off.' Through the fog one
day, near Swanage, Mr. B. McConkey also suddenly saw an
elephant, and he adds this piece of corroborative detail,
'Seated on his back was an "Indian" who hailed me with
"Guid mornin".' Mrs. Hollingsworth has a friend who, in a
mist on the Yorkshire moors, had to stop his car 'because of
an elephant having a rest' A quarter of a mile further on he
met a distracted youth who cried, 'Have you seen a stray elephant, Mister?' Mrs. E. W. Shawyer goes one better, for in a
Cheshire lane, she suddenly met '*two* elephants.' Mrs. Shawyer, in her turn, must retire in favour of Mr. E. M. Pyne. He

1

was tramping one of Surrey's beautiful lanes, about half past nine in the evening, when he suddenly heard 'a heavy thudding, shuffling noise—it was *four* elephants!' Another correspondent whose name has been mislaid, also met four elephants—in Windsor in mid-winter with six inches of snow on the ground. He adds that they had 'pads on their feet and bags on their ears.'

It was not on a winter but on a summer day that E. P. had his adventure. 'My daughter was driving me, in the depths of the country with not a house or soul in sight. We turned a corner and met an elephant. It walked slowly along the road past us. "I don't believe it," I said. We turned another corner and met two dromedaries. "This is serious," I said. "Alligator next, I expect," said my daughter. Round the next corner, a hundred yards away, we met first a camel, and then—the rest of the travelling menagerie.'

In the Western Highlands, at the head of a drove of cattle, I.M. met 'a man sitting on a camel.' And not a menagerie man. But the camel belonged to a menagerie. The beast had fallen sick in the far north, and had been left behind in the care of a drover who was 'skeely' in the treatment of animals. 'The drover cured the camel and got so fond of it he would not part with it and used it to ride when driving his cattle.'

But enough of elephants and camels. On the roadside between Maisemore and Hartbury, 'one July evening,' says Miss Mary Spalding Walker, 'I saw a large frog with its head wedged in the jaws of a grass snake, thirty-six inches long. The frog, released, hopped away.'

With snakes we get away from quadrupeds. Miss Leslie Wood's tale is of a biped: 'I was motoring along the crowded high street of Merton, when I saw a man riding a push bicycle, on the handlebars of which sat, calmly and apparently confortably, a fine swan.'

Finally, we have Mrs. Aikin, of Abbey Dingle, Llangollen: 'My brother-in-law, the late Dr. C. E. Aikin, told me that, with some friends on a walking tour, he turned off a main road into a field where the party sat down against a stone wall for lunch. Here one of the party discovered in the grass—a human ear. There was never an explanation of it.'

Doremy Olland also tells an ear story: 'A friend, in making alterations in a nineteenth-century house, brought to light an old oak cupboard door. On it was nailed a human ear, and on a shelf in the cupboard lay a rapier. Exposed to air, the ear crumpled away. Had some listener been punished?' W. H. Camplin describes how a hay trusser in his locality had his ear cut off by a hay knife. Miss Rossiter sends an account of a similar accident in Sussex.

Mrs. J. R. Gilmour speculates on the Aikin ear being that of 'the driver of a self-binder who had been pulled off his seat by the stumbling of one of his horses, and, landing with his head in front of the blades, had escaped with the loss of an ear. The self-binder could have tossed the ear some distance.'

A. J. Hartham has four shots: '(1) The ear had been bitten off by a dog or horse. (The sheep dogs and ponies on the Welsh mountains are particularly high-spirited.) (2) Some person fell whilst climbing over the hill with a knife or some similar tool in his hand. (3) The ear had been preserved as a charm by gypsies. (4) Dr. Aikin was a practical joker!'

This explanation is forthcoming from Lady Redesdale who writes: 'The explanation of the finding of the human ear in a field is simple. Dr. Aikin had on that day begun his holiday, but he had told his friends he could not start before midday as he was obliged to be in hospital to take a class of students in the dissecting room. He arrayed himself in white coat as usual, and when his work was over, washed carefully, put on his overcoat and hat and got into his car to join the walking party at luncheon, after which the car was to return with the chauffeur and the walk to proceed. As he walked to the rendezvous he kicked a little hummock, and out of his turned-up trouser fell a human ear—to be discovered later by another member of the party.'

R. M. Garnett imagines a practical joker surgeon friend of Dr. Aikin being of the walking party, and accuses him of being responsible for dropping the ear. The solution of the late E. V. Lucas was that Mark Antony was down that way burying Caesar, and one of the countrymen from whom he borrowed an ear forgot to claim it.

3

How Birds Sleep, *by Seton Gordon*

WE are all familiar with the roosting quarters of the sparrow in the ivy of our houses, but how many of us have seen the little blue tit at his sleeping quarters; how many of us know where the tree creeper roosts? In the bark of the Californian red-wood tree (Sequoia semper-virens) are often found small hollows or pockets. Some of us who are fortunate enough to own a few specimens of this stately tree have visited them at dusk to see the secretive little creepers in their roosting hollows.

Birds, like their human observers, do not all retire to rest at the same time. For example, the thrush is up later than the starling. At my home in the north of the Isle of Skye the starlings roost in a cave of an island half a mile into the Minch. In late summer, autumn, and through the winter, one may watch them winging their way in flocks across the land and then out over the stormy sea to their cave. One afternoon towards the close of summer I happened to be fishing for pollack round the island, and saw a peregrine falcon, which was perched on the top of the rock above the cave, making dives upon the starlings as they flew in. In the half-light of the early mornings also, when the starlings are flying off to their feeding grounds, that peregrine rushes in among them. Near us is another island sea cave where starlings roost. That small island is between two and three miles off the coast, and on a stormy winter night one may see the starling flocks flying out to see at a speed of well over a mile a minute with a following gale to aid them. Although in Skye starlings habitually roost in sea caves, this habit is not, I believe, a usual one.

Birds as sleepers may be divided into three categories: firstly, those which sleep from dusk to dawn, secondly, nocturnal birds such as owls, and thirdly those birds (and there are many of them) which sleep either by day or by night. To this class belong the waders. Their period of sleep, while at their winter haunts at all events, is determined by the state of the tide. If the tide is low during the night, and their feeding

---

Seton Gordon's pleasant and helpful books about wild life, chiefly of the birds of the Highlands, must number a score. He is also a Scottish mountaineer and an accomplished bag-pipe player.

4

WOODCOCK NESTING IN THE SNOW. New York State

HOW FARM ANIMALS GET UP

BUTTERMERE AND CRUMMOCK WATER FROM GREEN GABLE

GETTING THE COTTAGES

First Stage: *Conference in the village.* Second Stage: *Discussion at the Rural District Council Housing Committee.* Third Stage: *Opening day. On my left on the platform are Sir Stafford and Lady Cripps who generously made up the difference between the cost of building in stone and in brick and rough cast*

grounds are left dry by the sea, they feed at night. On a moon-light night there is as much activity as on a sunny morning. If low tide on a winter day is at ten, the birds will rouse themselves between seven and eight, and will feed until, say, one o'clock. As the water floods in over the feeding grounds they fly in to the sand dunes, or to the fields near the shore, and sleep there lightly for the next six hours, returning for a second meal between seven and eight in the evening. If there is no moon this second meal is searched for in the dark. Ducks also feed and fly by night as well as by day. The tufted duck of Fallodon, which were so tame that they fed from the hand (some of them pulled one's shoe laces if food was not forth-coming quickly enough), rose into the air at dusk, and *disappeared* on swiftly-driven wings, perhaps to some distant feeding ground. The life of the vast flocks of widgeon, which haunt the coast near the Ross Links not so many miles away, is less happy. These migrants have been forced to become night feeders. The shore gunners are daily on the watch, and the birds are obliged to pass the hours of daylight on the North Sea. Even at sea they are nervous, and it is an inspiring sight when they rise in their thousands and fly seaward over the white-crested waves.

There is a general impression that a bird sleeps with its head tucked beneath the feathers of its wing. The golden eagle does not, during the daylight hours at all events, sleep in this position. During several years my wife and I have watched eagles during many days in hides built only a few yards from the eyries. As the mother eagle gradually falls asleep on her nest, her proud eyes close and her head sinks forward until it is resting upon her breast. The eaglet sleeps like a dog. It lies stretched on its side, its head pillowed on the hard branches of the eyrie. The golden eagle is a heavy sleeper. One summer night my wife took an all-night watch in the hiding post, and before sunrise, when the eagle was sound asleep, a wandering blackbird unexpectedly alighted on the rowan tree beside the eyrie and began to sing. The strong liquid notes aroused the eagle with a start. She knew the ring ousel's song but this blackbird was a stranger. She glared at the singer. He continued to sing undismayed and when he had

flown away the eagle closed her eyes and resumed her interrupted sleep.

Birds roost on trees, on the ground, in caves, walls, and
hollow trees. Is there any species that sleeps on the wing? As
we all know, it has long been maintained that swifts on fine
summer evenings mount into the air at dusk to an immense
height, and sleep on the wing. Good observers admit that
swifts do indeed climb at dusk to immense heights, but believe
that they descend when it is too dark for their movements
to be observed, and fly into their nesting hollows.

Among sea birds there are diurnal and nocturnal species.
There are a few, too, which appear to be diurnal or nocturnal
at will. The Manx shearwater at its nesting islands is nocturnal, and yet it is often seen flying at sea in bright sunshine.
The shearwater lays her single white, polished egg at the
extremity of a burrow in the peat of some Hebridean island.
There she sleeps away the long hours of the summer day, and
an observer might walk over the colony, consisting perhaps
of hundreds of birds, without hearing or seeing a sign of life.
But almost on the stroke of midnight the colony awakes. The
birds on the nests bestir themselves, and their mates,
which have passed the daylight hours out at sea, begin to
arrive. For an hour or more an indescribable medley of sound
is heard—grunts, squeaks, moans, also sounds recalling the
crowing of cock pheasants and the hooting of owls, to the deep
accompaniment of the roar of the Atlantic surge. The darkness cloaks the birds, but from time to time one sees, against
the afterglow on the northern horizon, the dark form of a
shearwater appearing like some gigantic swift as it passes at
great speed on long narrow wings. Before the first Hebridean thrush has awakened, the last of the shearwaters' cries
have died away. Whether the birds coming in from the sea
take their turn on the eggs, or whether they fly in merely to
feed and visit their mates is not definitely known, for the
change over, if such it be, is made always during the darkest
hour of the night.

The storm petrel, Mother Carey's chicken, is perhaps the
most truly nocturnal of all British sea birds. It is no larger
than a swallow, and indeed in its flight closely resembles one.

6

As to its heralding bad weather, it is true that it does not fly abroad in daylight during fine sunny weather. Yet I have seen it flitting over the sea on a dark midsummer day, when no bad weather followed. Except for a short time in the summer, the storm petrel sleeps on the sea. When the young petrel chick is a week old, it is deserted by day by its parents. It is fed during the hours of darkness. By daylight its parents are sleeping on the sea perhaps a dozen miles, perhaps a great deal further, from their nesting island.

It is a remarkable thing that so small and delicate a bird should be able to sleep at all on the Atlantic during the winter months. Scarcely a winter passes but a number are found exhausted, sometimes dying, far from the sea. Their plight is due, not so much to want of food as to want of sleep. Picture their sleeping place out on the Atlantic, hundreds of miles from land. A gale has, perhaps, been blowing for days, even weeks. Immense waves, white-crested and menacing, hurry past. These breaking waves must render sleep impossible, except for a few seconds at a time. The small petrel, exhausted and longing for sleep, is aroused a fraction of a second before the wall of breaking water is upon it. It must struggle up into the air to escape being engulfed and this seemingly endless task of saving its fragile life continues, day and night, in stormy winters, for weeks at a time. The wonder is that any storm petrels survive.

Seabirds remain at sea, however hard their life is. They have the same mistrust of land as a land bird has of the sea. Watch the flights of gannets returning from a fishing excursion in the Minch to their home on St. Kilda. The Outer Hebrides rise between them and their goal. A few minutes' flight would take them across these islands and out on to the open sea beyond, yet, rather than trust themselves over the land, they fly along the east coast of the Outer Hebrides until they reach the entrance to the Sound of Harris. At any hour of daylight, from May until October, parties of gannets from north and south may be seen converging on the entrance to the Sound of Harris and passing west low over its friendly waters to the open Atlantic where, fifty miles on the western horizon, St. Kilda rises, faint and ethereal.

7

There is no sounder sleeper than the gannet. Tireless of wing, so that it thinks nothing of a hundred miles' flight to fish for its nestling, it sleeps after a heavy fishing so soundly that on occasion it can be caught on the water. Its ochre head is deeply hidden beneath its feathers; it is deaf, even to the approaching of a passing steamer, until the vessel is almost upon it. A Hebridean fisherman told me that on one occasion he had seen a gannet disgorge no fewer than seven mackerel before it was able to rise from the water. Presumable it even then retained a fish or two in its capacious crop!

Martin, who visited St. Kilda in 1697, mentions that at night, while on their nesting stack, the gannets post a sentry. Should this sentry be surprised all the flock are caught, one after the other, by the fowlers. 'But if the sentinel be awake at the approach of the creeping fowlers and hear a noise it cries softly "Grog, Grog" at which the flock move not. But if the sentinel sees or hears the fowler approaching he cries quickly "Bir, bir" which should seem to import danger, since immediately after, the whole tribe take wing, leaving the fowler alone on the rock to return home *re infecta*, all his labour for that night being spent in vain.'

But the gannet and the eagle are exceptional in the soundness of their sleep. It is perhaps because they have little to fear from sudden winged danger. In the bird world as a whole slumber is a very light and delicate thing. Watch a flock of godwits asleep in close ranks on the wet sand of the sea shore awaiting the ebbing of the tide to lay bare their feeding grounds. Each long bill is tucked away beneath the wing feathers. The bright eyes are closed. Then of a sudden comes uneasiness. It is scarcely alarm, but during that watchful moment many eager eyes suddenly open, glance around enquiringly, then (the position of the head being all the time unchanged) close again in the lightest of sleep. Heavy slumber, such as we humans know it, would be disastrous. Their enemy, the fierce peregrine, would be upon them before they could escape him.

'Tent the grass makes we so wet of a mornin'—'tis they bents!' explained old George.

8

Riding Song, *by Leonora Starr*

As I ride, as I ride, as I ride to the sands that are left by
    the tide
    There is nothing for me but the stride of my horse
and the scent of the thyme;
For the sun's on the hill and the heath, and the wind is a
    sword out of sheath,
And the hoofs that are thudding beneath have a rhythmical
    beat and rhyme.

If the arch of the sky were a stair, with the wind making
    songs in my hair
I would gallop the plains of the air, and the paths of the
    planets and stars,
And the eagles in terror would fly down the deserts and wastes
    of the sky,
And I'd shout my defiance and cry to the horsemen of Saturn
    and Mars.

Oh, the wind is unsheathed like a sword, and the gulls are
    a silver-winged horde,
And the sound of the sea is a chord of a song that is endless
    and free.
As I ride, as I ride, as I ride on the sands that are left by the
    tide
There is nothing in life but the stride of my horse and the
    smell of the sea.

*

'Yer grandfather 'ee wor right more offen nor no and he said you
must never no more put no drains there.'

In the cottage grannie was embroidering an exquisite bonnet for the
expected baby. The young wife, when her back was turned, took from
its hiding-place a tiny aviator's helmet, complete with chin-strap and
ear-flaps.

Picking up a pheasant which he had shot, the young peer pointed out
fleas to the keeper, who said, 'It's all right, my lord. The pheasant's
fleas won't bite your lordship any more than your lordship's fleas would
bite the pheasant.'

9

1—'I Walk', by the Earl Baldwin of Bewdley

The name Idbury strikes a chord. In 1906 I was beaten by a liberal at Kidderminster. I was disappointed because I wanted to be in the House with my father who sat for Bewdley. When spring came, I got the hump badly one day and I went off for a walk I took train to what is now Kingham and started off into space with no plan in my head I went I remember, up hill for some way and found a church with the place of the sanctus bell left: was it Idbury? In

in sun. I went on through Fifield to Tangley where a wagon had on it the wholly satisfactory name of Mervyn Wingfield. The Burford, and on to Minster Lovell where I had supper with Bonamy Price who had been headmaster of Westward Ho! thence to Witney where I lay the night

Oxford next morning, getting wet through, met Mackail on the platform and so home by train, forged and sown. I have never forgotten that day

Baldwin of Bewdley

Kingham, where Warde-Fowler, the scholar-ornithologist lived; Idbury which is in Domesday book; Idbury, it was, with the sanctus bell; Fifield, where the then Premier (Neville Chamberlain) planted the oak and it fell to me to propose a resolution of thanks; Tangley, where David Garnett's Lady turned into Fox and there is the hole in the farmhouse door through which a highwayman's hand was thrust and chopped off; Burford, where there is the house of Speaker Lenthall, who defied Charles I; Minster Lovell, where the heroine of 'The Mistletoe Bough' came to her death; and Witney, where the Earlys have been making blankets since Charles II—I reckon Lord Baldwin's walk to have been about 18 miles.

2—Seeing Scotland in Two Days

by Ramsay MacDonald

THIS is a rare problem that has been given to me. How would I choose, within the varied bounds of Scotland, a rout which in two days would give a stranger a good idea of the country? I doubt if it can be done, but let me have a look at it.

One day assuredly should be spent between the Border and Edinburgh. Here is the Scotland of romance, of the lyric, of the ballad, of a scenery which is the Scottish nature embodied in hill and howe and glen, of ruins domestic, military, ecclesiastical as interesting and fine as these islands have to show.

There are two possible gateways: one by the east, Carter Bar; the other by the west, Carlisle. Upon one's mood and the mood of the heavens depend which gateway will be the better to take. Take the former on a clear day; mount up to the summit of well over 1,000 feet; from the highest point of the road, with dramatic suddenness, Scotland lies to the north at your feet in a far thrown landscape of rich colouring and graceful expanse of hill and moor and farm—the revelation of a promised land. Impatient with speed, we dally down into the valley of the Jed with Sir Walter in company, rough-riding bands careering around North and South, the more ordered advance and glittering array (especially of those from England) of armies holding us up as we go. These shadow memories will never pass from this land, and a good Scotsman's foot will never hurry thoughtlessly through them.

When the road over Carter Bar has brought us down to the river valleys, we reach the land of the Abbeys, a great sanctuary of beauty and story. I advise that we take the way to Jedburgh, with its fine ruins of a Norman Abbey, in the close of which Sir Walter Scott first saw Wordsworth. In Jedburgh, even during a brief stay, we find a typical Border town, an atmosphere of remote peace, an exquisite ecclesiastical architecture, the footsteps of the infatuated Queen Mary whilst fascinated by that blackguard Bothwell. We have entered one of the richest corners of the whole world for song and story and lovely ruin.

Then our best way is to make for Selkirk (well signposted), and hard will be the tug of heart if the time allotted for this scamper prevents us from looking in at Melrose—'Marmion' in hand, or, very much better, on the tip of the tongue—and Dryburgh. We are scurrying through the native soil of Thomas the Rhymer, distinguished by such curious features as the cleft Eildon Hills whose triple-coned volcano peaks could be explained by our forebears only by imagining that the cuts must have been dealt by blows of the sword of the Devil.

From Jedburgh, we continue our road northwards till we join the Selkirk highway, where we bend to the West. Hills and woods and fields pass us and with judicious driving we see Abbotsford and the Tweed banks. The countryside is still studded with historical places and view-points some of which we can spare time to reach in our day's flight. On its shelf on the hillside the attractive county town of Selkirk bids one linger a wee and think of the Selkirk bowmen in green, Flodden Field and the 'Flowers of the Forest' and 'the Souters' (shoemakers).

Selkirk is comfortable and placid with its broad streets and well-to-do shops. Following the signposts, down the hill we go westwards by the battlefield of Philiphaugh and, across the river, 'the shatter'd front of Newark's Tower renowned in Border story' where Leslie shot his prisoners after Philiphaugh, and, a short distance on, we pass the birthplace of Mungo Park. Running on our left is Yarrow—'the dowie dens o' Yarrow'—the inspiration of those ballads which to this day stir the blood by memories of the braveries, the loves and the tragedies of the borderer. As we pass, we cannot fail to notice the square tower of Dryhope, the birthplace of 'The Flower of Yarrow', and, on a ledge to the right of the road, watchful eyes will catch a glimpse of the famed St. Mary's churchyard with the twelfth-century ruins of St. Mary's Kirk. By the side of St. Mary's Loch which mirrors the hills of Ettrick on its breast, we approach Tibbie Shiels' Inn, the scene of the nocturnal flow of wit and refreshment, when

13

Christopher North, Hogg, Scott, and the other cronies came together to enjoy each other's company. Hogg's monument stands on our right.

At this point the road we have come by meets that which we might have taken from Carlisle. As far as Langholm the road from Carlisle would have been pretty dull, but there we should have turned to the left over a bridge and gone into the moors by Road B 709. For thirty miles or so our way would have been over a truly magnificent moorland country— Eskdalemuir—affording wide views of hills including that noble peak of Ettrick Pen which dominates the whole countryside, and in the latter part we should have driven by gushing trout streams during the long descent into Ettrick Dale. This is one of the finest moorland roads in Scotland. Once in Ettrick we might have diverted for a short run to the left up the Dale to see Hogg's birthplace and the white church where the saintly Boston preached and which guards the quiet churchyard where Tibbie Shiels, Boston himself, James Hogg, the neighbouring Napiers, sleep, surrounded by generations of Border Shepherds like Will o' Whaup (the last of them to see fairies). Then we would have turned back, passing the Napier home to where the ruins of Tushielaw still stand gaunt on the hillside. Bearing to the left by the Inn, in a few miles, after the road has mounted to over 1,300 feet, we would have cut down between the Loch of the Lowes and St. Mary's Loch to Tibbie Shiels on its narrow shingly isthmus.

The road down Moffat Dale swings to the left from the Carlisle approach and goes straight ahead from Selkirk. It is a grand road along which are dotted farms famed in song and story. Hills rise up on both sides, and down them pour the waters of many streams. The most famous is the Grey Mare's Tail which issues from the hidden Loch Skeen described by Scott, haunted by hunted Covenanters when Claverhouse and Grierson of Lag were in the saddle. Lower down we come into Burns's country and pass the house where 'Willie brewed a peck o' maut an' Rob and Allan cam' to pree'. At Craigie Burn lived Jean Lorimer, the subject of about a dozen of Burns's love songs.

From Moffat we might finish the day going on to Edin-

14

burgh by the Summit (1,348 feet) and the famous Devil's Beef Tub (500 to 600 feet deep) described in 'Redgauntlet' as 'a damned deep, black, blackguard-looking abyss', and made all the more eerie by the part it played in a recent murder.

The district is still one of far-distanced mountain views and hurrying streams. In the days of the stage-coach the wild weather of the road was a sore trial to the passengers, and 'the tales of the road', whilst they told of many glorious summer joys, also recorded baffling and disastrous snow-storms, mists and hurricanes. On that well laid road and in a car, the tourist still feels that he is engaged in a fine adventure. Beyond this, we return to Covenanting country and to Border literature and history. We are indeed amidst the last haunts of Merlin himself—though he is of Caledonia and not of Wales. We creep up to the infant Tweed, and pass the site of that vanished weaving village with the unique name of Linkum-doddie. The road thence on to Edinburgh is as picturesque and interesting as any on the Border, and in Edinburgh we can bring the day to a close. From Carter Bar, we have gone 112 miles.

There are still 36 miles between us and Stirling and as that is to be the starting point for the next day it can be taken in a summer's evening. On the whole, it is a dull road made for speed, with occasional pit heaps. Linlithgow through which we pass has some interesting old houses, and was from the earliest times the residence of Kings. Its royal palace was the finest in Scotland. This regal abode, especially with the association of Mary Queen of Scots, is one of the proud shrines of historically minded Scotsmen, and will charm everyone who visits it. To rush through it is sacrilege, but here summer evenings are long, and ours is indeed a *tour de force*. A sunset from the battlements of Stirling looking over the Vale of Menteith is a panorama of natural beauty never to be forgotten.

Stirling is, next to Edinburgh, most sacred to the patriotic Scot. Almost at our feet, as we look down from the castle, Wallace fought the battles of Stirling Brig and Bruce fought Bannockburn. We must see the castle before we go, though we can do it only with apologetic haste. Everywhere there are memories—of youth in Queen Mary's Room, of tragedy in the Douglas Room. Its history grimly mingles the chatter of innocent children and the curses of doomed men. I know no place on earth more haunted by the innocency and tragedy of life.

And now, whither shall we go? Ben Lomond, the Cobbler, Ben Ledi, Ben Venue, are all enticing. There are so many ways I should like to take you, but one has always to remember that there is no coast road along the West Highland seaboard. If the sight-seer goes westward till he reaches the sea, he will have to retrace his steps when he wishes to pursue a northward journey through the centre. I have been all the ways, and clearly there is but one which the experienced traveller will choose. Gladly would I roam 'by far Loch Ard and Aberfoyle' with the 'Lady of the Lake' in my pocket, but the more direct road ahead has many shrines and charms, and by that we shall go. To-day, we'll 'gang the low road'. We pass on by Bridge of Allan and Dunblane, where, dropping into its cathedral a good many years ago, I heard 'The Banks of Allan Water' being played on the organ with a touch and a taste which I shall never forget. Whenever I approach the hillside on which Dunblane stands that fine old Scots melody begins to hum in my ears.

We are making for Callander and Lochearnhead over well laid mountain-shadowed roads, by lively bustling rivers and

UNKNOWN SCOTLAND, BY CAMPBELL KEITH

*Three young Haggis Romping, with a
Dirk overhead*

16

sheltered lochs—a land for dreaming in. Before we get to Lochearnhead, however, a finger post to the left will tell us that Balquhidder and Rob Roy's grave are within a couple of miles. We shall go and see the peaceful, unpretentious church-yard, of aged aspect and solemn remote air, on the face of the hill. Its ivy-covered church, of which naught stands but walls and belfry—an eloquently silent *memento mori*—is typical of many such graveyards in Scotland where one feels with simple directness that the dead have lain down to deep sleep. The flat stones at the east end of the enclosure mark Rob Roy's final abode, which he shares with the masterful Nell and a son who could not escape the hangman. Perhaps the stones were not cut and carved for Rob, but they are in keeping with his place in story. We may wish, however, that his protector, the wealthy member of his clan who erected the low railing which encloses the graves, had been less explana-tory about himself while doing a clansman's homage to Rob. One cannot help thinking of the dialogue between Rob and the Baillie.

We return through Glen Ogle, Glen Dochart, Strath Fillan—names of beauty and music and romance, as are most Perthshire names of ways through hills. When we reach Tyn-drum we go north to the Bridge of Orchy between those smooth, frequently wooded, but always graceful hill-sides which make the whole land an abode of peace and gracious-ness. How often are they like a comely human form reclining in the sun! If the Pastoral Muse has a dwelling place, it is here.

Our road runs by Loch Tulla to Glencoe and gives a fine idea of the Scottish moors—regally purple in the late summer; boggy and gloomy, but generally snow clad, in winter. No road that I know gives one a better sense of the eternal and illimitable, of the magic allurements of horizons, of the mystical colouring of Nature, than does this across Black Mount and the Moor of Rannoch. The gloomy sentinel mountains of Glencoe rise in front of us and we hurry on to meet them. By and by the white walls of the Kinghouse Hotel at the entrance of Glencoe appear, and—since the new road has been made for perhaps too much haste—we speed between the towering sides of the Glen which, in spite of the smooth road and the majesty of the hills, still retains the features of tragedy and sorrow. Give me snow and black snowclouds over the Glen so that the tale of treachery may be told to my heart! 'You have no idea of how convenient it is for getting to shops', said a friend of mine to my mournful remark that the Campbells made the road to hide their deeds of evil. That may be, and, in any event, it is a fine piece of engineering. We are through the Glen before we have time to think and brood as we used to do. God forgive me, for I am really a man of peace and forgiveness.

When we come out on the side of Loch Leven, an arm of Loch Linnhe, we turn to the right and go round the top of the Loch through a saddening aesthetically devastated industrial area. The whole land is haunted by ghosts and clouded by Highland tales of murder, hanging and strife. Every wooded mound and corner in the road has its eerie clan legend. But the grandeur and beauty of the scene banish these from the mind of the motorist who beholds in admiration the unfolding of the landscape. Fort William is soon reached under the massive bulk of Ben Nevis. Fort William, still known by the old people as 'the Garrison', is the meeting place at the beginning and ending of the summer and autumn, of people from the ends of the earth. In one day as I was passing through I met in an hotel, people whom I knew from New Zealand, India, and the Canadian West.

We can go but one way, avoiding tempting branching roads, to find our beds, and a noble way it is, for it takes us through one of the most famous avenues traversed by those who come to see Scotland, up the Great Glen alongside of the Caledonian Canal. I have flown that way by seaplane low down over the Lochs which go to make up the Canal, well below the tops of the hills which contain it, and would always go thus if I could. But the road (especially since it has been widened) will do.

By rushing rivers, over old bridges built before the days of concrete, we gradually leave the mighty dominance of Ben Nevis and enter the trough of the Great Glen, along which our road lies for sixty miles. It is a road through history, the characteristic history of Scotland. At once Inverlochy is seen on the left, and to this day, especially when the snow is on the ground and the mists are on the hills, one can see the great Argyle fleeing pell-mell from the avenging Montrose. The chain of Lochs keep with us all the way and the road is shaded by forests for the most part. There is hardly a dull mile. Rivers sing foaming over their rocky beds and a castle stands upon every point of advantage. We pass through the domains of most of the famous clans; their ruined homes, their battle grounds, their last resting places pass before us. We traverse the country where Prince Charlie lives on. They have long memories on this road.

Industry has conquered some of the beauty spots. It has subdued the heaths and hillsides of Foyers; it has woven the unseemly cobwebs of electric standards over hill and dale and it has a voracious appetite still to be appeased. Need the bread of life blast the glens?

May we not see the Monster where the pipe line comes down at Foyers? May we not have a cup of tea at Drumna-drochit whilst listening to tales of those who have seen it, and who induce us to try and believe by reminding us that St. Columba saw it on his way to Inverness and overcame it?

Some of the most beautiful spots keep their charm and will show themselves to you as you pass. Is not the scene from the summit of the level of the Canal at Loch Oich superb? Have you ever seen a more beautiful picture than that in which is set Invergarry—'Raven's Craig'—the ruined and deserted strong-hold of the MacDonnells of Glengarry, where Prince Charlie spent that first harrowing night after Culloden? Where does the spirit of Nature which makes this earth so beautiful, show itself in its unblemished countenance better than at Inver-moriston and at Glen Urquhart, where the twelfth-century castle stands?

From Fort Augustus to Inverness we go through a land of faery and legend, too rich for the speed of motors and too sacred for mere cataloguing. And so to Inverness, which you enter by that wooded hill like an upturned boat where the Inverness dead sleep in the keeping of their hills, soothed by the lullaby lapping of the Ness.

Here I must leave you, for you must be surfeited with the

19

glimpses which you have had in the two days we have been together. On this second day we have gone about 220 miles over excellent road surfaces. All I could do has been to put 'love on you' and make you return with 'The Road to the Isles' as your guide book and nothing but your 'cromak' in your hand and your knapsack on your back. These, at any rate, are still my chosen equipment for wandering in Highland places.

Although I had a number of interesting letters from this Prime Minister I never met him, and I regret very much that I could not accept an invitation to London which he kindly sent me before embarking on the voyage during which he died.

3—Natural History at Downing Street
by Neville Chamberlain

THE old garden between Downing Street and the Horse Guards Parade has existed for at least two hundred and fifty years, and perhaps it retains for that reason some traces of more rural surroundings. Only a few days ago, I was delighted to find resting on the trunk of a small hawthorn tree, a specimen of the beautiful, but rarely seen, Leopard Moth, its long, white, blue-black spotted wings folded over its back. The larva of this insect is a wood-borer, and, so far as I know, there is no tree in the garden which would be suitable for its food. Nevertheless, from its perfect condition, I am sure it could not have made any long flight, and it must have passed its earlier stages somewhere in the neighbourhood.

When I first came here in January of 1936, I at once affixed a nesting-box to one of the trees in the garden. Nothing happened for a long time, but last March I saw a pair of blue, or perhaps I should say, black tits, for they were a grimy couple, flitting about the branches of a lime tree. Shortly afterwards they were flying in and out of the box. I did not have time to make any examination till the week-end after I had become Prime Minister, when on looking into the box, I found the nest completed and three eggs in it. Unfortunately,

---

The writer, while Prime Minister, planted an oak in a village within view from my casements. In the eyes of the onlooking villagers, experienced with the spade, he did it with credit, his hat flung on the ground.

JOURNEYS END IN LOVERS MEETING
(*As a matter of fact the two photographs have no relation to one another*)

800-YEAR OLD NEW ZEALAND TREE

This photograph was sent to me by Lord Bledisloe when he was Governor-General of New Zealand. Lady Bledisloe is in the foreground

I saw little more movement, and looking again in June, found that the nest was deserted and the three eggs had been reduced to two. Now what is the solution of the mystery of the vanished egg?

Did the tits themselves carry it away, or did some marauder make off with it? I remember, long years ago, my mother's twin sister, a lady much beloved by me for her sweet disposition and her keen humour, related a conversation with her venerable gardener. Said my aunt, 'John, I see the blackbirds have been busy again with the cherries'. 'May be, Ma'am' the old man replied, and then with an indescribably sly chuckle, he added, 'but I fancy some *two-leggèd* blackbirds must have been round here'. I wonder if some animal of the same species went off with my tits' egg.

4—*The Prime Minister as Handy Man*

I CHERISH a fond but delusive hope that some day I shall retire and devote myself to gardening. At present, the exigencies of Parliament and the demands of weekend meetings deny me the possibility of acquiring the knowledge and skill and of giving the continuity of attention that the care of a garden demands, so that I have to cultivate by proxy. But the need for the relief which manual labour affords must be met. I find an outlet in acting as odd job man in my house and garage.

Without being in any way a skilled craftsman, I have a smattering of many crafts. I can manage the operations required in mending children's toys, broken furniture and china, electrical connections, defective locks and taps, and the like. I get most satisfaction out of the exercise of ingenuity in adapting unlikely odds and ends to new purposes. In the garden there are gates and fencing to be made or repaired, wire netting to be renewed and dead wood to be cut out. Last vacation I was more ambitious and made new laying boxes for the hens and constructed and glazed new covers to the cucumber frames. I get a lot of pleasure in effecting something

This was contributed to the *Country man* when Mr. Attlee was Leader of the Opposition. In giving his permission to reprint the article as written, he said 'You must have a wealth of interesting material to draw on'.

which, though not highly finished, is adequate for its purpose.

I have had many pleasant hours in the garden on these tasks. As I worked I meditated on political problems or, looking round, imagined a future devoted to the garden. Weeding the lawn is conducive to meditation, but I find that it is like many of our social problems; action has been taken too late, the weeds have got such a hold that nothing but a radical reconstruction of the lawn will be effective! I hope to get the opportunity of doing it some day.

A Butterfly Sanctuary
by L. H. Newman

THE requisites for it in your garden are sun, flowers and a feeding pad. Rock plants give nectar in the spring. Sweet arabis and aubretia are easy to grow. Then there are crocuses, snowdrops and hyacinths. Your sanctuary may have some of the common shrubs such as sallows and willows to provide not only nectar-bearing catkins but shade in the midsummer heat. As spring gives way to summer, flowers are in profusion everywhere. Red Admirals, Painted Ladies, Tortoiseshells and Peacocks will not leave beds of valerian, coreopsis, cornflowers, scabious, columbines, and mignonette. If the Holly blue should come she can be encouraged by permitting that old root of ivy to live. This butterfly lays its eggs on the blooms, and the caterpillars feed on the berries. On your buddleia the butterflies will feast so absorbedly that they will let you come quite close and perhaps even touch their wings. But there are days when butterflies seem to find it almost too hot for the sickly sweet of 'flower-honey', and welcome the artificial feeding pad—just a small piece of sponge or cotton-wool sprinkled with sugar and water. Keep it moist during the hot weather. When the first Michaelmas daisies wither, your pad may still expect an occasional visitor; the Brimstone or Sulphur may pause as she takes her last flight on a short sunny October morning. She will then return to her winter quarters, often a thick clump of ivy.

The well-known breeder of British lepidoptera. His latest Book is *Butterfly Haunts.*

Kitchen Paradise, *by Sir Miles Thomas*

I HAVE been asked to elaborate the suggestion to which I gave expression last year, that if a modern three-or-four bedroom house was equipped as it could and should be, 'any normal woman could keep it like a spotless paradise with one hour's work a day'. I am happy to do so, for unless there is a more general awareness of the immeasurable improvements now possible in our homes, the women of Britain must continue to be kitchen slaves. One pities the bird in the gilded cage. Our housewives are just as imprisoned, but their cages are begrimed with soot, covered with dust and thick with grease from out-of-date, ill-designed cooking equipment. One hears a great deal about young girls rebelling against the duties of the kitchen and clearing off into the world outside. It may well be that this is not so much a revulsion against discipline, and a weakening of character, as a healthy rebellion against an out-of-date way of living. There must be a clean break with the old and conventional, and everyone concerned—manufacturer, builder and householder—must think in terms of a new design for living.

Now what is to be the pattern of that design? I will deal mainly with the kitchen, for that is where there is most urgent need for change. As a basis there must be a drastic revision of lay-out. Just as any good works engineer saves thousands of man-hours in a factory by close attention to 'motion-study', so a little intelligent planning in the kitchen can save the busy housewife several minutes per job and leave her much less tired at the end of it. And it is not only in the placing of kitchen equipment, but in its actual design and colouring, that there are such infinite possibilities for improvement.

I wish it could be made compulsory for every builder in this country to visit the United States, or Sweden, or Canada, to see just what a gay and pleasant place a kitchen can be. There they would see the long, brightly coloured counter stretching the full length of one wall, under the window, and possibly running along a second wall also. Its surface is of

---

Formerly of the Nuffield organization; he is now Deputy Chairman of the British Overseas Airways Corporation.

23

stainless metal or plastic, so that it can be made spotless by the wipe of a cloth. Set into this counter, or at the ends of it, are the cooker and refrigerator. Under the window is the deep metal sink, supplied with water through a long, swan-neck faucet which pivots to direct water to any corner of the sink. The temperature of the water can be gauged to any degree from ice cold to boiling by one controlling handle.

Under the counter are drawers and cupboards, recessed at the foot about six inches back, with a three-inch clearance to allow you to tuck your toes underneath when working close up to sink or counter. Not all the drawers slide open; some let down on extending arms to form working tables or steps at varying heights, to make it easier to reach the top shelves and cupboards. The arrangement of cupboards and shelves is duplicated above. All have such a highly-polished surface that they need only a wipe with a damp cloth and a duster. All are heat-proof and dust-proof. Nested stools, in light tubular metal, with bright yellow washable seats, tuck away, one on top of the other, in a recess under the counter.

Every angle and corner is rounded so that there are no inaccessible dust traps. The floor is covered with a gaily coloured composition which can be made of a variety of materials—rubber, linoleum, etc.—but has the supreme advantage that it needs only about one-tenth of the cleaning expended on most old-fashioned English kitchen floors.

At half a dozen points round the walls are electric power sockets, all made to take exactly the same size and shape of plug which can be used in any room in the house, any house in the town, any town in the State. Electric service should never be as we know it here—a haphazard affair of varying voltages and different sizes of fitments. In the kitchen-as-it-should-be that ingenious device the thermostat takes over all manner of duties from the busy housewife. It controls the heating and ventilation of the room, it keeps the refrigerator cool enough and the cooker hot enough. Automatic time-switches watch over the cakes in the oven and the dishes in the washing machine. And let the housewife be happy at the progress in the design of the washing-machine. The latest models can be used, by a simple change of accessories taking only ninety seconds, to clean both clothes and dishes. They are smoothly and exquisitely finished, nothing to catch the dust—just one simple dial to set them silently working. They wash and rinse the dirtiest clothes perfectly—and *dry* them. They wash dishes, silverware, glasses and pots and pans.

In the kitchen department, electricians are already playing their part. When one realizes that the electric current, used to light out homes and give heat to our cookers, alternates back and forth in the wires fifty times a second, while in radio waves it changes direction millions of times a second, it is not difficult to visualize the possibilities when electronics are applied to the art of cooking. Bread, pies and joints of meat can be cooked evenly, without burning, in a matter of seconds. Even if this type of cooking is not generally developed just yet, there is, meanwhile, the pressure cooker, made of extra hard, thick, sheet aluminium, which cooks potatoes in eight minutes, peas in fifteen seconds and beef stew in a quarter of an hour.

The power-points conveniently placed over the kitchen-counter may be used for plugging in the dish-washer, potato-peeler, egg-whisk, iron, ice-cream freezer and the toaster. This toaster is of course automatic, needs no watching, makes the toast light, medium, or dark and crunchy, and even keeps it crisp and warm if necessary.

The modern, properly designed refrigerator has half a dozen compartments, each exactly the size to take the things it is intended to house (bottles of milk, etc.), each at its own appropriate degree of coolness and humidity. Some compartments are smell proof, so that the melon cannot taint the butter; some freeze, others merely cool.

The same thoughfulness in design should be found throughout the whole house. Heat radiation can now be produced by several far cleaner and more efficient means than the open coal fire. If the house is centrally heated, the boiler should be in a cellar or in a little outside boiler house, so that no dust and fumes get inside the kitchen. The boiler can be stoked automatically, and the fire blown up or damped down by thermostatic control. Bedrooms will be as warm and cosy as the kitchen, yet with air as fresh as in the fields outside.

All hot-water, cold-water and waste pipes will be routed through a central plumbing duct running from cellar to roof in the middle of the house.

The list can be augmented by a hundred items, but I have mentioned enough, I think, to demonstrate that the British home can, one day, and with proper efforts, be made into a gay paradise for the housewife, if only she will demand the latest and best-designed equipment and persist in her demands until she gets it. Even her food shopping may one day be made a tithe of its present daily burden. There are many big stores in America where it is now possible to buy fruit and vegetables washed and trimmed clean, ready for the table—but this is particularly of interest to townspeople without gardens —all packed in dust-proof wrapping and chilled to keep them fresh for the table.

These developments mean that the manufacturers are taking even more care to design their products to suit the customers' needs. It is a development that is spreading to this country. Many of the leading British industrial organizations are branching out in entirely fresh fields, using new light metals and modern techniques.

Master: 'How did your pig cut up, John?' John: 'Well, sir, it didn't weigh so much as I thowt it would and I never thowt it would nayther.'

A Scotswoman hearing of the death of a friend on a neighbouring farm summed her up. 'Eh, but she was a graand wringer out of a dish clout.'

An old roadman found walking to the market town, nine miles away and asked why he did not take the bus, replied, 'I never ahn't bin on nerra motor ner nerra bus, an' as long as I lives I never wunt.'

Little boy, to mother, outside a shop in North Leicestershire: 'They 'enna got non'. 'Wot did yo' say?' 'They 'enna got non'. 'Now yo' say it proper.' 'They een't gor' any.' 'That's better. I'll gie you "*enna*"!'

It is stated that a Sussex shepherd in old-fashioned villages, 'is still buried with a lock of wool upon his beard, in order that when he is brought up for judgment on the Last Day, and the Recording Angel reads out the number of Sundays on which he has been absent from church, the lock of wool shall bear evidence of the need of his calling, and he may be forgiven.'

Her Geraniums and Her Dog

New Letters from Miss Mitford

By the kindness of Miss D. H. Coleman, there came the opportunity of presenting unpublished letters from Miss Mitford which were written to Miss Coleman's grandmother, Mrs. George Price, who was a correspondent also of Leigh Hunt and Walter Savage Landor. Of three letters, two are written two years and the third four years after the publication of 'Our Village'. All are closed by a seal on which the word 'Thanks' is cut. The third letter is about the dog Jerry, brother of Elizabeth Barrett Browning's dog, Flash, to which, it will be remembered, the poet addressed a poem with a note, 'This dog was the gift of my dear and admired friend, Miss Mitford, and belongs to the beautiful race she has rendered celebrated among English and American readers'. The dog appears in 'The Barretts of Wimpole Street' and is the subject of Virginia Woolf's 'Flush, A Biography'.

July 2nd, 1834

My dearest Mrs Price

By to-morrow's Coach you will receive a little basket of geraniums, which I think & hope you will like—They are small plants because the large ones are such bad travellers & they are not so much of the sorts that are accounted the finest & rarest as of those that are my own peculiar pets, because of relying on your very kind & strong feeling towards me I have been afraid that you would rather have my favourites than the nice new flowers of the season which might be got at any nursery ground—I only wish with all my heart that you were here at this moment to see my collection in its full glory—for really it is from care & from high condition & from the contrast between our small cottage & our irregularly beautiful garden, the show of the county.

Such as it is, I am about to run away from it for some weeks. You will perhaps have seen an announcement in the Newspapers of my Tragedy of 'Charles the First' being about to appear at the Victoria Theatre, a small theatre near Waterloo bridge to which the legitimate drama (banished from the Great Houses to make way for Opera & Melodrama) seems to have retreated Mr Knowles having brought out his

Conserving the Countryside

by Thomas Derrick

I—Old English Architecture

last play there and Mr Serle(?) having a Tragedy which is to succeed mine in representation. My Play indeed could not have been done anywhere else, inasmuch as it pleased the pious & moral licensee M. George Colman to refuse to license it some years ago for Covent Garden. Why he did refuse it is best known to himself—inasmuch as the play is of so high-tory a complexion that I have been compelled to apologise in the Preface for some injustice done to Cromwell in the delineation of his character. At the Victoria however the licencee has luckily no power & it will be brought out with every advantage of getting up in scenery, decorations etc., they having closed the Theatre for a fortnight in order to bring it out with the greater care & having engaged a celebrated actress for the Queen, & a provincial actor of great talent for the part of Cromwell.—It will be produced Monday week—the 23rd inst.—& I am as you may imagine full of bustle & anxiety—having still my work to finish, which the necessary preparations for the production of this piece & the journey have greatly retarded. I told you I believe that having sent up my prose book in 1 Vol, Mr Bentley had requested me to add another—so that it will now come out in 2 vols. You may imagine that all this has hurried me exceedingly—& that if I fail at the Victoria I shall suffer much—If I succeed all will go right—for success does always set matters straight let them be ever so crooked.

I am quite sure of your good wishes & if you have any playgoing friends in London pray get them to see 'Charles the First'—It is by far the best thing I ever did. I hope you & Mr Price and my dear little girl are all as well & as happy as I wish you—Better and happier you need not be—My father is thank Heaven in excellent health—He joins in most affectionate regards & I am ever dearest Mrs Price

Most faithfully yours

M. R. MITFORD

July 3rd, 1834

My very dear Mrs Price

From the bottom of my heart do I condole with you on the illness of your excellent husband. I have myself so much faith

32

in youth & an unbroken constitution that I expect as well as hope that he may be restored to you. This summer—indeed the whole year—has been very trying—& many who have been invalided for months are now getting gradually better. That I sincerely trust will be the case with Mr Price. In the meantime be assured of our sweet sympathy.—What comfort as well as pleasure you must have in your dear little girl! We had no seedling this year pretty enough to bear her name— but this next season we shall I think have many—& the very prettiest together with a basket of the new geranium of this year shall be sent to you next May—God grant they may find you as well & as happy as my father & myself desire.

Many thanks for your kind congratulations on the success of my play.—It was a great triumph, having been more praised than anything else that I have written—& praised too by the best judges—But you will I am sure grieve to hear that the Manager decamped without paying me & that the Bill given in payment of the copyright has been dishonoured by the Publishers—so that my journey to London having been necessarily expensive has been a pure loss—& in addition to this grievance (which one who writes for bread cannot but feel) an actor of high genius a protégé of my own who played Cromwell and whose fine performance of that part ensured the success of the piece has been so ill treated by the Manager from a feeling of paltry jealousy that he has left London in despair—I apprehend that many of these evils are attributable to the circumstance of our having brought out the play at a minor theatre (which we were compelled to do on account of its not being licensed), but while it is a miserable exampli-fication of the uncertainties & losses of a literary life—one that I can answer for as being a long scene of anxiety & labour. But for this wretched circumstance of being cheated of the fair profits of my best work nothing could be more brilliantly gratifying than my visit to London—the most splendid of cities—in the very height of the season. I spent about a month there—& although I went to no show parties— nothing but select dinners—I yet for about three weeks dined out every evening with from 20 to 30 distinguished persons— 30 or 40 more coming in the evening—& at the end of that time finding myself in danger of seeing no public places I declined all invitations & went every night to plays & operas, the best private boxes being constantly reserved for me.— Every day I went about sight seeing with one friend & another—& my maid computed that our morning visitors averaged from 60 to 70 persons per diem—In short my dear Mrs Price I saw everything worth seeing in town (where except for a few days in the winter I had not been for nearly five years) & almost everybody—& if my physical powers had been greater I should have enjoyed the thing exceedingly —but it was the excitement & fatigue (for it is no trifle to have three or four clever men talking to you from the moment you get up till you go to bed) were so overpowering that I got to faint away regularly ever afternoon, & when by lying down & other precautions that dangerous habit was conquered, I still suffered so much from feverishness & lassitude that I really believe another week of the same exertion would have sent me home literally 'The Woman killed with kindness'— It was some time before I at all recovered—& even now I am suffering from nervous pains in the face & head which considering all that I have to do are exceedingly incapaci- tating—My dear father thank Heaven is perfectly well. He joins in most affectionate remembrances and good wishes to all, & I am Ever my dear friend Yours very faithfully

M. R. MITFORD

Sept. 14th, 1836

My dear Friend

By coach to-morrow you will receive a very pretty spaniel, Dash's very own relation of whom I can only say that if he prove to you what Dash is to me you will have gained one of the most faithful and intelligent companions in the world.

I sincerely trust that you and dear little May are well and Mr. G. Price and your mother are recovering their health and strength—My father who is quite well joins me in most affectionate regards. Ever my dear friend Most faithfully yours

M. R. MITFORD

The little dog who is going to you is Dash's own son Jerry by name—I would not have let him go to anyone else, but I know that you will be good to him for *his* father's sake and *my* father's sake—and mine—Heaven bless you my dear friend and let us know of Jerry's arrival.

Miss Mitford is again sending geraniums. Further particulars are given of her misadventures in London with her play, 'Charles the First'. We also hear of a novel which is nowadays very little read. It is news that Miss Mitford's preposterous father was a justice of the peace. As before, the author's punctuation is untouched.

Thursday, Dec. 18th, 1834

I so love myself to see flowers bud as well as blow, that I am tempted irresistibly to try the experiment of sending you seven or eight of our most healthy and forward geraniums, as carefully packed as we can to replace the ailing ones. They will show you the conditions of ours—and shall be sent (unless a hard frost comes on) by some one of the innumerable Bath Coaches that pass through Reading. I hope that I have not mistaken your feeling with respect to plants, and that these will prove an amusement not an encumbrance in your windows.

I wish I had a set of my own works to send with them—but I have only the one indispensable copy which every voluminous writer must keep as a book of reference to avoid the danger of repetition. I never have more than six copies in all—therefore only five to give away, and these I am always obliged to send as presents to celebrated authors—so that I never have the high gratification of sending them to the dear friends who would value them for their own sake and for mine.

The play of 'Charles the First' which was so great a success, the visit to London which was really a series of the most brilliant and most genial triumphs in which for above a month I averaged from 60 to 70 morning visitors every day—and saw quite everything and almost everybody worth seeing in that thrice beautiful London—this triumphant success has turned out a great pecuniary loss—the manager of the theatre a bankrupt past extrication when he brought out my play, ran off with the produce—and the bookseller who purchased the copyright has dishonoured his bill! As a climax to this vexation the actor who played Cromwell made so great a success in the part, by far the finest living Tragedian and a very interesting man with an encreasing family is from some theatrical intrigues actually starving in London!—You will not wonder that these calamities added to the loss of many dear friends during this unhealthy autumn should have greatly affected my health. I have been confined to the house these ten weeks with a complaint in my face which they call rheumatism on the nerves and which the least exposure to cold is sure to bring on. God bless you my dear friend. Ever yours.

M. M. MITFORD

My new work is at press. It is in two Vols., 'Belford Regis or Sketches of a Country Town'.

P.S. The plants are packed up, and will certainly be sent by the Reading and Bath coach which leaves Reading a 9 o'clock to-morrow (Friday) morning. I don't know where it puts up. They are well watered and I hope will go safe being ten of my very finest.

No! not musical at all—only very fond of hearing *expressive* singing.

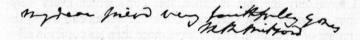

[*Postmarked Reading June 2nd, 1835*]

I received this morning my dear Mrs. Price, your pretty album, and have just written in it some verses 'to my own dear little May'—if you can guess who that may be. I shall send the Album on Saturday—as my father goes to the Reading Bench on that day and will be able to take the parcel himself and see to the booking. I shall send with it a copy of my opera which was less successful than it ought to have been on account of the being brought out in great haste and with disgraceful carelessness and perhaps to its being over-loaded with music good in itself but too monotonous in its character. I think that you will like the poetry and I am rejoiced to have

ARLEY HALL

SOME ENGLISH AND

SCOTTISH MILESTONES

OLD AND NEW, LAVENHAM

an opportunity of sending you one of my productions from the author. Belford Regis has been a great success—if you see it noticed in any paper review or magazine besides the following, it would be a great obligation if you could tell me of the Review, or Magazine and send me the Newspaper, for living out of London it is astonishing how few I see—I have only seen critiques in Tait's magazine—the Athenaeum—the Literary Gazette—the Spectator—the Atlass—the Morning Chronicle—the Morning Post and the Globe—and you know one is naturally anxious to see what the Press says of one's doings especially when as in the present instance one suspects —or knows them to have been well spoken of. I believe it to be better liked and better worth liking than Our Village. Your lady at the Horticultural gave a most pleasing proof of reputation and I thank you very much for telling so prettily so gratifying a story.

My geraniums have run away with all the prizes at our Reading Horticultural Show especially the seedlings—one of which I have called the 'Miss Price'—and she shall have a cutting as soon as I can raise one. It is a most beautiful white blossom. You had better cut down yours and not fresh pot them till the spring—or perhaps the autumn if you find them wanting fresh nourishment—but I should not cut them down until they are quite out of bloom—a month later will be time enough. I am ever my dear friend very faithfully yours.   M. R. Mitford.

The lad who manages my plants says that at all events the geraniums should be new potted in the autumn—when they begin to spring after cutting down—once again God bless you.

ℳ

Woman leaving shop with large parcel under her arm, disgustedly, 'Calls hisself a chiropodist, and says he cannot stuff my poor little dog.'

'A little bit of scientific may be all right,' said a farmer after the lecture, 'but it don't take much of it to spoil a decent farm.'

An old fellow, noted for his nearness, had a journey to make across the moor. He took his boots, a new pair, off, slung them round his neck, and walked bare-foot. In the course of the journey he stubbed his toe against a stone, cutting it badly. All he said was, 'Thank God I hadn't got my boots on.'

The Badger

Tame, by Alys, Countess of Essex

I GOT my badger when she was about a week old, covered with fleas, but after one good dusting with insect powder I never saw a flea on her all the time I had her.

She was the sweetest pet and soon took to her bottle and thrived amazingly. I kept her with me in a box all the time that she was small, taking her wherever I went, and at night had her to my room in order to feed her during the night. She soon learnt to trot about after me, was absolutely clean in the house and had no smell at all. She got on very well indeed with all my dogs and cats, and played the wildest games with a terrier pup much older than herself. She had a passion for coffee, sugar and chocolate cake for a time, but got bored with it, and, towards the end of the time that she was with me, lived almost entirely on cooked beef and raw bacon.

She was always entirely free and came and went in and out of the house as she liked. She made an earth under a tree not far from the house and came in every night for her food. Whenever I wanted her I only had to call down her earth and she would come up.

I had her for fifteen months. One day she did not come in as usual and I have never seen her since, but I have heard on good authority that she has been seen some miles away with a mate. There were no badgers near us, so I suppose she went in search of one. I live in hopes that one day she will return to me, perhaps with a family as charming as herself.

Wild, by Alexander John

I HAVE spent many nights watching the elusive brock. I remember one night an old female badger came up to the mouth of the hole to see if all was clear for her young ones to come out and play. She sat listening, and waving her nose in the air for some time, clearly rather uncertain. Some dogs were barking at the farm, and I thought I heard the closing of the yard gate. Still she sat with raised head, testing the air. Then, like a flash, the badger was down her hole. Not a sound did she make; she just vanished. Five minutes later a man came by, walking quietly away from the farm; he was neither smoking nor singing, yet the badger had become aware of him.

Badgers can be extraordinarily quiet, despite their great size and weight. This fact was well illustrated to me one evening when I arrived rather late at the sett. I was just in time to see a badger cover about twenty yards to his hole over ground strewn with sticks, dead leaves, and chalk-rubble. He moved with a curious gliding action. However when brock believes himself to be unobserved he scratches loudly, and, if old, grunts to himself as he hunts for snails and other delicacies among a large heap of flints behind his front door. The young badgers are even more noisy. They roll and fight on the ground like young puppies, snapping at each other and emitting high-pitched yaps, which remind me of the clucking of a coot or moorhen, or of the first few staccato notes of the blackbird's alarm call. I have never heard older badgers make this curious sound, though I have heard their mating call which is eerie on a dark night. Some of the trees growing in the vicinity of an old sett are scored and torn about two feet from the ground, particularly a yew tree and a whitebeam. One damp night I saw an old badger leave his earth and wander round to the whitebeam, where he stood upon his hind feet and sharpened his foreclaws on the trunk, afterwards playfully tearing away the loose bark, and, incidentally cleaning his teeth.

☙

About a local difference of opinion in Devon: 'There wor a proper upstore in th' village auver it'.

'I canna get no profit out o' mine,' said a cottager about his pig, 'but there I have the muck and the company.'

Said a country paper in an obituary notice, 'She was in her 84th year, and leaves a grown-up family.'

A Cumberland woman was shaking a mat outside her cottage door, in a lethargic manner. The passing cowman cried out, 'Divvent kill't.'

A dispute having arisen as to when a local lad went to Canada, the oldest inhabitant thought for a few minutes and then said, 'Why noo, if they've tonnuped (turniped) t'land as they ought to ha' done, it'll be fowerteen year since.'

Countryside Crack from Scotland
by the Duke of Montrose

OUR WEATHER. It is dominie James Buchanan who keeps the school rain gauge, and wee Erchie, the dux of the school helps him. Just as the cloak of Elijah fell on Elisha, so, benefiting by the wisdom of the dominie, Erchie has come to be recognized as the school weather prophet and professor. Erchie says that on January 2 and 3 1932 we had a rainfall of 3·14 inches; and then to rub it into his class-mates he explains that if all the heavenly water that fell on those two days in the glen (which is 39,000 acres in extent) was collected into the minister's glebe (which is two acres) there would be a loch 3,925 feet deep, and if that loch were frozen into a solid block of ice it would reach to within 150 feet of the top of Ben Nevis (4,266 feet high). My! he is gey gleg in the uptak is wee Erchie the dux.

As a matter of fact this rainfall, heavy though it is, is by no means a record for Scotland. One of the heaviest downpours known was that which occurred between 5 a.m. on August 3, and 5 a.m., August 4, 1829, in Morayshire. There they had 3¾ inches in the 24 hours. Indeed they had 7·36 inches that month and suffered one of the worst floods ever known. The heaviest rainfall does not always cause the worst flood. Much depends on the state of saturation of the soil previously. In October 1827 they had in Morayshire nearly the same rainfall; it was 7·13 inches but the floods were then nothing like the same as in August 1829 when there had been a perpetually wet July.

One of the crofters in describing his experiences of that dreadful night said: 'We pat the wife an' her bit wean and the bairnies into the bed, and the rest got up on to the kists and tables. We pat the girdle on the crook i' the lum an' stuck the lamp on the wa'. But the water soon drooned oot the fire an'

'Its gran' tae hae wark tae dae in these times', writes the busy Duke as this book goes to press. These pieces of his illustrate not only his happy relations with the Doric but some of his many interests. Holder of a title which goes back to the fifteenth century, he has a master mariner's certificate, is vice-president of the Institute of Naval Architects and president of the British Institution of Marine Engineers, the inventor of the first naval aircraft carrying ship, designer of the first heavy seagoing motor ship, and maker of the first film of a total eclipse of the sun.

rose i' the bed. We then pat twa chairs i' the bed, an' pat a
door atween the twa chairs back, and set the wife an' the wee
anes aboon that. But the water it raise and raise till aboot twa
o'clock o' the morn, when it drooned oot the lamp and left
us a' i' the dark. In trowth it was an' awesome nicht yon,
what wi' the roar and ragin' o' the water, the howlin' o' the
win', and the blattering o' the rain without, and the greetin' o'
the wife an' bairns within. A' the kists an' brods were floatin'
aboot, an' a basket o' linen went oot o' the windie foreby an'
aye whammled afore oor een. Aye, we was a' on the brink o'
Eternity yon awfu' nicht'.

In the Isle of Arran we have a yearly rainfall of over 60
inches. It has more than once been as high as 80 inches, but,
because the steep hills slope straight into the sea like the roof
of a house there is no flooding. In Stirlingshire and the middle
counties there are 40 inches a year, and the Carse certainly
'gets saft'. But away on the East Coast in North Berwick and
Nairn 23 to 27 inches will cover the annual rainfall and so
they can and do

> Gowf—an' gowf a' the day,
> Dae'n nothing whatever ava,
> But runnin' aboot wi' a bag o' sticks,
> Efter a wee bit ba'.

WILD GOATS. I was discussing wild animals with Geordie,
my byreman, when he said, 'Yon ramstam camsteerie deevil
frae India is no the on'y body as haes goat's milk tae his
parritch'. As a matter of fact, I believe the Mahatma Gandhi
never took porridge, confining himself solely to fruit and
goat's milk, a beverage which is undoubtedly very rich and
sustaining. In Scotland we have had herds of goats and wild
goats for many generations, but a clear answer has never been
found to the question, 'What is a wild goat?' Between years
1600–1700 droves of goats used to pass through Ross and
Sutherland and Caithness regularly, many beasts being sold
to the cottars as the herds moved along. Some of these
animals escaped from time to time and became wild such as
those on Ben Venue, on Slochd or a Flichity, and their descendants of to-day are erroneously called wild goats.

Undoubtedly there is a genuine wild goat, as there are genuine wild cattle, like those at Cadzow Park in Scotland or at Chillingham in Northumberland. These real wild goats are pure white and can only be seen now in one or two places such as on Creag Mhor, on Ailsa Craig or on the Holy Isle near Arran. The skin of the real wild goat is much sought after for use as an apron for the big drummer of a Highland Regiment. Like the blackcock's tail in the piper's bonnet, it gives distinction and a national atmosphere.

THESE COUNTRY DANCES. Have you ever battled your way through a 'Meg Merrilees', or nearly been flung off your feet in 'Rory o' More', or collapsed on a seat after twenty minutes of 'Strip the Willow'? If you have you will know the beauty and the happiness, not to mention the physical benefit of belonging to a Country Dance Class. We have quite a lot of these classes in Scotland, and Lord James Stewart Murray is the energetic president of the movement. Classes are got together anywhere, and competent instructors or instructresses to teach the proper movements are provided by a central organization. Branches flourish in Edinburgh, Glasgow, Perth and Stirling, and dances have been held in many a neighbouring village. Ladies and gentlemen, the right side of forty and the wrong, battle together through the mazes of 'Jenny cam doon tae Jock', 'The Fight about the Fireside', 'The Eight Men of Moidart' or 'The rock an' the wee pickle tow'. These square dances, or processional dances, certainly offer a splendid change from the two-step, the waltz or the reel. I have seen a programme with eighteen different dances on it, and the variety did not detract in any way from the pleasure of the evening. On the whole these dance clubs give a lot of fun, and elderly persons with a spark of life in them get an opportunity of joining with younger members of the community on festive occasions. The country dance class movement deserves encouragement in all rural districts and it helps to preserve ideas and customs.

Ancient farm worker, invited by his mates to contribute to a discussion on the pros and cons of marriage: 'What I says is, a wife's there if you want 'er—and she's there if you don't want 'er'.

The First Migratory Bird Marking Station in Britain, by R. M. Lockley

WE had long considered how we could best get to know individually the small birds of the island. Experience in putting numbered rings on the legs of our swallows had already proved that these birds had deceived us in the past. We had ringed our breeding pair and their brood one summer, expecting them to come back as usual the next year. With April, the swallows returned, thousands of them streaming northwards, unheeding the open windows of the pony's stable, on a beam in which last year's nest still lay unharmed. Then, in May, a pair suddenly swung in and out of the little shed, in a day or two carrying mud pellets to build a new nest at the other end of the beam. We let them settle down to egg-laying before closing the windows one night and catching them with the aid of a torch and handnet. I had not brought any rings, only my notebook to jot down the old numbers of the rings of last year which they would surely be wearing. It proved, however, that only one bird wore a ring, and the number of that ring bore no relation to the numbers of those placed on the legs of last year's pair of young! The number on it proved the bird to have been ringed as a passing migrant (a juvenile too!) caught in the wheelhouse in the previous August! The other bird was an individual quite new to us.

The value of ringing grew to be more and more obvious. It seemed to us essential that we should know every pipit, wheatear, hedge-sparrow and blackbird on the island, or at least be able to distinguish them from passing migrants of the same species. Was the hedge-sparrow that stole crumbs from the kitchen doorway the same bird each day? We became uneasy about even this, detecting imaginary differences of poise and behaviour. When a tail-less hedge-sparrow began to alternate with a normal individual the point was considered

Some of Lockley's earliest work appeared in the *Countryman*, and extracts from it are to be found in his widely read books, among which may be mentioned *Dream Island*, *The Island Dwellers*, *Island Days*, *I Know an Island*, *Island Farm*. He is an authority on shearwaters, on which he has written a volume, and on other sea birds. This article was written in 1934.

proved. We determined henceforth to catch all the birds that came to the house and garden, and to mark them with rings. At the same time we longed to be able to catch and ring the many migratory species that used the island garden as a halting place. The percentage of recoveries of birds ringed in the British Isles is round about three. We argued that we had only to ring one hundred to get our first results. Actually the sea-birds we have ringed have given better results, our cormormants leading with 40 per cent recoveries, chiefly reported from France. But would the small warblers be so profitable? We should see.

How to proceed? To-day the number of traps for catching birds is legion, whether we look at the ironmonger's catalogue of the bird-catcher's requirements or at the extensive 'bird-banding' literature of America. The average trap, however, does not come up to the standard required on a storm-swept island. It must be proof, not only against gales, but against sheep, ponies, and above all, goats. This was our first problem. There were two solutions, both rather disquieting: either to erect a four-strand barbed wire fence around the contrivance or to place the trap in our garden. In my mind I had already chosen the second solution, but as yet I dare not be bold about it to Doris. I could not see quite how to avoid breaking up her flower beds. I had as well the rather absurd idea (as I think now) that the flaming red and pink and white of the Shirley poppies, the orange and purple of the nasturtiums, the yellow and gold of the marigolds, and the azure and deep blue of the borage and love-in-the-mist would act as so many warning colours to the birds I wanted to catch, and so frighten them away. (Is there anything in this notion? We all know that finches will devour the seeds of brightly-coloured garden flowers, and sparrows will tear the petals of the crocus, but readers might well consider whether they have ever seen small insectivorous birds frequenting vivid flower masses). Our garden is so small that every inch is planned out and I was planning to drop into it a contrivance as large and as ugly as a small bird aviary at the zoo. It was indeed to be our small bird aviary, with this difference, that the birds could fly in and out at will, only that in return for the shelter and food and

44

water provided they must wear a ring for the rest of their lives.

I feel that it was a strategic move to suggest that if we placed the netting of my contrivance over the currants, gooseberries and strawberries the fruit would be more sheltered than ever from the salt wind, from the occasional incursion of leaping goats and from the birds themselves. I even suggested—shameless hypocrisy—that when the fruit was ripe we could shut the trap altogether and so save the fruit whole from the birds. This proved too transparent, for Doris knew well enough that there were only two blackbirds and their youngsters to eat our summer fruit. I did not pursue this line further or mention that at night my dreams were of the migrating armies of green and yellow warblers which were to swarm to the currants inside the trap and be caught and ringed.

The next thing was to decide on the shape and size of the contrivance. Something on the principle of the Heligoland trap seemed the only thing, a contrivance with a wide entrance leading to a roofed-in funnel, this in turn tapering to a box into which the birds are driven. It would be, in fact, a miniature of that famous trap, but much adapted to the peculiar shape and lie of our garden. I sought advice from other ornithologists. There was no Heligoland trap yet erected in the British Isles. In the end the scanty knowledge I could glean came from the few books loaned by friends.

The greatest height at the entrance is eight feet. The cost of the one roll of $\frac{5}{8}$-inch six foot netting 22-gauge, which we used, was £2 14s. 8d. Add to this the cost of staples, nails, tying wire, hinges, plate glass, etc., and the figure of £4 covers our total cost in materials. All the wood came from the sea. For the guiding fence I used some one-inch mesh netting.

By the time Doris and I had sunk the posts—it was a hot August day in hot 1933—our hardened skins were scorched and blistered. All the white willow warblers had fluttered about us, perching on posts and tools alike. Now when we threw down spade and saw at 9 p.m., they dropped away one by one to sleep in the bracken beyond the wall and perhaps to rise up in the night and fly on to Africa. 'To-morrow, if they are here,' I declared, 'we'll catch every one of them, as soon as we get the netting laid.' The willow warblers seemed to be waiting for us to finish, so tame were they. The gaunt skeleton of the trap, with the bushes beneath, was to them the nearest approach to a spinney the island could provide. Curiously enough, as the netting-over drew near to completion they appeared shyer. Towards evening the few that found themselves enclosed grew more and more agitated and at last escaped through the open ends. So does the wild bird fear restraint! It was dark when the last selvedge was nailed home and the last stone laid upon the netting where it touched the wall (for we had economized considerably by using the garden wall along the whole of one side of the trap).

August 6th proved so hot and still that it was the hardest fight not to go on with the work. But there was no wash on the rocks; even the Wild Goose Race was scarcely rippled and there were obligations to holidaying friends. We spent the whole day with the gannets on far-off Grassholm. Refreshed, the morning of the 7th saw all hands on the island at work. The construction of a suitable catching box involved

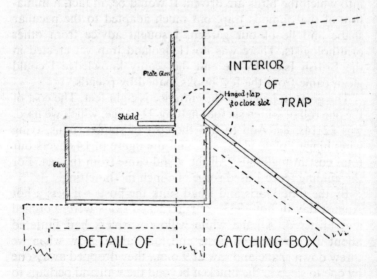

much discussion. The detail of the catching-box shows how we made it in the end. We proposed to work the trap after this manner. All the birds possible around the house and buildings having been manœuvred over the wall and into the garden, three or two of us entered the garden. We walked down into the mouth of the trap, gently stirring the bushes and vegetables in front of us with bamboos as we advanced. The birds flew ahead of us and under the netting and, finding their retreat cut off, continued down the avenue to the glass above the box. Fluttering against this they dropped down through the slot into the box itself. One person followed up and, as a precaution against birds attempting to double back or refusing to enter the box, dropped the trap door in the roof behind him, thus enclosing himself and the birds in this narrow end of the trap. He made sure that all the birds were in the box by first shaking the bushes about him and next by lifting the flap over to shut the slot over the box. He then re-set the trap by hitching the trap door up to the roof again, and made his exit by the side door.

It remained now to collect the birds. The box containing them was gently pulled out until the slot was exactly under the wooden shield (whose purpose—to cover the open slot temporarily—is obvious). In this position the special slide was inserted in the grooves of the box. The box was now bird-proof and could be moved clear of the shield. The slide was opened sufficiently to allow the insertion of the operator's arm, this aperture being controlled by the other hand, and the birds were easily caught as they fluttered against the glass in the box. In theory one carried the box into the house to do the examining and ringing. In practice we found it better for the birds and simpler for us to put our captures in a special pocket I wore in my jacket and to reset the trap there and then. This was done without re-entering it. The slot flap was thrown open from outside, the box slide drawn and the box

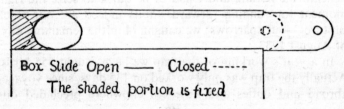

Box Slide Open ——— Closed ------
The shaded portion is fixed

placed beneath the plate glass once more. I always carried the birds into the house in my pocket, to examine and ring them behind closed windows, since if they escaped before ringing they would fly to these and be re-caught at once. In the dark recesses of my pocket they were perfectly quiet.

Actually it was eight o'clock that evening before we were ready for the inaugural drive. Willow warblers had been conspicuously scarcer but a beat of the ragwort and nettles outside the garden put up several. Five were foolish enough to take cover in the garden and were gently driven into the mouth of the trap. They flew down over the bushes, fluttered against the glass and dropped into the box as to the manner born. G. C. S. Ingram ringed the first bird and declared open this the first migratory bird marking station in the British Isles.

In the succeeding days of August we caught five or six birds each day. I did not strive to catch faster than that, remembering the cost of the rings. Neither had I the time to sit in the windows of the house and wait all day for birds to visit the garden. We just looked at the trap every time we passed the garden and ringed what we could walk up into it. I could also watch from my bed each morning. Soon after sunrise the roof netting of the trap would bristle with birds supercharged with morning vigour. Pipits would run over the fine mesh at great speed, snapping up the drowsy flies as they rose from their sleeping places in the folds of the currant leaves and collided with the wires. In their exuberance the birds chased each other, the pursuit often ending up inside the trap. This was my opportunity. I would leap out of bed, run down the loft ladder and out into the garden. Often the pipits and wheatears beat me; they are so volatile, disliking cover and able to rise perpendicularly. They would flash playfully in and out beneath the netting and I had to be quick to seize the right moment for running forward. Pipits indeed are our stock captures—our sparrows; we caught 74 in the remaining days of August 1933.

In a year's working of the trap we have caught 555 birds. Actually the trap was only worked on 135 days, since voyages abroad and duties and absences elsewhere precluded our working it oftener. The exact figures for the various birds caught are 164 meadow pipits, 93 hedge-sparrows, 83 rock pipits, 35 wheatears (including a few of the large Greenland race), 32 chaffinches, 30 willow-warblers, 25 blackbirds, 22 whitethroats, 14 robins, 7 white wagtails, 6 sedge-warblers, 6 wrens, 6 chiffchaffs, 5 spotted flycatchers, 4 pied wagtails, 4 greenfinches, 4 stonechats, 2 black redstarts, 2 song thrushes, 2 pied flycatchers, 2 yellow wagtails, 2 water-pipits, and one each of ring-ouzel, garden warbler, yellow bunting, cuckoo, and turtle dove. Several young puffins, shearwaters, and storm-petrels, struggling towards the sea at night, blundered into the trap and hid themselves inside the catching box during the day. These were not counted officially in the trap records, but were entered elsewhere in our lists of sea-birds ringed. We released them in the harbour where they eagerly splashed into the sea, their only safe refuge at fledging time.

The situation of the trap at the far end of the garden in full view of the windows of the house was ideal (from my point of view). At meals one sat with the windows wide open, ready to spring through them whenever a bird appeared in the currant bushes. On rainy days I was not unnaturally looked upon askance for my muddy boots when I returned with my captures to the house. To obviate this it became necessary to lay the stone walk from the window to the trap (see diagram). At the end of the walk we sank a shallow concrete drinking and bathing pool. This brought us the wagtails. It was a pleasure to handle several of the beautiful and rare white race of our common pied bird, to ring them and to wish them good flying on their journey from Iceland to tropical Africa. Other happy moments were experienced on the capture of a fine cock ring-ouzel, splendidly adorned with white gorget and all his brown-black feathers ringed with grey. The turtle dove was easily walked into the trap; the cuckoo took us nearly an hour to manœuvre into the bushes. But an adult cuckoo in the hand is worth all that trouble—and more. The water pipits were our greatest rarities. Had it not been for our taking them in the trap they might have passed unnoticed among the hundreds of other pipits in the island, since we caught them in the autumn when their distinctive pinkish underparts, grey head and white eye stripe are inconspicuous or absent.

We quickly ringed the residents—blackbirds, dunnocks and meadow-pipits. After being caught three or four times in as many days they became more wily. They saved us the trouble of handling them by shooting out over our heads as soon as we approached the trap. Hence we knew that any bird escaping so brazenly was already ringed. In walking round the island six months after the erection of the trap it was interesting to find that almost every small bird wore a ring. Even the habitués of the lighthouse gardens, a mile from ours, were labelled, proving that they, too, had paid their respects to our garden. We learnt much from this, and, had we had the time to spare, would have made a study of these local movements by using Mr. Boardman's coloured rings to identify individuals in the field.

As an experiment the trap has been very successful. There is an ideal spot in the sunk ground below the island well where we think the erection of a full-sized Heligoland trap would yield four times the number of birds we have caught, but we shall move cautiously in this matter. We in the British Isles are not blessed, as are the workers on Heligoland, by a benevolent Ministry of Education which finances such research and ringing schemes and maintains a scientifically equipped and staffed bird observatory. In contrast with the far-sightedness of the German Ministry, our own recently withdrew the only contribution it has made to the study of economic ornithology, leaving it once more in the hands of struggling private enterprise. It is all the more encouraging, therefore, to find that under Mr. Witherby's 'British Birds' Marking Scheme, British workers have ringed as many birds as have the Germans at Heligoland and at the several places in Europe where Heligoland rings are used; while the percentage of recoveries of British ringed birds is higher than that of Germany. We need, however, to emulate our Continental friends by establishing permanent ringing stations in this country at places on the coast where migration is most in evidence.

Fifty-one ringers marked between 100 and 1,000 birds each, and others ringed under 100, making up to 1933, 38,441 birds ringed.

Work at a migratory bird marking station is extraordinarily interesting. A second station has been opened by R. M. Garnett who has commenced to trap migrants at Blakeney in Norfolk. A third has just been established on the Isle of May by permission of the Commissioners for Northern Lights who own this lonely island in the Firth of Forth. It is being run under the auspices of the Midlothian Ornithological Club, two of whose members (H. F. D. Elder and E. V. Watson), together with W. B. Alexander of Oxford and the writer, spent a fortnight in October 1934 erecting a Heligoland trap there. It took us a week of solid work to complete the structure, which, although larger, is as far as essential details are concerned, a replica of that on Skokholm already described. In anticipation of having to cope with large rushes of migrants, the catching box was made larger, with a grill to prevent hawks from mingling with smaller birds. The whole is excellently situated at the higher end of a valley sheltered from the prevailing west winds. Birds may be driven some three or four hundred yards from the lowest part of this valley towards and into the mouth of the trap. If and when the bushes of elder, currant, furze, gooseberry, raspberry, etc., which we planted grow, the trap should be a great attraction to weary migrants. For the time being we have provided temporary cover in the shape of branches of deciduous and evergreen trees, their ends thrust into the ground, grouped together, both along the approaches to and inside the structure. Since all the materials for the May trap had to be bought the total cost of the structure will not be far short of £20. This sum and other amounts for the maintenance and working of the trap have to be raised by voluntary subscription. The Midlothian folk hope to arrange for a sequence of volunteer observers to man their station at the migration periods.

The Isle of May is ornithologically renowned for the work of the Misses Rintoul and Baxter, who, over a series of visits in past years, have 'secured' a number of birds rare and even new to the British list. Probably none deplored this systematic shooting more than these Scottish naturalists themselves, but it seemed inevitable if the valuable study of migration they had set themselves to make was to be carried out thoroughly. However distinct the races and allied forms of a single species may be in the hand, they are often difficult to distinguish in the field, but in the past far too many 'doubtful' birds have been shot in the hope of securing one rarity, by the snipers among ornithologists. To-day the excuse to shoot no longer exists at a bird marking station. The bird must be worked into the trap, examined, ringed and released. Under this modern and humane method the study of birds becomes a pure delight.

During the last few days of our stay on May we were able to operate the trap. Although owing to a strong west wind, there was little movement among the birds, we caught migrant goldcrests, stonechats, a Greenland wheatear, robins, wrens, rock pipits and a brambling. We also ringed the resident blackbirds, thrushes and hedge-sparrows. One of the latter proved, however, to be of the Continental race, the salient points of difference so obvious in the hand that we began to feel that, with a little more experience, we should soon detect them in the field. If the west wind kept away the hordes of winter migrants from Scandinavia expected to reach May at that time, it did at least blow to us one very rare visitor from far north-western shores. We had frequently seen mealy redpolls. For a week two of them, very tame, frequented one of the lighthouse gardens. One of these was both larger and darker than the other, and we were frankly puzzled. At last, it came to the trap, entered the avenues of artificial cover and was swiftly driven into the box. It proved to be a Greenland redpoll, the first to be recorded on the east side of Britain and doubtless the first to be ringed and released on British soil. In these two instances alone the May trap justified its existence within a few days of its erection.

*

An extra farm hand was noticed eyeing a ladder. Said the foreman, 'That's a bit heavier than the one you pinched, Ned.' 'I didn't pinch un,' was the reply; 'I only took un.'

FRANK TWEEDIE AND THE BIRDS
(*From the painting by G. W. Lennox Paterson*)

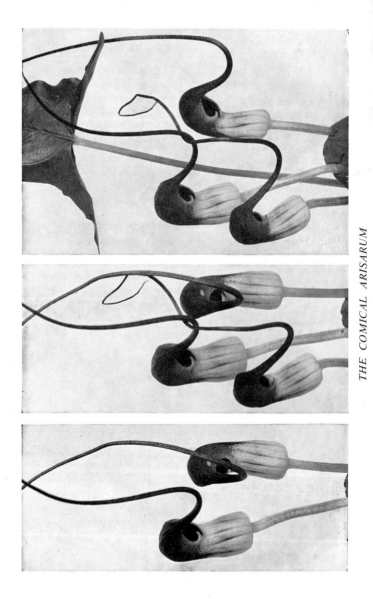

Elegy, by Sylvia Townsend Warner

HERE, where the ale and pewter stream
Pours its strong limbs along the rock
And dives into the pool,
To bask beneath the netted gleam
Of airy woodland breathing cool,
The charabangers flock.

They lay themselves about the sward
In a constraint of ease, unpack
Face-powder, food and drink.
Some read, some stare, some smoke to ward
The flies away, some from the brink
Call the charmed children back.

Small peace of mind is theirs, and when
The given hour has gone they climb
Meek on their monstrous coach;
For the spirits of mechanic men
Feel inwardly as a reproach
Weight of unmoving time.

Yet as the wheels devour the road,
Out of their cloister-cage of speed
Already they look back:
It seems there was unloosed a load,
Released a dream, made good a lack,
Souls with free water freed,

Where, when the sensitive resort
With chiding foot they thrust away
Torn flowers from field and moor,
Crumbs, paper, orange-peel, the short
And simple annals of the poor
Who've spent their holiday.

The home of this charming, spirited, plainspoken writer, who lived for a time at Idbury, is in Dorset. Her books—who does not know *Lolly Willowes, Mr. Fortune's Maggot* and *Whether a Dove or a Seagull* (with her friend Valentine Ackland)?—are like no one else's. It is characteristic of her to put in front of the list of her novels and poems in *Who's Who* 'Member of Tudor Church Music Editorial Committee and Member of Executive Committee of Association of Writers for Intellectual Liberty'. There is an article of hers on page 136.

My Cottage and My Garden

by Sir Austen Chamberlain

I

MY own cottage and garden in Sussex are, alas! mine no longer, though I am glad to know that they have passed to the possession of another garden lover who cherishes the little garden as I used to do. The cottage stands where two lanes meet. Its framework, if you could see it, is exactly like that of the farmer's great barn opposite—huge oak timbers such as went to the building of the old wooden navy, some straight or bent with age, some curved by the natural growth of the tree, but all hewed and squared with the axe and adze; no saw or plane has spoiled their beauty. Between the balks of timber it is wattle and daub, but one side has been clapboarded against the south-westerly storms and the opposite one, facing the lane, is half-brick half-tile. The old tile roof sags and wavers with the yielding of the beams. Just to the right of the cottage and shadowing the north-west corner is a magnificent old yew. As we pass in through the little wicket gate and up the short brick path, you will see, in spring, hyacinths or polyanthus in the narrow borders on either side, to be followed later by some bedding-out plants—almost the only ones I allow myself, for the garden is to need as little labour as possible—out of which will rise in turn two healthy groups of scarlet martagon lilies and another group of the new hybrid martagons which tempted me at one of the Royal Horticultural Society's shows. Over the front of the house ampelopsis and wistaria creep, a pyrocanthus breaks the line and cotoneaster horizontalis, beloved of the bees, half hides an ugly water-spout; but what I pride myself upon is the narrow border, scarcely a foot wide, which runs along the house. Snowdrops (Elwesii) and winter aconite give me my first flowers here; then comes a clump or two of narcissus; but the moment to see it is when it is one mass of anemone apennina with primula cashmeriana thrust-

Sir Austen was Foreign Secretary 1924–1929. The article was written in 1932.

ing up its purple globes among their blue stars.

Under the yew tree, by adding some good soil and plenty of old mortar rubble, I have flourishing colonies of cyclamen coum for spring and cyclamen europeum for autumn, when its scent carries me in fancy to Italian woods about Bologna where I have picked up great bunches of them to brighten up the old Brun's hotel. Hepaticas, our own wild wood anemones and crocuses, help out the seasons. But come round to the southerly side of the cottage. Here against the clapboarding grows wistaria again, but the nurseryman sent one so pale in hue that it scarcely shows against the white paint and reminds me that flowering plants should be selected when they are in flower. A good Pyrus japonica gives on the other hand a blaze of colour and a purple clematis, which I cut down nearly to within a foot of the ground, is covered with blossom twice in the summer. The yellow jasmine nudiflorum flowers in January with iris stylosa at its feet and a white jasmine scents the rooms in mid-summer. Here too I find room for Carpenteria californica and choysia and the Californian fuschia (Zauschneria).

The flagged terrace is supported by a low wall of loose stone not more than two to three feet high. Amidst the flags grow thyme and pinks (D. deltoides and graniticus) campanula pusilla, hypericum coris; grape hyacinths and other things have found their way along the cracks from the narrow ribbon border that tops the low wall.

The border at the top of the wall is kept for low and early flowering plants. Here you will find Iris pumila in four or five shades, I. histrioides and reticulata and tulipa clusiana and linifolia with mossy saxifrages to follow. There are just two bushes of Daphne mezerium to break the low line, and a fine specimen of D. cneorum, which later loads the air with its scent of honey, and a little bush of plumbago larpentae carry on the interest later in the year. The wall itself is kept mainly for saxifrages of the pyramidalis type which did extraordinarily well, but the male fern has seeded itself in the crevices and threatens to become a nuisance.

I know nothing more lovely among tulips for the rock garden than the two species which I have mentioned. The scarlet linifolia increased with me and I grew it from seed, but T. clusiana had a sad tendency to 'dwindle', as a farm-hand I once knew used to say of his young turkeys. I retain, however, a warm affection for it, which is partly a tribute to its own delicate beauty and partly to my own vanity.

When I first went to Geneva, in early March, 1925, to represent Great Britain on the Council of the League of Nations, I visited Dr. Correvon's famous Alpine garden. It was too early for flowers but a gardener loves to see plants growing only one degree less than to see them blossoming. Whilst walking round I happened to remark upon a group of T. clusiana whose leaves were pushing up, though the buds were not yet showing. Later the same day an English lady went to see the garden and Dr. Correvon mentioned my visit. 'Ah!' said the lady, 'you have had the Minister for Foreign Affairs here? It is a great honour for your garden.'

'Minister of Foreign Affairs, pooh!' exclaimed the Doctor. 'There is a Minister of Foreign Affairs in every country, but there is only one who can identify Tulipa clusiana by its leaves.'

The story spread (shall I confess? I helped to spread it) and my reputation was made. There was one subject at least of which I knew more than my colleagues!

A second terrace, grassed this time and supported by a rather higher wall, finds room in the border at the top for half-a-dozen species of Cistus. These lasted through several winters, but it is wise to take cuttings every year or two and nurse them through the winter in a frame lest a spell of specially hard weather destroy the established plants. Here I had a bit of luck. I thought this would be a good place to put a plant of Hypericum (Hookeri, I think) in my first autumn and found when I dug my hole that I was among roots which in my inexperience I did not recognise. They turned out to be a darkish orange Alstroemeria and grew up through and around the Hypericum, making a colour combination on which I received many compliments.

The wall below this terrace was kept mainly for aubretia, alyssum, helianthemums and erodiums, but some white foxgloves seeded themselves between the stones at one end.

I am not going to show you my rose-garden in front of the oast house, for it was not very successful, nor my border of flowering shrubs and trees, for though I dug the whole of it (and it lay on a belt of stiff clay) three times over with my own hands in one year, I could never rid it of the squitch, bindweed, ground elder and all the other poisonous weeds with brittle ramping roots which had taken hold of it in war time. I have only one word of advice to give to anyone so situated. Clear the border, summon all your patience, disregard appearances and plant potatoes on the ground till you have got it clean; and do this before, not after, your cherries, pyrus, crabs, lilacs, berberis and the like have begun to grow and make shapely bushes or trees. Once that has happened, you will never have the heart to disturb them. By the thorough policy you will eradicate the weeds. Nor need we linger at the herbaceous border. Let us go straight to my rock garden, or, as I would have you call it, my Alpine garden, for my purpose was to grow the Alpine flowers, not merely to repeat the aubretias and alyssums of the wall.

II

It must be nearly forty-five years ago that, one Sunday morning, when my father and I were visiting Kew Gardens, under the auspices of the late Sir Thistleton-Dyer, he took us into one of the enclosures where, he said, he had something new to show us. The novelty was an unheated greenhouse filled with pans of Alpine plants. I remember saying to my father as we drove back that if I ever had a garden of my own, I should not attempt to grow orchids but that I must have an Alpine house. Thirty or more years passed before I owned a garden; by then much more was known of Alpine plants and their cultivation, and I determined to have a rock, or as I prefer to call it, an Alpine garden instead of the house. A house would require daily care and watering, and I could visit my cottage only at week-ends.

Thus when I obtained my cottage the first thing to decide was where to place the Alpine garden. Below the terrace, the lawn, whose earlier use as an orchard was recalled by two old apple trees still standing in its midst, sloped down to a hedge

57

in which a stile gave access to a small field. But the hedge was not parallel to the house, and the shrubbery border on one side of the lawn was not parallel to the yew hedge which divided it from the kitchen garden on the other, so that the lawn formed an ugly rhomboid. This was corrected at the sides by the realignment of the shrubbery border, giving room for a herbaceous border in front of the flowering trees and shrubs, and at the bottom by planting a yew hedge parallel to the terraces, in front of which we placed a herbaceous border, broken in the centre by a wide grass walk leading to the stile. Between the two hedges there was now an elongated triangle. To the right of the grass walk my wife made a small sunk garden filled with polyantha roses; the left and larger section I chose for the site of the Alpine garden which would thus be hidden from the house by the yew hedge as soon as it had grown about four feet high.

There, then, was the site, not perfect but not a bad one. The next thing was to make the garden. My first attempt was a failure, though I put up with it for two or three years. I did not know what I wanted beyond the fact that I wanted a rock garden. I did not know what was necessary except rocks. I called in a local man and said, 'Make me a rock garden and let me have rocks, not pebbles'. He fulfilled my requirements with good-sized blocks of the local sandstone, and at first I was very pleased with the effect. I visited spring shows, pored over catalogues and planted enthusiastically and optimistically, but my plants did not grow. I could repeat the easier successes of the terraces, but the things which I most wanted to see succeed dragged out a miserable existence or died upon my hands. Only two things do I recall as making really fine specimens; these were a Lithospermum prostratum, heavenly blue, for which I chanced upon just the right position at the top of a big rock with a cool root run down the back of the stone into deep earth. In two years or so it had covered the top and hung three feet or more down the rock face. The other success was provided by two plants of Anemome sulfurea which will appear again in this story. But of drainage and soil and how to place the rocks I had thought little and knew less. It was all to begin again. The experiment had cost something,

58

but it had taught me much. I wrote some articles, was fortunate in finding favour with a generous editor and accumulated a sufficient sum to start afresh. This time I knew what I wanted and I found the right man to understand my ideas and supply my deficiencies. The rules for an Alpine garden are:

1. See that the drainage is good.

2. See that the soil is suitable and that in different places you have the various kinds which you will require.

3. The rocks should be large. Like icebergs, only the smaller part of them should appear above the surface.

4. Let the soil be well rammed down around and between them so that no holes are left in which the roots as they grow fail to find sustenance. The builder knew all this as well as I did, and it was a pleasure to see him and his foreman handling and placing the great rocks. The largest weighed nearly 15 cwt.

I chose weather-worn limestone for the stone and I express my desiderata as follows:

1. I must have a cliff-face with northerly or cool exposure.

2. I wanted a peat-bog.

3. There must be a low Alpine meadow and

4. A high Alpine meadow.

5. There must be a moraine or scree.

6. The new garden must somehow be built around my beautiful Anemone sulfurea. They were doing too well to be disturbed.

I rejected the idea of a pool, for I felt there was not room for one, but I jumped at the suggestion of a rhododendron forest. In the end the garden was all my fancy had painted; but here you must use your imagination. My rhododendron forest consisted at first of two, later of three R. ferrugineum and three dwarf Himalayan hybrids. Daphne Blaygayana flourished among them. Give it a cool peaty root-run and throw a stone at it whenever you pass. It likes these rough love-makings and will reward you for them with its sweet waxy flowers in early spring. Androsace lanuginata trailed over the rock in front.

I had not one but two cliffs, each some three feet high, and at the bottom a peat bed kept moist by drainage from the rocks and path. In the ledges and crannies of the cliffs I grew Primula marginata, Wilsoni, viscosa and some garden varieties, but Wilsoni never, I think, survived more than three winters. In the peat were P. rosea (this seeded itself freely and would grow in any damp shady spot in the path at the base of a rock), P. chionantha, involucrata and others, besides Orchis foliosa, Cyprepedium calceolaria and Pyrola rotundi-folia, both collected by me in Switzerland, and Parochaetus communis with a leaf like clover and a pea-shaped flower of the blue of G. verna. I name only enough flowers to give an idea of what I was striving for and the results obtained.

The low Alpine meadow, say 12 feet by 8, made a good place for Alpine crocuses and tulips and a small scilla collected on the cliffs of Newquay and Brittany. These were followed by Anemone fulgens, and a marvellous magenta-coloured variety brought home by Lady Chamberlain from Palestine. Later came A. narcissiflora looking like apple blossom in bud, A. Alpina and sulfurea, and the yellow globe flower. The first time I saw A. sulfurea it was a single plant in a pocket of a great moss-grown limestone boulder beside a flooded mountain stream in the Pyrenees and my heart leapt with delight. The first time I saw A. Alpina was when making an excursion in the Jura with Dr. Correvon. It grew so thick that in the distance I took it for a large patch of snow. Then I added the great yellow gentian and other plants of like size and similar habit. There was hardly one of these which I had not collected myself, and the memory of the places in which they were found added to one's delight in seeing them grow and flourish.

The high Alpine meadows were on a smaller scale; they were intended first and foremost for G. verna, but I always tried to get a succession of flowers if possible, and I convinced myself by experience that except in the case of those which live in some tight cranny of the rocks, it is a mistake to plant one's precious things apart, as, in his anxiety for their safety, the amateur is apt to do. Think of the close short turf of the high Alpine meadow where you find G. verna in masses. It is never alone; it has to fight its way up and down through the turf itself and in and out among G. acaulis, Primula frondosa, violas and I know not what other small beauties. They grow so thickly that you cannot put your foot down without treading on several kinds, and they will be more likely to succeed in your garden if you make them fight for existence with plants of their own size as nature does. I planted Narcissus minimus, Androsace carnea and chamaejasme, viola bicolor, Dianthus neglectus and such-like things with mine. But G. verna is notoriously contrariwise. After all the best patch I ever saw in cultivation, two feet across each way and a sheet of blue like cloudless Italian sky on a summer day, grew within five miles of the centre of Birmingham. I asked the gardener how he managed it. 'I grow them from seed,' he said, 'and prick them out.' He did not appear to be aware that he had accomplished anything out of the ordinary. He had boxes of the seedlings in a frame. There is a variety of G. verna called angulata, which is a trifle larger in leaf, though otherwise indistinguishable to anyone but a botanist, which I found easier to grow.

There are few joys like a garden and in a small garden none which gives such constant interest and light occupation as an Alpine garden. In my own every plant after the first twenty or so was planted and tended by me. It is the amateur's garden par excellence, for after this first making it requires no heavy spadework, whilst the plants have character and individuality and require constant attention and skilled treatment.

III

It is astonishing how much there is to say about a small Alpine garden. I have yet to deal with my screes, for in the end there were two of them, one less exposed to the full sunshine than the other. Both contained more chips than earth (indeed, I suppose the proportion was at least as ten to one) with limestone and granite mixed in varying proportions. Obviously the scree is the place for the Kabschia and Engleria saxifrages and many other treasures. Here, too, I grew Drabas, Hutchinsia alpina, Ranunculus Seguieri, a lovely thing, Geranium Plyzowianum, to be watched closely lest it spread too far; its clear pink flowers prolong your flowering season. Papaver alpinum, orange and white, and Linaria alpina flourished in the scree and seeded regularly. Wahlenbergia Pumilio with its grey leaves and lovely purple flowers sitting close down to the ground was another favourite, easily increased by cuttings. In the scree too I tried Omphalodes Lucillae with its grey-blue leaves and feathery tufts of forget-me-not flowers of the palest porcelain blue shot with pink lights. The precise spot between two rocks had been specially made for it by an expert, but it slowly faded away. Then I found that admirable gardener, Mr. Hay of the Royal Parks, growing it as a bedding-out plant! He was kind enough to give me some plants and reveal the secret of his success—stiff loam and well-rotted cowdung. Yet the plant comes from the hot limestone mountains of Greece and Asia Minor. To the four things which the compiler of the Book of Proverbs did not understand, he would, had he been a gardener, have added a fifth: the way of rock plants in cultivation. The best plant of Douglasia Vitaliana, a peat lover, which I ever had, grew into a fat cushion five or six inches across from a tiny slip which in ignorance or absent-mindedness I planted at the head of my limestone scree. Indeed I am disposed to say that whilst the scree is no place for any coarse thing, it is worth while to try in it any precious plant which has refused to do elsewhere.

It is a great advantage if you can water Alpines and especially the scree plants from below. In their native haunts, some sit in crevices on a steep rock-face where no rain lies and draw their moisture from the cool stones into which their roots penetrate deeply. Others sleep all winter under deep snow. They burst into life and blossom with amazing rapidity when the snows melt, but all through the hot summer their roots draw moisture from the water trickling just below the surface of the ground. In this country it is not possible to reproduce these conditions exactly; the raw damp days of February when the air is cold and laden with moisture are apt to be particularly deadly, especially to plants with hairy leaves. But something may be done to lessen their trials; a sheet of glass in winter is not a pretty object, but it is not at that time that you take your friends to admire your rock garden and the gardener in those months may well decide that safety first is his appropriate slogan whatever it may be for a political party. In any case let him try underground watering. If he has the conveniences or does not mind the cost, let him lay a leaden water-pipe with a few pin-prick holes in it under his garden. If, like me, he has not the convenience and is unwilling to face the expense, there is a simple alternative within everyone's means. Get a few two-inch agricultural drain-pipes; sink them vertically in the ground till their tops are only an inch or less above the surface, and hide them with a rock—the only one allowed to lie loose on the surface—or by a larger plant and, when watering, turn the hose or the spout of your watering-can down the pipe. A little care in the disposal of a few stones and some chips under the pipe will ensure the proper flow of the water and you can water at any time without danger of sunburn or of rotting out the crown of the plants. Incidentally, if you have not a convenient or sufficient rain-water tank and are dependent on the water company's mains, your water percolating through the soil will be more palatable to the plants.

Here you have the outstanding features of a rock garden as I conceive it. It will of course need larger patches of colour to prevent it looking patchy. For these you can choose the dwarf Phloxes and Iris, the finer Aquilegias, the mossy Saxifrages, Anemones, Aubrietias, Helianthemums and the like. Once the garden is started, fill in gradually with other plants acquired from friends or growers (you need never pay more than a few pence except for special rarities) or best of all plants collected by yourself. In a short time you will be searching for space in which to bestow some newly acquired treasure and will be thinking which plant you will sacrifice to make room.

A word about collecting. In these days, if he can afford a trip to Switzerland, anyone can reach the Alpine plants, however poor a walker he is. I was past sixty before I saw the Alps in early summer and, coming straight from heavy office work, I was in no trim for climbing. Yet there were in my garden many plants which I had myself collected with Dr. Correvon or other friends in the week's holiday which I used

to take after the sitting of the Council of the League of
Nations in early June. Not an hour from Geneva I found a
white Cyclamen europaeum which Dr. Correvon in all his
rambles in the Alps and elsewhere had never lit upon. Another
day he took me a drive along what is called the International
Route (for it crosses the Franco-Swiss frontier more than
once) and showed me a grassy slope where every outcrop of
rock had its patches of Daphne Cneorum. I had other
glorious days with him in the Jura and yet others at Zermatt
where the Professor of Botany at the University of Lausanne
kindly made himself our guide. We went up to the top of the
Görnergratch by train and before I could take my eyes from
the glorious panorama of snow peaks and glaciers, he had
found me a piece of Eritrichium nanum, the heart's desire of
every Alpine grower. As we walked down, we passed through
all the seasons from the places where the snow still lay in
half-melted patches through which the earliest flowers were
just peeping till we reached high summer in the meadows of
the valley. That day I first saw Androsace glacialis and next
day the Professor showed me a spot where the scarce Asplenium septentrionale was to be found.

Of course I had my disappointments. I lost my E. nanum by
too much coddling when at home and neglect when I was
absent. (I saw a capital piece only the other day growing in a
stone trough in scree mixture in Sir Clive Wigram's garden at
the foot of the Round Tower at Windsor Castle) but the
Asplenium grew well in a crevice where it had Penstemon
Davidsoni for neighbour and the majority of my plants lived.

For collector's tools, a fern trowel with a long blade not
more than one and a half inches wide and so firmly fixed *in*
the handle that it will give you good leverage and an Alpine
ice-axe suffice. If any of the plants are short of fibrous root,
plunge them in a bed of wet sand placed in the shade. It is
amazing what root they will then make in a few weeks.

Reluctantly I end, for even to write of these bygone delights
is itself a pleasure. There are few joys like a garden and the
Alpine garden is par excellence the garden for the amateur.

P.S. A cure for sleeplessness. If you find that after the
worries and excitements of a busy day, say after winding up a

debate in Parliament at midnight, you are too excited to sleep when you reach your bed, if then counting sheep passing through a gate proves as with me of no avail and you share my incapacity for thinking of nothing, visit your rock garden in imagination. I have put myself to sleep night after night in this way before my head had been five minutes on the pillow or I had covered six paces of my small garden.

P.P.S. With regard to a question sent to me about pruning clematis, I cut back those clematis which would stand pruning in March, but I certainly did not mean to imply that this is a wise treatment for all of them. I did not find the horticulturist's catalogue a safe guide on this point and had to learn by experience which plants it suited. I believe it is a good plan to keep the plants mulched in winter to protect them from frost and in summer to keep their roots cool.

*

Gladys, Chimney Sweep

IT began during the War, when her brothers were called up and her father broke his leg. For fifteen miles there was no chimney sweep and it was the spring-cleaning season. There really was nothing else to be done, Gladys must help. She began by going to one or two houses quite near her home, and the thing becoming known, she was pestered by the housewives to come to them. She found she could sling the brushes and the sack for the soot on her bicycle, or over her shoulders, as the men did, and that, although she might be less expert than her father, every job she went to she did better. So she made up her mind to continue, especially as her father's leg did not set well, and gave him constant trouble. And one of the brothers did not come back, and the other married a girl in a distant town and started work there. She now has her printed postcards for appointments, and her motor bicycle.—*E.W.*

*

Dear old cowman, milking: 'You see, ma'am, I nivver lets me nose drip in the milk pail; I wipes it wi' the back of me 'and, so, and then I wipes the back of me 'and down the backside of me smock, so. It's cleaner'n handlin' a hankiture.'

Guide to Up-to-Date Farming
by Campbell Keith

With Illustrations of Three Breeds which are New to You

THE FOXOOSE

Costs little to keep. Often brings home a Rabbit. Good protection for other Poultry. Lays a large, hairy Egg

THE HENABBIT

Lays a fine Easter Egg with Rabbit inside. Good Table Bird

THE SHEPPIG

Makes a lovely 'Shoulder' and 'Ham' Animal

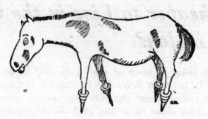

Old Horses with Dibbers for Potato Planting

Kind-hearted Farmers have Fattening Mirrors for Shorn Sheep

Mechanical Scratching Birds give Hens more Time for Laying

Keep Turkeys' Minds off Christmas

Is it Cheaper to Live in the Country or in London?

Shall I go on living in town or shall I buy—if I can—a house in the country? Shall I enjoy a fuller life by staying in London? Alas, many people in the towns whose thoughts are turned towards the country are under illusions about rural life, while many people who have to live in the country but think they would like to be in London imagine vain things about urban life!

If town life is given up for rural life, and rural life turns out a failure, it is the woman who pays! It seemed worth while, therefore, to ask a few women in the country—the date was midway between the wars—to be good enough to help women readers in cities and towns. The letter writers include a number of women who have houses both in the country and in London. And there are some who, though they live in the country or in London, have 'tried baith'. The writers include peeresses, authors, an ex-M.P., an M.P.'s wife, the wife of an artist, the wife of a secondary school-master, two squires' wives, a primary school mistress, the wives of a gentleman farmer, a yeoman farmer and a tenant farmer, housewives in small country houses and cottages, and the wife of the founder of 'The Countryman'. The pre-War luxury, amusing now, is retained.

LONDON AND SUFFOLK.—Country living is definitely more economical. In food, even if one pays as much as in the town, one gets a much better pennyworth. Clothes one spends less on, because one does not need so many, and they stay clean longer. And one spends less money on distractions and whimwhams. Housework in the country is child's play to what it is in town. The country dirt is honest dirt, not grime. Cooking is slightly more arduous in the country. There is the food question instead of a gas stove, and one cannot rush out at the last moment and buy something ready-cooked, or retire to a restaurant. Balancing housework against cookwork, I should say town draws with country under this heading. Country servants do very well if one does not expect too many graces and refinements. It is worth noticing that every good housewife in London tries to get country servants. A Sentry or Ideal boiler is a great help. In town or country, if you want catering done well, do it yourself. Even if one can't afford a cheap car, transport is getting easier every day with buses and charabancs.

SPRING CROCUSES

THE VILLAGE THAT WON VISCOUNT BLEDISLOE'S PRIZE
Stanton, Gloucestershire

FAKED CASTLES
At Bath, Dinton (Bucks), Steeple Aston (Oxon) and Brislington

THREE STAGES IN CLEARING A DITCH

Regarding recreation and social life, (a) have a job of some sort and don't depend on your neighbours for a *raison d'être;* (b) entertain your friends for week-ends. They will enjoy it too. A scheme I should like to see tried out would be a co-operation among neighbouring parents to teach their united children. On Monday the children would gather at Mrs. Tomkins and learn from her what she feels best fitted to teach. On Tuesday they go to the Manor where Professor Grubbins (retired) does his bit, and so on. As stars differ in their glory, it is probable that any group of parents would also differ in their distribution of talents: one could teach French but not mathematics, etc. But everyone could teach something. Older children would go to school presumably, as town children do. The great merit of my scheme would be that it procures for nothing in £ s. d. what is very expensive in the country, and very important anywhere: a variety of teachers. It bores children to learn everything from one person.

There is one general comment I would like to make. One talks of town and country. There is also the country town. Of the three estates, this is perhaps the easiest. It supplies gas, and perhaps electricity from the local works; it simplifies shopping and transport; and it gives one's servants more society and pleasure. To live on the outskirts of a small country town seems to me the ideal state: from the woman's point of view it is much easier than living right in the country and certainly quite as economical.

OXFORDSHIRE.—Which do you like best—your father or your mother? Economical? Neither country nor town is economical. A parsimonious person can get out of spending in a town without being found out or being made to feel guilty. Country life is open, and no niggard can hide there. Country people know you for what you are. If you live in the country because you love it, but have a rooted interest in fine music and good drama, you will scrimp and scrape to get to town for special concerts and plays. But that will not prove that you are a town-lover. It will only prove that our civilization punishes the artist who will pay the price to breathe flower-scented air and lie on clean grass.

What is economy? True economy is spending recklessly on things that matter, such as clean linen, good roses, fine books, to share with your friends who come to visit you. It is having an open hand for the mother whose baby's needs are greater than her husband's wages, or for the old man or woman whose pension even when supplemented by the sacrificial offerings of a willing family does not run to Ovaltine or rubber hot-water bottles. Economy is rejoicing in the number of things you can afford to do without, such as dinner parties, cigarettes and the very best kind of dress. It is no good having fine clothes that will outlast their mode; the country demands plain, durable clothing.

You can spend less in the country on things that towns-people think they must have because of the contagion of spending, but you will find that the country sets a higher scale for other kinds of expenditure. The chief economic difference between life in town and in country is that you get better value in the country for your spending. You can have country sweetness, flowers, the song of birds and pure food, and by outlearning some of the heated desires of town life, have enough in hand to go to town for its real pleasures. How dead must be the human being who is insensitive to the tingling joy of mixing in a city crowd, of sharing a laugh with thousands of other people, of singing in the Albert Hall when it is full. You cannot get *that* thrill in the country. But, as to music, the wireless has completely changed our rural condition.

Like 'Old Meg' whose 'brothers were the craggy hills, her sisters larchen trees', I have no children and should not speak of schools. But the country is the place where all children ought to learn. It will need a new social structure to bring this about. Elementary teachers are excellent instructors, but the rural child is often soul-starved, deprived, smutty, and the boys are ignorantly cruel to birds. To mingle daily with these children might hurt for life the outlook of a happier-born child. Three labouring class children in a school of the children of a more fortunate class might make all one, but three better-off children in a school of the really poor might make snobs of the three and cause needless envyings

70

and heartburnings in the envious majority.

In catering for speed, convenience, variety and generally for price, the town has it every time. But the country house-wife, though she has to work hard for it, can get, if she will, pure food, fresh eggs, vegetables and fruit, etc. It is much dearer than in town unless the housewife is herself something of a smallholder who counts neither her own not her hand-maids' labour.

The town grocer may be a sort of a machine with a steel face that grinds off the parings of your costly victuals and picks out the smallest and dingiest of his good things to make the balance almost touch the notch. In the country your grocer is your tried friend who shares in your public works, goes to personal inconvenience to supply you with a sudden 'corner' of needed bacon when unexpected friends arrive in their car for a week-end. Your country grocer expects to be asked and does contribute to your village outing or other fund with tea or sugar or other good things. Your butcher charges you a high price, but you may take your meat from his cart blind-fold. The woman who does your washing is your friend as well as your neighbour, so it is easy to love her. Your maids have planned to work for you while they were still at school, and a waiting queue of fourteen-year-olds is for ever yours if you but 'take an interest' in their welfare. There is no servant problem in the country to a woman with a heart who has learnt to give as well as to take. As for public ser-vice all true country people are community helpers, and there is always room for the right folk on the rural district council.

For dignified, wholesome, clean home life with such natural pursuits as gardening, botanizing or the hundred other practical or studious interests, the country is the normal place for normal folk. But it is lived in to-day at a high cost. The town has allurements and conveniences that are un-gettable elsewhere. Why otherwise should people make cities? Where a few are gathered together there is common security of things to eat, heat, light and wear, to hear and to see. But the price of town life is that your aims and ideas become standardized, as also do your dress, your food, and your friendships. The country is more individual; therefore, for me, the country has it!

SUSSEX AND OXFORDSHIRE.—Life in the country offers many attractions, particularly if there are children. One of the chief attractions is the much less strenuous battle with dirt, which makes one of the great difficulties of life in London. The woman with a small income can have more space for her children in the country, a larger house for the same or less rent, and best of all, a garden. I do not think servants are harder to get in the country; there are usually girls to be had in the villages, or a widow who wishes for daily work. The social life is much what you choose to make it, and the motor-car and motor-bus have revolutionized country life in its social aspects. To anyone who has no car, neighbours are usually more than kind in giving lifts. There are many excellent grammar schools up and down the country, such as provided education for Shakespeare and Nelson in days gone by, and many of our most successful men to-day. Opportunities in plenty exist for public service. There are the Women's Institutes, Girl Guides, Church and political organizations, all prepared heartily to welcome the willing worker.

SURREY AND DEVON.—In Surrey, twenty miles from London, practically everything is at London prices. At my other home, near Exmoor, and in sight of the sea, prices are quite as high as in London. I think things may be a little better in the winter months, but I am not there then. Of course, if people know how to keep a garden and work it themselves, or at any rate with only a moderate amount of labour, they can grow what they please and find it economical. In the two neighbourhoods I have described, the scarcity of servants, or rather the excessive demand which is the root of the trouble, prevails, so that I find it easier to recruit my household in London. In real country neighbourhoods, however, where I have relations living, it is not difficult to get young girls going out to their first place, and also occasional day help is easily got. I rather think that the really trained and experienced maid servant is scarce everywhere. Men are easier to find, also boys. If you wish to live in the country with a small household, I beg you not to think of attempting to do so in an isolated place. You will find it almost impossible to get or keep servants, and you will have all sorts of difficulties in the way of household provisioning. If your household is large and includes indoor men (also gardeners, grooms, chauffeurs, etc) then you can live where you please, but small households should always put themselves near a village, where women servants can find friends.

HERTS.—Success in home-making in the country is, to an even larger extent than home-making in towns, the result of a trained mind, unfailing foresight, freedom from certain conventional ideas and the power of giving one's soul an interesting time. This last point is probably the most important one. The country gives time, space, and quiet—one can survey the whole world and its activities in a far deeper manner than one could in any kind of town. There naturally the noise and the hurry make tremendous inroads upon our sixteen hours of daily living.

I have seen more homes that have been failures in the country than in the town. I hesitate to recommend the country to any married couple if the wife is not absolutely the right type. The husband does not matter so much. He is generally satisfied with the place that satisfies his wife. Life in the country can be infinitely more economical, but only to those who can rid themselves of conventional notions, who understand how to plan a house, who have not become hypnotized by too much rusticity and the charms of 'picturesque old houses'—those dirt and labour producing traps. Life in the country can be extraordinarily expensive if one follows the rules laid down even to-day in English novels, with hunting and shooting and the country house atmosphere. A small income must be coupled to a free mind. The servant problem is easily solved by getting one's maids locally and taking care to establish a good reputation for fairness and understanding. It is fatal to try to bring town-bred maids out into the country. Of the purely practical problems, water supply seems to be the most important. If you ignore that you are courting sheer disaster. Electric light is not so important. There are many good oil lamps on the market nowadays. The Aladdin lamp, for instance, is almost perfect. Gas has a marvellous substitute in the Valor-Perfection stoves. In the kitchen we have the modern continuously-burning coke range that produces neither dirt nor labour, while its twin brother, the boiler in the cellar, hall or corner of the kitchen, warms the whole house without any fuss. Living in a cold house in the country is even more disheartening than performing that unnecessary feat in town. For the rest, one can have as many open fires as one finds pleasure in looking after. House-keeping in the country must needs be done with a resource-fulness and forethought that can be dispensed with in town. But that brings its own reward—the methodical and looking-ahead housewife is generally the happiest one. The stream of tradesmen at the back doors is a peculiar English curse.

The bus services have solved our transport problem beyond our wildest dreams. The social life? Well, is not that what we make it ourselves? The village hall is an institution that has no equal in other countries, but it must be entered in a right and a humble spirit. If you think that it somehow doesn't suit you because you got your musical education in Vienna, then all that can be said is that you didn't suit Vienna either. As for the Women's Institutes, they are on the same level as the Boy Scout movement, a perfect product of the English mind at its highest. So-called social service is not so much needed as town folk may think, and in any case no service can equal that of setting a good example of order and industry, simplicity and culture, reverence for the soil and good cheer. Schools? You can sit for a week writing about that question and in the end nobody is wiser. Town and country have both special advantages. The village school has produced many of the American Presidents, but up to now only one English Prime Minister. And until we have a line of the latter we shall probably go on making a fetish of the public school and do our utmost to give our children 'a chance', as we say.

LONDON.—I only know that if I lived in the country the town would see me no more, as I should never find courage to spend the reckless amount of money which the railway demands for carrying me to and from London. As for the hardihood of a woman who lives still farther away and spends £1 to come to the sales and 'save' on buying the various things one can't do without, I give her up. Then there is the fallacy that if you have a garden you live for nothing. I've eaten eggs in the country which must have cost at least 3s. 6d. a piece owing to cost of the fowls' food. It is perhaps true that you get cheaper service in the country, but generally you have to 'break in' the 'breakers', and so lose as much in china and temper as you save in actual cash. For timid people who cannot dare, town is the place. There they have no great emergencies to face. They can, if they are really poor, get a great deal for nothing. Free sights if they are young enough to stand and see them. Delightful enjoyment in countless museums, assuming they have minds in need of nourishment. Our town sunsets leave nothing to be desired. We never run short of water. We have parks with sheep in them if we want to feel 'rural' and now that the dwellers in the country have 'listening in' to make their lot more varied, the scales are equally balanced between us and we have only to envy the countryman perhaps the quiet which is sometimes his during the nightwatches but very seldom ours. Sorry to give no help, but if I did have an income and a car I'd choose the country.

LONDON AND SUSSEX.—Life in the country is more economical than life in town in the following respects: (1) Lower rents and rates. (2) Facilities for recreation and exercise and fresh air generally and consequently the better health of the family. (3) Gardens and the keeping of a few hens help with the housekeeping expenses. There is usually a fair supply of young girls and also daily help, but the more experienced servant is very difficult to get. A cheerful village with a good Women's Institute helps to make the servant problem easier if the W.I. is able to persuade the local authorities to give more and better classes in cooking. It is useless for urban women 'looking forward to living in the country' to base their wish to do so on the beauties of the country as seen perhaps for two weeks every year on the occasion of a holiday. They must be prepared for certain disadvantages such as (1) more irregular and less accessible transport, (2) earlier hours, (3) possible difficulties in the obtaining and delivery of fuel and other things on certain occasions, (4) certain problems as to catering. The family caterer is dependent on local supply. Variation of dishes is more difficult. This is just a matter of getting used to local conditions and a certain amount of organization.

BUCKINGHAMSHIRE.—If you live (as we do) anywhere within the radius of the delivery of the big London shops, the prices of groceries, etc., in the local shops are no dearer than town prices. Meat and fish are slightly dearer. Vegetables, if you grow them and pay a gardener are certainly dearer but infinitely nicer. Fruit we have free.

The servant problem is infinitely harder in the country. So far as I can make out, the people in town who keep one or two maids can procure a succession even though they may be incompetent. In the country the difficulty is to get anyone at all. In this district and anywhere where there are factories in the neighbourhood the girls naturally go to them. Such servants as there are tend to go to big houses where a large staff is kept. The offer of a large salary makes no difference for the recipient of a big wage does not expect to do the rougher work. There are a certain number of married women or widows in this neighbourhood who go out for daily work, but they are quickly snapped up and the new generation has no training in housework. Of course there are some women who like posts in the country as 'working cook housekeepers' single-handed or with help, and I myself have been lucky; but they are few and far between and I should advise anybody going into the country to be prepared to do housework themselves, and not to be over fussy or over scrupulous about standards of housewifery. There are a great number of 'lady cook housekeepers' advertising for places, but they almost invariably require a girl under them and the problem in the country is to get that girl.

I should not advise anyone to put in a plant for electricity unless they (a) have a regular gardener or handyman to run it

76

or (*b*) are prepared to spend a good deal of time over it themselves. I think on the whole it is worth while. It may cost rather more than oil lamps but it saves eyesight, saves cleaning and enables me to use a vacuum cleaner. But in the winter the engine is running for at least three mornings a week.

Failing electricity, Aladdin lamps seem to me the best. We used them before putting in our electric plant. Electric bicycle lamps are excellent for using about the house and outside instead of candles or the old-fashioned lanterns. I should advise anyone who could afford it to install central heating because of the problem of service. With two heaped fire (Brott and Colbran) grates, two anthracite stoves [Fancy!] and the kitchen fire, we keep our house warm, but the problem of getting the two grates lighted in time is a difficult one, and when an anthracite stove goes out it means a lot of work. Doing fires is the job in housework that is most disliked, even though your grates may be the best labour-saving ones.

WORCESTERSHIRE.—My husband and I, when we married, found the choice between London and the country difficult; but, after much consideration, we turned our back on the allurements of country and elected for the town, largely because of its sociability. We could not bring ourselves to separate from our numerous friends and acquaintances. We had not to consider ways and means. Those who have will make a note, among other things, of the greater facilities in the country for keeping and maintaining a small car. With regard to service, there is no doubt that the country is cheaper. Village maidens on leaving school may with tact and patience be trained into excellent servants. But here heredity and environment come in. One should be careful to choose the daughters of mothers who have in their youth been in good places and kept them. In such cases the little girls of fourteen come to you with astonishing ideas of good housewifery. The garden may be an expense or otherwise. Anything between half an acre and an acre should be made to supply a moderate household of six or seven with ample fruit and vege-tables in addition to flowers. But after all is said there remains the question of sociability. Here the town has the advantage. And I should strongly dissuade anyone who is dependent for the enjoyment of life on a large circle of congenial acquaintances from living in the country. To be happy in the country one must have resources in oneself. One ought also to have a passion for mother earth and an interest in all her gracious happenings as the seasons go by. Then there is a final consideration, which must appeal to those whose circumstances have undergone a change, who for some reason or other are condemned to live on less than they have been accustomed to. They may have had a dignified house in town, the upkeep of which has become impossible. They look at smaller houses, a flat being impossible unless they bring themselves to part with most of their possessions. The smaller houses which coincide with their income are commonplace, badly built and frequently suburban. It is only in the country that they can discover a dwelling with some dignity and distinction.

SOMERSET.—To people willing to forego the sophistication of town life and cheerfully to adopt the simplification rural life demands, rural life can be distinctly more economical than life in town. Highly trained servants are not easy to procure, but there is no shortage either of women to do daily work or of young girls to train in domestic service. A car, though by no means a necessity, is naturally an asset in the country. Most villages have a carrier cart and bus services. And one does not realize the usefulness of a bicycle until one lives in the country. The country can rarely offer so fine a choice of schools as a town. But most country towns have a grammar or secondary school, and few villages in England are more than fifteen miles from a country town. Thus higher education of a sort is available everywhere. With regard to public service there is a growing tendency to welcome women on parish and district councils, boards of governors of schools and public committees. The town fear of finding country life dull is without foundation; the difficulty is rather to cope with the crowding engagements.

LONDON AND BEDFORDSHIRE.—Rents and rates are

cheaper. Vegetables, fruit, eggs, etc., save cost of food. Life is usually simpler and old clothes can be worn. Health is undoubtedly better, so doctor's bills can be lessened. The peace of a country home must save nerves. I should not like to say that the servant problem is easier, so many girls preferring town life. I have never had any trouble in getting servants myself locally: there are still many mothers who prefer that their young daughters should not go to the towns. Young girls are usually to be had and village women are often glad of the chance to give 'help' when wanted. Most large houses now are centrally heated, a simple matter once installed.

Nearly all country places have regular calls from tradesmen with motor vans, and catering is as easy as in a town. A motor-car is decidedly a necessity though the bus service in most places has revolutionized country transport. Social life is much the same as in a town, though country people think less of distances to go for their social activities. Schools are rather a problem. Children are usually sent to boarding schools, unless within reach of a good day school, but this, I think, applies equally to towns.

I am certain that all things considered money goes farther in the country than in the town. Having spent my married life of twenty-two years, the first twelve in a town, the last ten in the country, wild horses would not drag me back to the former.

❧

Country Honours, by C. J. M. Turner

I LOVE the happy fairground of the wood
that wears its colours not remembering
the world looks on to see if it is good.
And gold in plenty's mine at harvesting,
and dignity enough behind the plough,
and praise enough from singers in the bough.

❧

'Don't seem as if they'd anythin' to say to us,' was the explanation given of why there were so few people in the churches.

Mr. Ducket's Mode of Cultivation

by His Majesty, George III

Everybody has read that 'Farmer George', under the name of Ralph Robinson, his Windsor shepherd, contributed to Arthur Young's 'Annals of Agriculture'. In the British Museum are the whole forty-six volumes of the 'Annals', George III's own copy, by the way. The 'Annals' began in 1784 and ran until 1809, and His Majesty's first contribution is dated Jan. 1, 1787. It is headed, 'On Mr. Ducket's Mode of Cultivation,' and, like many contributions to the press of that time, takes the form of a letter. It begins:

SIR, It is reasonable to suppose that your laudable efforts for the improvement of husbandry by publishing the 'Annals of Agriculture' must in time be crowned with success; therefore it seems incumbent on all who think they have materials on this interesting subject worthy of inspection by the public to transmit them to you who, if you view them in that light, will give them a place in that estimable work.

Without further preface I shall mention that the dispute which has lately risen on the subject of summer fallows had made me greatly wish that Mr. Ducket, the able cultivator of Petersham, in Surrey, would have communicated his thoughts, not only on that subject, but would have benefited the public, by a full explanation of that course of husbandry which has rendered his farm, which has now been above 19 years in his hands, so flourishing, though his three predecessors had failed on it. As you have compleated your sixth volume and I find his great modesty prevents his standing forth among your correspondents, I will attempt to describe his mode of cultivation, rather than it shall longer remain unnoticed in your pages.

And His Majesty does so cogently and technically to the length of about four COUNTRYMAN *pages, concluding:*

I shall not take up more of your time than to assure you that I am, Sir, your most humble Servant,

RALPH ROBINSON

To which Young adds an editorial note: 'I have at various times during the last fifteen years viewed with great attention

the husbandry of the very ingenious Mr. Ducket. I took notes of what I saw for my private information but did nct publish them as I thought I perceived a disinclination in that gentleman to have them so brought forward. I am glad to find by this memoir (for which the publick is much obliged to the author) that he has relaxed in this particular. I wish that Mr. Robinson would proceed, and in particular give his courses of crops; and explain in particular his utter rejection of fallows, and his very significant mode of treating a field when full of couch grass.'

Thus encouraged Mr. Ralph Robinson obliges again with a communication of almost equal length, under date March 5, 1787. He begins.

The early attention you have given to my attempt of laying before the public through your channel Mr. Ducket's system of agriculture, fully entitles you to expect from me a compliance to the request you have intimated in a note at the end of that publication.

The courses practised by the ingenious Mr. Ducket are detailed, and the article concludes with a paragraph in reply to the Editor's request about couch grass or twitch:

The method he constantly pursues for destroying couch grass is by trench ploughing into the ground when it dies when it is buried deep; that left on the surface is destroyed by hoeing. Grain of quick and luxuriant growth sown on the ground, also assists very much towards destruction; but a change of rye, tares and turnips when produced by this mode of culture will the most effectually destroy couch grass.

The article concludes:

I have wished to be as pointed as possible in attempting to answer your enquiries, which may have led me into greater length than I should have wished.

This time there is no editorial note at the end of the letter, but Young has a small type footnote at the bottom of the page: 'I am obliged to this gentleman for so readily answering my enquiries.'

Old woman, to lecturer after talk on 'Bird Song' at women's institute in Surrey: 'There's a bird in our garden. 'E's always alone an' 'e do roar. Would 'e be a robin?'

A Curious Rural Sect In Sussex
by Earl Winterton, M.P.

IN a corner of the Weald of Sussex, due north of Petworth, lies a quiet woodland district the inhabitants of which do their farm work in summer and copse-cutting in winter, untroubled from year's end to year's end, by railways or the big military camps and red brick villas not so many miles away over the Surrey border. It is in this district, which may be said, roughly speaking, to comprise the parishes of Wisborough, Northchapel, Kirdford and Lurgashall, that a little-known sect has its headquarters. In 1850, a London shoemaker, John Sirgood, came to live at Loxwood, a small village in Wisborough, and started the Society of Dependents or Cokelers. By 1861 a considerable proportion of the farmers and labourers in the district had joined, and this seems to have alarmed the parish authorities for a notice was served on Sirgood and his followers informing them that unless they discontinued their unlawful meetings they would be prosecuted according to law. The notice was accompanied by the following letter signed by a gentleman who was deputed by the vicar and churchwardens:

Mr. Sirgood—Sir, I went to your house on Thursday evening for the purpose of giving you the enclosed notice, but found you holding one of your unlawful meetings. I am glad I did this because I have now myself witnessed two of these unlawful assemblies there, and could without difficulty procure your conviction in two penalties and these two could probably be easily multiplied. It is a very general opinion that your illegal proceedings have been allowed to go far enough, and that it is quite time they should be controlled.

No action was taken, however, by the parish authorities, and soon afterwards the repeal of the Conventicle Act left the sect free. Meanwhile, Sirgood was establishing branches of the sect in the neighbouring villages and in more distant places.

The article was published fifteen years ago, but Lord Winterton writes, 'the situation has changed little. Save for a couple of "displaced persons" camps we have resumed our pre-war rural existence. The Society of Dependants still flourishes but the sect itself continues to diminish'. American readers may be interested in knowing that Lord Winterton is the Father of the House of Commons in which he is eligible to sit as he is an Irish not an English peer.

Early in the 'sixties a chapel and burial-ground were acquired. In several of these places, notably at Warnham, Loxwood and Northchapel, a sort of store was built so that the flock should be commercially self-sufficient. When in 1885 Sirgood died he must have had nearly 2,000 people under his influence. The reading and committal to memory of large portions of scripture form a considerable part of the Cokelers' services, and members speak as the Spirit moves them. They differ from almost every other Christian sect in that they do not use the Lord's Prayer, asserting that it was given merely as a model for other prayers and that its brevity proves its inadaptability for use. Of an evening, in a quiet Sussex lane, one may suddenly come upon twenty or thirty Cokelers driving in waggons to their chapel, and chanting a sort of psalm, the men being dressed in dark clothes and the women in black dresses with poke bonnets. Total abstinence is no longer, as formerly, insisted on among the Cokelers, but it is encouraged. The sect, while recognizing the necessity of marriage, does not encourage that estate. It also eschews dancing, music, except of a religious nature, and flowers. A more honest, industrious and clean-living set of people it would be hard to find. The vicars of parishes which contain Cokelers are almost unanimous in their praise. But I should not think that the Cokelers now number more than 900 all told. Besides their chapels, the Cokelers have stores at Norwood, Warnham, Shamley Green, Loxwood and Northchapel. At Northchapel, a small village six miles from a railway station, with a parish population of 700, the Cokeler store consists of three departments and employs thirteen saleswomen and assistants, besides delivery-cart drivers. The red-brick emporium with plate-glass windows is flanked on one side by the Cokeler meeting house and on the other by the sect's steam mill. At another store, at Loxwood, even bicycles, gramophones and motor accessories are dealt in; indeed a motor is let out for hire, and I believe one could buy a motor. The labouring class among the Cokelers is much better off than its neighbours.

It is noteworthy that the members practise mutual assistance not only in commerce but in agriculture.

The Cottage and Smithy that went across the Atlantic

THE experiment made by Henry Ford in transporting a Cotswold house to Dearborn, which some readers, unacquainted with all the circumstances, may have deprecated, justified itself. Indeed it cannot be called an experiment exactly. Many of us have visited or know of the Open Air Museums of Scandinavia, composed of ancient cottages, farmhouses, farm buildings, windmills, well-heads, etc., brought carefully from sites on which they were doomed to destruction.

In the vicinity of Detroit, at Dearborn, Henry Ford, who was a reader of the *Countryman*, set apart forty acres or so of pleasantly wooded land for the preservation of buildings and machinery of historic interest and value. He had re-erected there some of the humble dwellings of the pioneer settlers. There is a series of buildings in which the young Edison lived and worked in the early days of the phonograph and electric lighting. There is an old-time American railroad and depôt, with an out-of-date engine and cars. There are typical old frame buildings—dwelling-houses, school houses, a court-house, a store, a post office, toll house, tin-type photo store and a church. The Ford collections will be specially interesting in showing the evolution of English and American machinery, early examples of pumping gear designed by Watts, and also primitive forms of gas, oil and fire engines, having been secured over here. Visitors are transported to and fro in old-time coaches and buggies.

The Cotswold cottage was transported from Chedworth. It stood in an isolated position not far from the famous Roman villa. It consisted of two seventeenth-century dwellings used as labourers' cottages, knocked into one, and there was also a barn and stable. The place had not been occupied for some time and was in a bad condition. Indeed, there was very little hope of anything being done with it, for the walls were rotten and bulging, and much of the timber was decayed. The task of first putting the buildings to rights

84

THE COTTAGE THAT CROSSED THE ATLANTIC

FOUR GENERATIONS

COME AND JOIN US

and then taking them down and despatching them to America was given to Mr. Cox Howman, a Cotswold builder known for admirable restorations who had been a local magistrate for a generation. The cottage had had wooden windows put into it. These were removed and the old stone mullions were replaced and the casements fitted with old glass. The old pigeon holes were uncovered, an old oven was restored, the cement that covered the walls was cleaned off, bad timber was replaced, and a special feature, winding stone staircases and fireplaces, was cared for. This was two months' work. Then it took seven weeks to pull down and pack. All the important stones were numbered, and Mr. Cox Howman's careful drawings included a survey of the trees and the garden with the name of every flower marked. Not only the garden walling but the crazy paving and the stone edges of the paths were sent to America. The total weight was 475 tons, and the material was conveyed in a special train of sixty-seven wagons to Brentford, where it was barged to the London docks. The building stone was in bags and the freestone and stone slabs in crates.

To re-erect the building with the assistance of American workmen, Mr. Cox Howman sent a mason and a carpenter, two men who had been responsible for the pulling down. The mason had been with him since his boyhood. They left home on the last day of May, and were back on December 7. Work began on July 8 and finished on September 23, without one rainy day. By September 23 everything was in place, including the cider-barrel indoors (containing cider), the flowers and roses in the garden, the well complete with well-head from Chedworth (but, though thirty feet deep, there was no water) and a horse and cow in the barn. In reconstructing the house every conspicuous stone found its old place and the indoor plastering was done in the old way with chopped straw. The flooring had, of course, to be new, but the oak boards had come from the Cotswolds. All the work was done in the best possible way, copper nails for example, being freely used. Of the success of the reconstruction the photograph offers evidence. Indeed, towards the end of the job the new buildings looked so much at home on their new site that the workmen could almost fancy they were back at Chedworth. For the furniture and equipment of the cottage Mr. S. B. Russell, who is known for his remarkable restoration of the Lygon Arms*, and as the founder of the workshops at Broadway, was consulted.

Henry Ford was frequently on the site, sometimes even three or four times a day, during the reconstruction, and the English craftsmen formed a high opinion of him. When staying in Broadway last October, he went over to Stow-on-the-Wold before breakfast one morning to talk with the families of the workmen who had directed the rebuilding, and had the kind thought of having photographs taken of the exiles' home circles. And he sent the two men to Niagara Falls before their return home. The men were struck by the way in which Mr. Ford insisted that everything should be left in apple-pie order at the close of every day. They particularly noticed the cleanliness of the windows of the Ford Works. Photographs of the progress of the re-construction were taken every other day. Mr. Ford repeatedly expressed himself well satisfied with the job, and Mrs. Ford gave a luncheon party in the cottage, the food being cooked in the old oven. Mr. Cox Howman was also pleased with Mr. Ford's quiet, unassuming ways, his physical fitness, mental alertness and fine visual memory, and his delight in Cotswold scenery. Mr. Ford continued to own the land at Chedworth from which the cottage was taken, and by his instructions all the rubbish of the demolition has been removed, so that the little paddock still remains a fair part of the Cotswolds.

Some time ago the present writer was at Snowshill, a perfect Cotswold village, where he saw an old smithy which had been shut up for close on twenty years. The interesting tools and equipment were rusty and partially buried under a deep coating of dust and mortar from the fast-decaying roof. It was on the death of the widow of the last smith, who lived in the smithy cottage, that the property was bought by Mr. S. B. Russell, a resident in the village. Snowshill can no longer provide a living for a village smith. Even had this been possible, a large expenditure in repairs and renewals of

*See his article on page 243.

86

hearths, bellows and tools, many of which, from their age and interest, were only fit for a museum, would have been necessary. Many unsuccessful efforts were made by the new owner to preserve somewhere on the Cotswolds, the contents of this old-time smithy. A careful examination of the building was made by a Cotswold architect of experience and skill, Mr. Thomas Rayson* with a view to using the forge building as a living room for the tiny adjoining cottage, but the roof had holes in many places, the roof-timbers were rotten, and the walls were bulging, and without damp course. To comply with building regulations for occupation as a dwelling house it would have been necessary to re-build. When Mr. Ford was staying in Broadway, it was suggested to him by Mr. Russell, to whom he has been known for many years, that he might like to look at the contents of the forge, with a view to preserving them in his museum at Dearborn. As a result, they were purchased, with the decayed building, at a price that almost covered the cost of the living-room to the cottage, erected in true Cotswold character in its place. Mr. Ford became so much interested in the contents, that he paid many visits to the forge, looking over and sorting out the tools, and getting much begrimed in the occupation. So Mr. Cox Howman has had another task to his mind, and the smithy and its contents—all nicely cleaned and labelled with their local names—were soon in America, with his mason on the scene again to undertake the work of reconstruction. This time the stone of the walls were not packed in bags, but in crates and clamped barrels—Mr. Cox Howman made a purchase of one hundred old beer-barrels. Fifteen tons of timber were also sent across the Atlantic.

Some years afterwards a transatlantic correspondent visited the Cotswold cottage in its new setting. 'I was greatly delighted with it and its flower and vegetable gardens and its stone wall and everything as if it had always been there,' he wrote. 'It really is a remarkable thing to have done. I was greatly struck by the old furniture and the old kitchen utensils. I was shown all the outbuildings, also brought from the Cotswolds.

*See his article on page 272.

Making and Blowing One's Own Trumpet, by Captain Wylie Kettlewell, R.N

FOR the first time in my life I have learnt to blow a trumpet which I have made myself and I am a proud man in consequence. My wife and I have known Miss Margaret James for a good many years now and when she started her experiments with bamboo whistle-pipes for school children, we very soon heard of them. This led to the starting of a week-end school of pipe-making and playing for adults here in Burford and although I was not a student, it was not long before I found myself set to work whittling an A pipe out of a length of curtain rod bamboo. After it had been shaped, I must needs cut the finger holes and tune it. This necessitated fingering up and down the scale, clumsily at first, but before I had made six pipes I found myself, almost unconsciously, playing elementary tunes. This pipe-making and playing business is far from being just a pretty novelty, it is one of the most ingenious games for the education of the hand, eye and ear, all at the same time. For, not only does the pupil have to perform the hand-work of cutting-out and hole-boring, which necessitates the use of saw, chisel, file and knife, but the ears and fingers are exercised in the getting of pitch and tuning. After that comes the actual playing in unison and in parts, and, finally, if the spirit so moves one the finished pipe presents a splendid medium for freehand decoration, whether in carving or in painting or both. Blowing one's own trumpet has ceased, indeed, to be a term of reproach.

ø

'Wonnerful 'ow the weather changes d'rectly they goes about altering the proper time,' said the horseman on the advent of Summer time.

'Read notices on cabbage trees' was the instruction to visitors to a New Zealand gathering. The cabbage tree is Cordylina australis.

Scene I. A market. George: 'What dew yew give yar old cow when she's sick, Jimma?' Jimma: 'Tarpentine.' George: 'Ah!' Scene II. The same, a week later. George: 'What yew say yew give yar cow, Jimma?' Jimma: 'Tarpentine.' George: 'Tha's a rum 'un! So I did mine. But she died a-Thursday.' Jimma: 'So did mine.' George: 'Ah!'

On Spiders and Harvest Bugs
by the Duke of Bedford

SPIDERS are among the most harmless and interesting of the smaller animals—they are not insects—and are certainly among the most useful to us. Few, if any, even of the tropical species, possess the venomous properties with which they are credited. I should not like to assert definitely that all spiders are incapable of inflicting a dangerous bite, or unwilling to do so under provocation; but the unpleasant aptitudes ascribed to the Italian tarantula are, for all practical purposes, mythical, and even the huge and forbidding American 'bird-eating' spiders can be handled gently almost with impunity.

Certain foreign spiders provide examples of protective mimicry unsurpassed, even in the insect world, in strangeness and perfection; with some kinds the males perform a courtship display as striking as that of birds; while strange and elaborate uses of the web for insect catching reach their climax in the methods of an Australian spider which fishes in the air for moths by casting with one leg a line with a drop of sticky secretion on the end of it!

Some of our own British spiders are not unskilled in protective mimicry. One small orb weaver, not uncommon in gardens, and often found on yew bushes, has its abdomen strangely formed and coloured to resemble the dark portion of a bird's dropping; and to heighten the illusion it arranges some streaks of whitish silk immediately below where it sits in the centre of its web. The same of another species, when slightly alarmed, begins to shake its web so violently that it disappears in a blur of invisibility.

These actions are to be attributed to instinct rather than to deliberate reason, but a spider is not wholly devoid of intelligence, nor is it the automaton that some scientists assert. A few years ago I read in a scientific book that if an orb-weaving

---

The Duke, whose close interest in the rare animals in his park at Woburn Abbey is well known, has been a frequent contributor of natural history articles to the *Countryman* from the time he was Marquis of Tavistock. He is the author of *Parrots and Parrot-like Birds*, and I have heard of him once, while staying in a cottage on a speaking engagement, skilfully setting the leg of a canary.

spider be interrupted in the construction of its web it is unable to finish its work and is obliged to begin the whole process again from the start, first laying the outside framework, and then constructing the spokes and finishing with the sticky cross meshes. To put this assertion to the test I interrupted in the middle of her web-making a half-grown specimen of a little pinkish-grey orb weaver, common on the walls of houses. After the custom of her race when frightened, she dropped from her web, feigning death, but left a communication line by which to re-ascend. When her fears subsided, up she came, spent a few minutes in performing her toilet and then set herself to complete her unfinished work. *She* was not going to be labelled an automaton, anyhow! Under normal conditions the females of this spider live for about a year, the males dying after the breeding season in their first autumn and taking very little food after they become sexually mature. The young hatch about May and are fully grown in late summer or early autumn. After mating, the females deposit a cocoonful of eggs and in rather poor condition prepare for winter, spinning webs in the hope of catching a stray insect during every spell of mild weather. With the return of spring and better feeding they fatten up again, but nature is remorseless in requiring further maternal duties, and as soon as they are plump and strong a further batch of eggs is deposited, usually leaving them too weak to spin again. As an experiment I once tried to prolong the life of a female by feeding her on dead flies until she regained sufficient strength and condition to make her own living. As a result she laid, at intervals, five lots of eggs and survived until the early autumn of her second year, when she disappeared and, I have little doubt, died. A certain proportion of the eggs in her last cocoons were infertile.

The same species of spider and a little ichneumon fly figured in an amusing incident I once witnessed. The ichneumon, though a very tiny and slender insect, was equipped with a pair of sharp jaws and ability to use them to some purpose in an emergency. She was flying about in a myrtle bush when she chanced to blunder into one of the numerous spiders' webs hanging in all directions. Out rushed the spider, counting on an easy prey; snap went the ichneumon's jaws on her enemy's front foot, causing the latter to back off hastily. With a few wrenches and bites at the detaining threads, the ichneumon had cut herself free, only to fall plump into the web of the spider immediately below. Out came the owner of this web, snap went the ichneumon's jaws on *her* foot too; a few more struggles and the ichneumon sailed off in triumph, leaving two extremely discomfited spiders ruefully sucking their bleeding 'thumbs'. The whole tableau lasted about fifteen seconds only!

Critics of spiders are fond of commenting adversely on the alleged habit of the females of devouring their often smaller and weaker husbands. Certainly cannibalism is common in the spider world, and death may overtake a too venture-some suitor, but it is a gross libel to call the occurrence common. In very many species the females are quite gentle to their partners, and with those inclined to be hasty when dinner is late the experienced males are too well aware of danger to take unnecessary risks. I have often watched with amusement the approaches of a little male spider to his large and voracious lady. He endeavours to soothe her by continu-ally pulling and shaking the web, a proceeding which one might have thought more likely to irritate than charm the fair one, but presumably he knows what he is about. If they get to close quarters and she is inclined to be aggressive he backs away, trying to keep her at arm's length, and saying as plainly as anything by the language of touch 'Now, now, my dear, pray be calm; I am *not* a fly and I really do admire you immensely!'

Male spiders appear to possess the power of discovering, at great distances, potential brides, rather after the amazing fashion of certain male moths. The moment the female is ready to mate the male arrives, apparently from nowhere. Quite recently an immature female of a rather rare spider established herself in a room in my house, an unusual situation for an outdoor species. Immediately after her last moult, however, a male arrived, spent three days with her, disappeared, and, rather to my surprise, returned to her again a fortnight later.

Certain spiders, like certain birds and mammals, have adapted themselves with strange exclusiveness to man's handiwork. There is a rather large spider, related to the garden spider, which makes its home in tarred fences and tarred wooden buildings and is never, apparently, found anywhere else. Not only is its colour blackish, like tar, but its body is strangely flattened and adapted to the narrow crevices which are found between boards and in iron railings. Is this natural or 'unnatural' selection?

Another little spider appears to live exclusively in the flower and seed heads of rhododendrons, where it constructs an irregular web of threads running in all directions. The rhododendron is not a native British plant. Where did it live before there were rhododendrons in Britain, and what did the tarred fence spider do before there were modern fences and tar? Moreover how does the tarred fence spider reach (as it often does) the only tarred fence or building within miles of untarred country?

The common house spider, owner of a flat, sheet-like web, is, in many ways, an interesting creature. In the first place it may live for several years and in certain localities is capable of attaining an enormous size. The largest I ever saw used to live in the back premises of the college boathouse at Eton. I should be sorry to guess their exact measurements without a specimen, for fear of being put down as a romancer, but they were enormous: I never dreamed that such spiders existed outside the tropics. After I was grown up I returned and captured a pair. The female was only of normal size but the male was a real big fellow. He was in every way a perfect gentleman. He had a very small appetite and treated his mate with much gentleness; indeed when I returned him to her after he had got loose in the room for some days he seemed quite pleased to see her, quivering his abdomen and settling down contentedly beside her.

Owing to the nature of their haunts, house spiders have to be content with few and scanty meals. It is said that they can live without eating for nearly two years, and although I have never been brutal enough to impose a test fast, it is certainly the fact that captive specimens can go without eating for two months, not only without much loss of condition, but with benefit to their health.

A peculiarity of the house spider is its inveterate wander-lust—a fact which should be borne in mind by anyone who keeps a specimen in captivity. They need very roomy quarters, and, if possible, a change of quarters. Most animals are attracted to a place where the food supply is plentiful: not so the house spider. Feed a wild specimen until she is plump and portly, and within a week or two you will find her web empty. Nothing has disturbed her, but a restless instinct has driven her forth from the land of plenty to wander where meals are scanty and watches in the web-mouth long and vain.

The spider's poor relations, the mites and ticks, are, as a tribe, far from respectable and contain a number of highly disreputable characters. Still, there are exceptions: the little Hydrachnidae, the water mites, which, as a boy, I kept and studied for years, though without any literature to enlighten me as to species, are both beautiful and interesting. When immature they are parasitic on water insects, and I was never able to rear to maturity the six-legged young that hatched from sheet-like masses of eggs attached to the side of the toothbrush dish I used as an aquarium. The adults feed on minute crustaceans, or on the larvae of small gnats, and some have a tendency to cannibalism. One of the commonest scarlet species feeds on the lowly organisms which encase themselves in jelly-like masses on pond weeds during the summer months. A larger scarlet mite was a most curious creature in that its body was very soft, had no particular shape and remained crumpled into whatever form its last adventure happened to leave it! Notwithstanding this odd physical peculiarity, and the fact that it never appeared to feed, it was one of the hardiest of my mites; and plodded stolidly about the floor of its home for years! One of the most interesting peculiarities of the water mites, particularly of the river kinds, is their extraordinary variability. Not only do individuals of the same race often show great differences in colour, but almost every stream seems to have different species or sub-species which run into one another in the most bewildering fashion. Some of our ornithologists love making a new sub-species of every bird whose wings measure two millimetres more or less than the common form, or which appears a shade lighter or darker: what field days they could have if they took up the study of the Hydrachnidae!

Of the land mites, the little scarlet 'money-spider' is the best known. When adult he leads a blameless existence, scampering wildly about in a fearful hurry to go nowhere in particular, and refreshing himself on aphides in his few spare moments. In his youth, however, he is suspected of parasitic habits, and, in the disreputable guise of the 'harvest bug', of burrowing into our legs at blackberry time. The torture can be avoided by thoroughly smearing the legs with carbolic soap before entering the mites' haunts and allowing the soap to dry on the skin. Another familiar mite is the queer long-legged Harvestman or Shepherd Spider, usually mistaken for a true spider as he wanders about among the grass in late summer and autumn, often minus some of his extremely spindly and fragile legs, or uncomfortably adorned with minute scarlet parasites of his own family. What he lives on is a mystery to me. The only one I ever saw feed joined a shooting luncheon and partook of roast beef and plum pudding!

Of the ticks, like the famous aboriginal tribe it can only be said, 'Manners they have none and their customs are very beastly.' They are parasites of the worst kind, capable, in certain mountain and moorland districts, of conveying cattle diseases after the fashion of their relatives in tropical countries. One tick of the genus Ixodes can, in the autumn months, be a terror to the aviculturist who keeps foreign birds at liberty or in large thickly planted aviaries. So vora-cious and poisonous are these ticks that a single specimen can kill, not only a finch, but even a bird as large and strong as a Barbary dove.

🖉

Hedger in East Devon, describing an encounter between an adder and a frog: "Twor back-along in th' zummer time an' getting proper dimpsey-like, an' as I wor going home-along up auver th' knap, I zeed alongside zum brim'els, one o' they long cripples wi' a girt big twoad in's mouth, a-trying for to swaller 'en, so I hit 'en a clout auver's back an' thiccy twoad scrabbled out an' hopped away.'

I Go on Tramp and Thieve

IT was a dispute with my employer, a shipper in St. Mary Axe, concerning the reality of a slight indisposition which lost me my job. I was not worried very much. I had had many jobs—selling shirts to Jews, loading compressed hay with bare hands in Southampton Docks, shifting coal, working barges, among others. And I found myself with about 11s. and a week's rent paid in advance. The money quickly went, fortified though it was by the sale of clothes, medals, etc. For the medals I got half a crown from a Jewess in Leman Street. In the matter of food I was helped by the existence of Lyons' tea shops and the possibility of sitting near the door and slipping out when opportunity occurred. I knew from a waitress friend that the waitress did not suffer by this practice, and I was more concerned with my immediate needs than with my duty to Capital.

Unfortunately my landlady would not give credit. She gave me a day's notice instead. I don't blame her. My prospects were not bright. I found that the Labour Exchange as a means of providing employement was a waste of time. One might queue up for an hour and a half, only to be told 'Nothing to-day'. On some days, I would call on sixty or seventy different firms—a heartbreaking job. From haunting the City and West End I had to take to the suburbs. My clothes were getting shabby and my shoes down at heel. The process of demoralization had set in. I became less and less particular. I remember noticing a distinct tendency to walk on the kerb or in the gutter and the effort required to combat that tendency.

I renewed a previous acquaintance with common lodging houses, usually dark buildings with a lamp outside announcing, 'Good beds, men only'. The prices ranged from 9d. to 1s. 3d. For 1s. 3d. one obtained the use of a cubicle and the company of the insect inhabitants. For 9d. one slept in a large low room and shared the bugs, fleas, lice and cockroaches with—I counted one night 199 other people, and also the stench on a wet night and the steam rising from men's bodies. I used to spend half the night sitting up catching pests and the other half cursing the waste of 9d. for a sleep I did not get.

One could also listen to men talking in their sleep—in a very interesting way sometimes. Frequently there would be an inspection by the police for suspects or 'wanted' men.

I determined to go on the road. The first thing necessary was an overcoat. This I got by seizing an opportunity of lifting one from a car outside the Everyman theatre at Hampstead. I did not get it without a shock for as I put my hand in the car I must have touched the button of the electric horn. Every minute I expected someone to rush after me, but I got away. Reaching the Heath I tried the coat on. Alas, the sleeves just about reached my elbows, while the bottom of my coat did not come to my knees. It was useless, so I hid it under a bush. Next day I took another coat from the telegraph counter of the West Strand Post Office. This coat was as much too large as the first was too small. However, I made it do and had quite a comfortable night on the Heath.

The first night I was on the road I got a little farther than Barnet and slept in a large packing case filled with straw which I found in a nearly completed house. Next morning how to get food became a problem. I was rather lucky for I got away with a loaf of bread and a bottle of milk standing outside a door. How quickly one's notions of *meum* and *tuum* go by the board!

I determined that I would subsist as far as possible by getting odd gardening jobs. Despite many rebuffs I was quite successful. At one house at which I called, hoping for some odd job, a sweet old lady had no work to offer me. I asked for some water—I was really feeling rather ill—but the reply was that the rector had warned her against giving anything away at the door. My hope was that water might not be forthcoming when the parson tried the next world. In the same village, without being asked or spoken to, a young man and his wife took me to their cottage, gave me plenty of hot water for washing, a good meal, a shakedown and a packet of cigarettes. The man was an agricultural labourer earning 30s. a week. In a village near Stilton, an old man was mending or sweeping the road very early in the morning. He also took me to his cottage unasked. He gave me a jug of tea and an enormous breakfast.

Between Doncaster and Selby, policemen roped me in three times. On the third occasion, the policeman took me to a small pub, and, after questioning and searching me, paid for some tea, gave me a two shilling piece and walked off wishing me luck.

In one lodging house, I made a shilling by betting some of the men that I could move my ears. It is a somewhat unusual accomplishment. I was amusing the place for a couple of hours for the shilling.

In a lodging house in Leeds a fellow lodger took a fancy to a waterproof groundsheet which I had acquired. However, in the ensuing up-and-downer my application of the 'policeman's lift' left me in undisputed possession. As to sleeping on the tramp, sheaves of corn well arranged make a comfortable and warm bed. The drawback is that in the morning one is usually covered with uncomfortable tiny white insects.

There is a woman near Pontefract who should have been a taskmaster over Israel. I did her mangling, chopped her wood, cleaned her steps and windows, polished the brass and enamelled her bicycle, all for threepence and a sweet smile.

Haystacks, I found, are over-rated sleeping places. Barns are preferable, although one has to be out and about early to dodge the owners.

New houses were springing up all over the country and it was always an easy matter to get through a window of a nearly completed one. Here one could usually make up some kind of a bed, and sometimes, make a small fire between some bricks for tea.

As to the things that people give one, I have had Bibles, tracts, Testaments, tins of milk, tea, sugar, chocolate, cigarettes, boots, shoes, matches, and all manner of clothes.

Gradually I came not to worry much about trying to get a decent job. At first I used to visit the libraries of different towns to study the advertisements, but after being turned away from one, presumably on account of my not very clean appearance, I didn't trouble. I was getting experienced, too. Like the regular tramp, I learnt that it was better to avoid the larger towns; country folk and rural police are much better disposed than urban.

For a while I made my headquarters in a bungalow near Lincoln—doors and other openings carefully closed, except, of course, for the bathroom window. From here, in company with another man, I went to the races, where by the expenditure of much lung power and the appropriate costume of my partner, namely leggings and breeches, we were able to assert our intimate relations with leading trainers and owners and to sell the results of their supposed confidences to not a few people. Our method was to write the names of many horses in each race on slips and thus be fairly sure of including the winner. On the first day we shared about fifty shillings and should have divided more on the last day had not my partner left me to get a 'wash and brush up' at the station and found himself on the train for London with my share.

My next job was with a Jew in the market-place of several little market towns. His speciality was the sale of a wonderful tonic. He helped it along with an offer to restore silver to a new and brilliant condition. He made the restoration by the simple device of dipping the article into a jar of acid. This process, worked in front of labourers and small farmers, seldom failed to establish the efficacy of the medicine. It was my job to move round the crowd after my colleague's preliminary remarks and sell the stuff—'9d. large, a "tanner" small'. If, at the start, no silver article was forthcoming, the orator would appeal to me and I would produce a carefully soiled watch-chain which he had previously given me. This job didn't last long. We parted company owing to my knocking over the wonder-worker's jar of acid and to the mutual recriminations which followed.

✍

Mistress of remote manor to new maid, 'Isn't that someone at the door, Ethel?' Ethel, 'Can't be nobody, mum, the postman's bin.'

Wiltshire coachman inquiring for a cooper, 'Tisn't n'ere a cupper in Devizes is it?'

The J.P., examining mental powers of alleged mental deficient in a rural poor law institution, asked: 'Now, my girl, if you had a pound and bought 5s. worth of groceries, how much would you have left?' No answer. Finally, the master intervened and urged Jane to give her answer. Jane, with an offended air: 'If this old fool doesn't know, I'm not going to tell him.' J.P., delighted, 'She's all right.'

The Country in London
by Sir Timothy Eden

IT is an odd and pleasant thing that London's heart is green. Her head, in the City, may be full of money and noise, she may stretch her ugly limbs to Tottenham, Ealing and Woolwich, she may dabble her dirty fingers in the Thames at Rotherhithe, but her heart is green. It is this greenness which makes her the natural, sympathetic capital of England, a land where attention is still given to the quiet influence of grass.

Hyde Park and Kensington Gardens are generally regarded together and are sometimes even confused by the casual visitor. But to anyone with more than a passing acquaintance with their moods and atmosphere, there is a vast difference. Hyde Park, at the first glance, has many advantages. Against the dead sweetness of Peter Pan and the insipidity of nursery-maids, it can set the living Epstein, Rotten Row and the heady orators under the shadow of the Marble Arch. To Hyde Park, moreover, belong all the glories of the past. In Kensington Gardens we can only think of Queen Caroline, and we are not quite sure who she was. In Hyde Park long ago, the monks of Westminster enjoyed a day in the country, replying to the song of birds with psalmodies and Aves. Here the burly form of Henry VIII burst—swearing, no doubt—through the greenwood in pursuit of the deer. Here the Moroccan ambassador and his suite raced past on their fleet Arabs, flinging and catching their javelins in the air. Here Henrietta Maria walked in sack-cloth to Tyburn. Here duels were fought to the death. Here masked highwaymen lurked for the hurrying traveller. Here, in more peaceful days, was the elementary pitch of a dignified Georgian cricket.

But the true lover of the country is little concerned with the past. For him the world is all coming and going. Death and life are both over in a moment. There is no time for lament. Yesterday's sorrow for the passing primrose is forgotten in the triumph of to-day and the scent of its lilac. So what do we

Sir Timothy is the author of *Five Dogs and Two More* and *The Tribulations of a Baronet*. He is the elder brother of Mr. Anthony Eden, M.P., ex-Foreign Secretary.

99

care, as we walk through Hyde Park, for the memories that lie there and the woodland that is no more! For the present we have grass, and sheep, and the Serpentine with its gulls, and a police station, and Ajax defying the lightning, or Achilles, or an Italian horse-tamer, as he has variously been called. We have also a few good trees, but not enough. Here Kensington Gardens score heavily, though there is a pleasant little grove of birches which they cannot claim.

Rotten Row has associations for a countryman, whatever air of unreality there may be about this wide country sport so carefully limited to a ribbon of artificial dirt. There is something unnatural in the sight of these horses pounding steadily round and round like animals in a circus.

We have still two beauty-spots to visit before we leave Hyde Park. The first is the Serpentine where people bathe; but we are come to see bathers of another sort. We are come for the gulls, and the cross-looking geese, and all the gay varieties of duck which we try laboriously to identify with the help of coloured plates thoughtfully displayed for our guidance.

My second beauty-spot is the bird sanctuary, in the very centre of which is the hated Epstein. So let me say at once that I like it, that I admire it. At least you will admit that it is beautifully placed; the semi-circular background of shrubs and trees, the stretch of clean green grass, the bird-baths, where sparrows and other birds dip and flirt their wings. This is one of the quietest spots in London. Whether it be Mr. Epstein who scares the people away, or because it is on the way to nowhere, I cannot tell, but I have never met more than a very occasional passer-by. So here you can lean against the railings and hear nothing louder than the singing of birds, with the faint drone of distant traffic for their accompaniment; you can look at trees and grass and poor Rima with her large welcoming hands. If you will lean long enough, perhaps her quietness and simplicity will suddenly impress themselves upon you, and forthwith you will cease to worry about her proportions and her ugly face, and you will see that the thought given to her goes very deep indeed.

Kensington Gardens are more lovely and friendly than

Hyde Park because of the trees. There are, no doubt, more beautiful trees elsewhere. There are older trees, and larger trees, and rarer trees, and altogether more remarkable trees, But there are none which seem to the Londoner, when he comes to them for refuge from the traffic and the pavements, so representative of all that is best in trees, so absolutely satisfying—in shape, in number, in their distance from each other, in just the proper quality of 'tree-ness'. It is partly the sharp contrast between the trees and their surroundings which so appeals to us, between the tiny leaf and the motor-bus, between the bustling woman with her arms full of paper bags and the green serenities that meet above her head. But much of our satisfaction is due to the skill of the planter, or to the wind, or the taste of the man with the axe; to the fact that here is one of the few spots in England where one may see ornamental trees properly spaced, not overcrowded, and unencumbered by an underworld of shrubs. Here we are troubled by no fussy bits of laurel or of holly, such as catch up the travelling eye in almost every garden of England. Here are vistas and compositions, unimpeded and in endless variety, of bare sepia trunks on the short green grass until, in the distance, enchanted by the light which seems to drop before them like a curtain, the trees are floating blue on a sea which is grey.

Perhaps it is, above all, the peculiar light which has placed these trees in a category by themselves. The light in Kensington Gardens—and in Hyde Park, though in a slightly less degree—is a light of which you can see the colour, less a light than a luminous haze, which in the morning is of the palest blue, with the softness of grey in it, which changes to amethyst as the day wears in, and in the evening turns to violet of such pure blue and such deep intensity as to seem unreal. It is a light not only to see, but almost to feel, like an airy cloak about the shoulders. Coming from Oxford street, in the evening, on the top of a bus, we dive suddenly into it as into a sea, while the lamps are being lit all the way down to Notting Hill and the common macadam road is become a high-road through a dream. And I suppose hundreds of people have walked through Kensington Gardens and noticed nothing remarkable in the air at all!

What does appeal to them? Peter Pan, of course, and the children, and the dogs, and the flowers. The flowers in Kensington Gardens. People stand, yards deep, gaping at the dahlias, about which the gossipy newpapers go into ecstasies. Individually there is nothing to be said against these flowers. They are magnificent specimens. But collectively? As arranged? Scarlets side by side with mauves, blues and pinks and oranges all higgledy-piggledy, and here one, and there one, scarcely ever two of the same colour or the same shade together, and so all the beauty of the individual flower not only lost, but transformed into an aid to billiousness, through lack of the most elementary taste! How much more beautiful that corner looks when the dahlias are gone and the eye rests contentedly upon a patch of bare brown earth! The way of beauty in gardening is to mass, all your blues with all your mauves, all your yellows with all your oranges, and then your scarlets, if you must have scarlets. This is not the way of the gardener in public parks. Yet I must admit that people like the gardener's way. They think it bright I suppose, because they have seen no better. The Flower Walk—the famous Flower Walk in Kensington Gardens—is as bad, or even worse. In the country we have herbaceous borders. And even here are a few mangy delphiniums which make us happy for a moment. Why may we not have more of them? Why may we not have a herbaceous border here? Come! Let us walk away from the Flower Walk! Let us hurry to the Round Pond!

Here are neither trees nor flowers, but excited, barking dogs to greet us, and children who crane and topple on the edge of the water, and great yachts sailing artfully in the teeth of the wind. They make a pretty picture. Yet there is something a little irritating in the spectacle of heavy grown-up men, without a smile on their faces, trimming toy sails for hours on end.

The grey squirrels in the gardens are the delight of wandering old men. There is something artificial about the tameness of these animals. There is too much presumption of immunity; in spite of the dogs that rush at them and send them scampering back again, up the boles of the elms. These cheeky little grey brutes have none of that wild shyness which makes the English squirrel, flashing high up in a red-brown streak, so attractive in his native woods. And the wood-pigeons here move like aldermen after a feast, puffed and gorged with food, oblivious of the existence of a shot-gun. But what delights do they miss besides the perils of a wilder life—the long summer days in the cornfields, the flight home in the darkening, windy sky, the final sweep and clutter into the rusty friendliness of an old Scotch fir! It is better to risk the flash of a gun out of the darkness than to be chased, after dinner, by a yapping Pekingese.

✑

A Bailiff's Notions

'THERE are many sorts of rogues up country,' said a farm bailiff, only he spoke in his dialect, 'but, wherever people farm, you find two of the worst. You'll never keep horse dealers or lawyers from taking the hard-earned cash of the honest farmer, little though there be to take. If you've got five shillings, one or other of them two people will have it sooner or later. The way they find out what you've got shows their cleverness; the way they get it shows their knavery. If you're a mile to the east of 'em with a west wind blowing they'll scent what you're worth. And when they've found that you've got five shillings they'll persuade you that the only way to make another five bob is by giving them what you've already got. Or else they'll say that the way prices are going and what with the weather you'll lose what you've got anyhow, so you might as well let them have it with the chance of getting something back than to see it disappear with nothing in return.'—*R.F.G.*

✑

Whisper at women's institute after peeress visitor had delivered her address. 'You'd never know she was a Lady.'

'Fine lot of beans,' the visitor said over the wall to the best farm-worker in his village. 'Aye,' said Samuel, 'I could bide up all night a-atin on 'em.'

103

Characters

by Viscount Charlemont

PATRICK SMITH has just been here, looking (he said) for something for his shest, the Cuckoo Winter (April 20th) being known to be a sore time for shests. The price of whiskey is, however, far sorer to Patrick than any cuckoo could ever be and some relief in this direction was what he was really looking for. As I watched his queer little figure going shambling (but cheerfully) down the drive I remembered that Patrick was never anything but odd and a wanderer who couldn't stay more than a month anywhere. During that month he was an excellent specimen of the casual labourer who could turn his hand to anything, but only so long as there was supervision. If that was lacking one never knew what Patrick would do. On one occasion I had him weeding a path some distance from the house by the side of a stream—it was in the summer. I went to see how he was getting on; his tools were there but Patrick himself was missing. I called him and there was a gurgle from the stream in which I found Patrick reclining in the weeds with only his mouth and nose showing—he had his clothes on too!

'I just took a wee while off to get cool', he said, rising slowly and with dignity; 'watther's good for the skin, so it is, and it'll dry on me.' A few days after this he told me he wanted to go somewhere else as he had been told there were badgers in the wood nearby—'I wouldn't be working on my lone there with all these sthrange bastes about', he said.

My earliest recollection of an odd 'character' was of a carpenter employed by an uncle of mine; he wiped his paint brushes in his hair. Any doctor would tell you that this would be a bad thing to do, producing eruptions and maybe lead-poisoning, but Ned was an extremely healthy old man, though his hair was unlike anyone else's hair, quite solid and varying in colour according to, the paint he was using.

Most of these 'characters' were agreeable, but I had one disagreeable gardener. He was good at his job but always full of complaints about the way in which Nature fought against

104

him; much more here, he said, than in any place he'd ever
been in before. 'I'd do well with the fruit here if the bül-
finches didn't have it all desthroyed on me. And then squirrels, God knows they have all the peas ate and the garden's
polluted with rats, so it is.' It was impossible to catch him
out. He was always comparing Drumcairne with Dromore,
his last place. If I complained about anything I was told I
ought to see Dromore, that was a wonderful place, it was a
pity he'd ever left it. But on going over one day to Dromore I
thought it was very inferior to Drumcairne in every way (I
would think the same of Windsor Castle or Chatsworth) and
on my return I told this to Johnny. 'That's what I've always
been telling you,' he said; 'a man who could be a gardener at
Dromore could be a gardener annywhere.'

I suppose most people have suffered from old servants in
one way or another, but there's a directness of speech in the
Irish variety that is disconcerting and difficult, if not impossible to deal with.

In my childhood I knew a Colonel Smyth who had been in
the Indian Army. Curry and a hot sun during many years had
produced a very short temper in him and he was rather an
alarming man in himself. One day I lost my fear of him, for
I heard him conversing with his old gardener whom he was
scolding, with that picturesque language that one acquires in
the East, for something done or not done. 'You damned old
fool', Colonel Smyth was continuing, 'you won't do what I—
dammit, you're not listening to me!' 'I'm listening to you,
Master Reggie', was the reply, 'but I'm not heeding ya.' I
expected a frightful explosion from 'Master Reggie', but
evidently he knew only too well that he could do nothing;
there was a deep silence for a minute or two and then a
remark to the effect that rain might be beneficial to the crops.

By far the oddest character I ever employed was Barney
McQuaid. He was a very tall and thin old man with very light
blue eyes with a queer dancing light in them; he was a bit
eccentric, I knew, as it was his practice in summer! to put
his donkey, of which he was very fond—he called it 'a bould
wee ornament'—in his bedroom while he lived himself in his
wood-shed. 'She is annoyed with all them flies', he said. I

was a little disconcerted one day, however, when I found him gazing at the view from the terrace here in the intervals of scything the grass. 'The two finest prospects in all the world', he said, 'are from this place and Edenfield Asylum.' 'Were you working there?' I asked, 'or were you—living there?' 'I was just putt there', said Barney simply; 'I was there for a wee while—something to do with a scythe.' He was with me till he died, and he left me 'the bould wee ornament', and I have her still. Barney believed thoroughly in fairies, from whose attentions he had suffered to some extent, he said, but he had one story of his childhood which proved that eccentric characters in the old days were found in all classes. 'When I was a wee boy we all lived in a little house down at Bellmont. It was a quare wee place and it had no chimbly, and no window would open, and we all had sore eyes in the winter with the smoke, and my mother was always at Mr. Bell to make us a chimbly. Well, we all thought we'd die of old age before we got a chimbly, but Mr. Bell came down one morning with an ould gun and bags full of cartridges and didn't he sit on a creepy stool (a small stool with three legs) and fire at the roof all day till he'd blew a hole in it. "There's you chimbly", he said, "and now you won't be bothering me anny more about chimblies." God rest his soul but he was a quare man, so he was.'

They say 'characters' are dying out, but I don't suppose this is really so; 'characters' almost invariably belong to a previous generation to oneself while one's contemporaries appear common place. If I can manage to live for another twenty years I have some hopes of becoming a 'queer character' myself!

Seeing two second-hand books, a novel and a recent popular study of Casanova, being picked out from the medley of a general shop in a small market-town, the proprietor said apologetically: 'That one'll have to be a shilling, seeing it's a story, but'—brightening—'the other's only ninepence, being educational like.'

Jan earned his living by driving a wagonette. On one occasion, somewhat overcome by the hospitality of a fare, he slept by the roadside. Waggish friends took his horse out of the shafts, and on waking he was heard to say, 'Be I Jan Stewer or be I not? If I be Jan I've lost a horse, but if I bain't I've found a wagonette!'

Why Do Dogs Like Motoring?

Every owner of a dog and a car must have wondered why most dogs like motoring so much. Professor Julian Huxley, when asked about it, replied: 'I wish I had any inkling of the answer, but I could only make guesses and my guesses would have no biological basis.' A letter from Professor J. B. S. Haldane, showed what a wide subject the question opens up. 'The following questions, could they be answered, would help us to solve the problem: 1. Are there differences in this respect between dogs which habitually hunt by sight and by smell? 2. Do dogs which have lost their sight still enjoy motoring as much as other old dogs? 3. Why precisely do men and women enjoy motoring?' Here are other replies:

Sir Frederick Hobday of the Royal Veterinary College: 'I am quite sure that many dogs do derive intense and intelligent satisfaction from riding in a car, quite apart from whether they are in the company of their masters or mistresses. Naturally, owing to the 'palship' which exists between a dog and its owner, it causes greater pleasure to the animal if that beloved owner is also present; but I am quite certain, from personal observation and consideration, that the motor riding in itself gives many dogs very great pleasure.'

Principal A. W. Whitehouse, Glasgow Veterinary College: 'There is no doubt that most dogs enjoy motoring very much more than I do, nor is their pleasure due to the consideration that the inside of a car is the only comparatively safe place on a country road. As far as I can see they are reckless little beggars and really like speed—the faster the better. They like to look out and pass other dogs; but on the whole it seems to me that their feelings are much like those of their masters or mistresses: it is the rapid change of scene that appeals to them, and they are always ready to show their feelings. I am one of those that can see no difference in kind between the minds of animals and human beings, only differences in degrees.'

Dr. O. Charnock Bradley, Principal of the Royal (Dick) Veterinary College, Edinburgh: 'The answer is made none the easier by the recollection that we have dogs apparently unmoved by the privilege of motoring, evincing neither special pleasure nor definite dislike, while others decidedly do not like the experience. Incidentally, also, though this is of

---

These three authorities are, alas, now dead.

minor moment in the present instance, we have perhaps reminded ourselves that it is not difficult to fall into error when trying to translate animal behaviour into terms of human language. This danger is probably at its minimum when dealing with the dog for, having been associated with man for thousands of generations, he has become the most 'humanized' of all animals, and expresses his feelings in a fashion that is scarcely likely to be misread by the person he owns. But even if we frame the question very cautiously: Why do most dogs display a desire to ride in motor cars, and exhibit what we humans regard as signs of pleasure when permitted to do so? a satisfactory answer is not possible without considerable reservation. It is quite possible that many will immediately think that speed—an essential faculty of dog, the hunter—is the attraction. And, in the days before the advent of the motor car, dogs liked to ride in a trap or carriage, the speediest road-vehicle of that time. But dogs did not, and still do not despise the homely, plodding farm-cart. It would be an interesting experiment to allow him the choice of farm-cart, trap, and motor car, and see which he would prefer—always providing conditions absolutely, including experience, equal in each case. There is a subsidiary question. Does the dog prefer the open tourer or the closed saloon? And, from what one has seen, the dog in the open tourer has far and away the jollier time.

'The dog's world is a world made up very largely of smells, and the closed saloon contains few of those in which the dog is really interested. The open tourer brings to the dog hundreds of wildly exciting and enchanting odours every minute. And the dog is a creature that is either sleeping or hunting for smells. Few normal dogs, when awake, will choose to remain indoors if they can get out, and when out they are constantly investigating odours. Does elevation above the common herd play any part in the matter! Without doubt a primitive instinct in the dog is to get into a position from which he may observe the approach of friend or foe, or become informed of the possibility of replenishing the larder. The domesticated dog likes to get on to a wall. And when on the wall—or in the motor car—he is not over careful of the language he addresses to other dogs less favourably placed. On the ground, and therefore on a level with his fellows, he may be a silent and very discreet person, but otherwise, otherwise. There are other secondary questions that might be asked, such as, Does the dog regard the car as a detachable part of his home, and therefore a place of safety to which are added the advantages hinted at above? Doubtless every individual will hold his own opinion as to the correct answer to the primary question; and, equally doubtless, different individuals will hold different views—all possibly more or less correct. It is one of the things without number on which it is not safe to be too dogmatic.'

Mr. Frederick W. Cousens, M.R.C.V.S., editor of 'Sewell's Dog's Medical Dictionary', for twelve years honorary consulting surgeon to the Zoo: 'This very interesting question has often fascinated me. The vast majority of educated dogs enjoy motoring in very much the same way that we enjoy it. I have known only one dog, a griffon, that did not find pleasure in going out in a car—the vibrations made the little lady sick. My own dogs, a rather large variety, bloodhounds, Irish wolfhounds, various terriers, French bulls, Pekingese and Brussels griffon, all clamour for a ride. Several will jump into a private car if the door is open and the car standing anywhere near my house. These dog passengers see most of the things we see and enjoy seeing them. They feel a bit superior to the pedestrian dog, and, according to disposition, show it, some by barking, some by airs and graces, particularly Pekingese. The larger breeds love the passing through the air rapidly. Of course the windows must be down for perfect enjoyment, so that they lose nothing, not even the rain unless it be violent. Scenery and locality, if known to them, are immediately recognized. They prefer a smooth running car to one that bumps or rattles. Nothing is too fast for them. Very little escapes their notice in fields adjacent to the highway—rabbits, hares, game, but not so much cattle or horses, and yet deer excite attention. One of my Irish wolfhounds sits on an outside seat, front legs on floor of car, head out of window, only occasionally looking round to let me know how he is enjoying every moment: people, things, places, town or country, all come in for minute inspection. The dog looking out of a car is higher up than when on his own legs and sees more than usual; that is part of the fascination undoubtedly. I fancy that comparatively few dogs like motoring alone.

'Hunting dogs, as you know, are not very generally used to travelling in cars with their owners or with those who would be likely to notice the differentation in enjoyment. In the case of all the dogs which have come under my notice in the circumstances you name—and for forty years I have nearly lived in a brougham or a car, and have nearly always had one or more dogs with me of my own—the nose had the advantage every time. As to old dogs, all the senses are dulled in them, and although, in the vast majority of cases, sight and hearing are affected more and earlier than smell, yet the loss of sight in the average dog would materially affect his enjoyment of motoring. Over against this I could give cases among my own dogs and among my patients in which blind dogs— some totally blind—have been so expert with their noses that they have hunted on the flat with little inconvenience and few mistakes. These dogs appear to develop another sense to aid them. If it is not so, one cannot give a sufficient reason for their extraordinary facility in surmounting difficulties which would ordinarily be considered insurmountable. When a dog's sight goes fairly early in life and the life is spared and time and patience (a lot of it) is spent, quite extraordinary results are obtained if the animal has the gift of scent highly developed. My personal knowledge of this is confined to bloodhounds which have been used for tracking, always with the clean boot. I have written to two of my old clients who I know well have blind friends of the hunting breeds and have asked them to let me know at their early convenience, exactly what they have experienced. You shall have their reports. I will also put you into communication with two professors.'

Mr. Joe Walker, author of 'My Dog and Yours' and 'That Dog of Mine', being puzzled to find an answer to our question, questioned a friend of his: 'Master has asked me to try and tell you why I like to jump into the car when it comes round. Well, in the first place, to watch folks go off anywhere without you is pretty mournful; partly because one hates to be left

110

behind since one never knows what excitements one may miss in consequence, and, naturally, also, one always wants to be close at hand to protect "them" wherever they may be. For my part, give me a good walk, with lots of time for routing round on my own, in preference to a ride in the car, but I like the latter, too, very much because *one sees such a lot all in a heap*, and wooshing through the air is very exhilarating and makes biscuits taste extra good when plate-time comes round. Again, it's rather fun to see pals trotting along the path on their four legs and to watch them look up suddenly when you call out "Cheerio!" as you rush past. Not that one feels superior, exactly, but—(Master says this means I'm a "snob" —whatever that is, but I'm sure he's wrong.) One great advantage of a car is that, being perched up so high, you can see a long way in front and also over the hedges. I notice this especially because I'm short-legged. (Hopkinson says I'm low in the chassis.) As to *what* I see—well, I dunno that it matters much in a way for mostly one is moving too quickly to distinguish things very clearly. "Hullo, that's a cat—wasn't it?" is the sort of thing that keeps occurring, but one doesn't mind for there's sure to be some other excitement in a moment—either another cat, or a new smell blows along, or Hopkinson toots 'cos somebody won't get out of the way, or we have to pull up with a jerk at cross-roads. Yes, the great thing about a car is—*there is always something happening*.'

Miss Mazo de la Roche, author of 'The Portrait of a Dog': 'I think the dog's pleasure is only partly due to the outing in the company of master or mistress. My Scottie refused to go for a walk with a friend of the house, but she would joyously accompany any stranger who drove a car. On one occasion, after she had become totally blind, she escaped from the house and climbed into an immense van which was removing our furniture to another part of the town. She established herself on the driver's seat, and sat there awaiting the departure with an air of ineffable satisfaction. She always delighted in motoring and this delight increased with her blindness. She had been a great hunter and, in my opinion, she recaptured something of the exhilaration of the chase in the swift movement of motoring. The car could not go too fast to please her. If it slowed down she would utter whines of protest. If it actually stopped, the whines would almost become howls. She never sat down in a car but stood, braced tense, facing the wind. Now and again she would turn her face toward me with an apologetic expression as though to say: "I have not forgotten that you are here but there are certain pleasures I cannot share with you." Her nose never ceased its sensitive quivering.'

Lady Kitty Ritson, author of 'Dogs: an Illustrated Handbook', ' A very great percentage are far too car-sick to like it, and they never do get used to it. On the whole, smaller breeds such as dachshunds like it better than bigger dogs, but as dachshunds are remarkable for their sense of smell and so are Alsatians (who are very often very sick) I do not associate the two conditions. I believe small dogs get a sort of drugged feeling. My two dachshunds always begged to come, and as long as the windows were shut and it was very warm, they would lie with their heads hanging down, never moving for hours, and apparently insensible. But if I introduced a little air, they were furious! I think that dogs often like motoring more because it means that they are accompanying their master or mistress than because of the actual motoring. On the other hand, they may feel soothed, as personally, nothing soothes me more than driving myself on a good day along a pleasant road. With twenty years' experience of dogs, I am not convinced that they are so universally fond of motoring as is sometimes imagined.'

Miss Frances Pitt: 'That dogs do take pleasure in a motor ride no one may question, even those dogs on which the motion has dire results! I have known several dogs that were invariably sick after a few minutes in a car, yet they were none the less keen for a ride. Nor have I known any dog, once used to a motor car, that was otherwise than pleasurably excited at the prospect of getting into one. In some cases the pleasure may be due to being able to see and smell so much that is new, but anyone who has seen foxhounds delightedly scrambling at the close of their day's work into a closed van, whence they cannot see anything or smell much, would conclude that the pleasure lay in the prospect of a ride. Recollections of, as a small child, climbing into farm-carts for the joy of riding in them makes me wonder if the dog's emotion is not similar to the joyful excitement I then felt, the pleasure being in the ride, just the riding in the cart and nothing else!'

Mr. E. Douglas Wolff, M.R.C.S., L.R.C.P., has kept dogs ever since he can remember and now breeds Labradors and golden retrievers: 'Dogs are very much given to forming associations in their minds with things pleasant or otherwise and these things stick in their heads. This is the basis of dog training. The most obvious reason why my dogs like motoring —I have kept dogs ever since I can remember and now breed Labradors and golden retrievers—is that they associate going in the car with going to shoots. But all dogs are not gun dogs, and I know a local terrier, belonging to a doctor, which loves to go in his car on his rounds, though it never as much as gets out while he sees his patients. An old Labrador of mine often goes to sleep in the car and does not even look out, though on one occasion when she was awake and looking out, a hare committed suicide, and the instant I pulled up she was out and back along the road and retrieved the hare to hand. Others of my dogs sit up and look out the whole time and notice things, such as game getting up or other dogs on the road side. One little cocker sings during the whole journey. In his case I am sure it is anticipation of shooting as he will do the same in the house if he has the least idea that I have gone out with a gun. Some dogs are always car-sick and I am sure they do not love motoring. I am certain that the dog's mind differs only from the human in degree. It is not true that the dog is entirely a creature of instinct. The dog has more pure instinct and less reasoning power developed than the human, but it is only a matter of degree. Many humans like the sensation of speed. This may have its counterpart in the dog. Most dogs in an open car like to hang their heads out in the wind. But then again, my dogs like to get into the car when I have come in from a run, just to be driven twenty-five yards round to the garage, and that possibly in low gear—not much rushing through the air here! To sum up. I am not sure that the explanation is not as follows. Dogs first like going in the car for obvious reasons, i.e. companionship of master, getting to a shoot, etc., and so form an association of car and pleasure in their minds, and later on rejoice in motoring as being a change from rather boring monotony. But how is it that if the car should be going down to the garage when all the dogs are having a good romp in the park with my wife or myself, they will rush down to get in?'

Mr. A. Croxton Smith, author of 'About our Dogs', 'Tail Waggers', etc.: 'No doubt several reasons account for the signs of pleasure shown by most dogs at the prospect of a ride. Probably the chief is their love of change. They appreciate variety, and are almost as capable of suffering from boredom as we are. See how delighted the average healthy dog is with a walk. Certainly it is not that he is aware of the benefits of exercise, but because it means doing something fresh. Another reason may be almost as cogent. A dog loves to feel that he is one of the family, and as such is permitted to share in whatever master or mistress may be doing. He would be miserable if he were left behind, and the thought of going with master or mistress fills his cup of joy. He is an intimate of theirs, privileged to be in their company. It is possible, too, that he enjoys the sensation of rapid movement. Our own dog looks forward to a motor ride or journey by train, and once or twice he has left us to run into a station. Some dogs, by the way, are sick when travelling. Mr. A. J. Sewell in "The Dog's Medical Dictionary" recommends giving them chlorotone in a capsule about an hour before starting, the dose being two grains for the smallest breeds, five grains for the biggest, and intermediate quantities according to size.'

The late Mr. Harry Price, National Laboratory of Psychical Research for the Scientific Investigation of Alleged Abnormal Phenomena: 'Wendy at home and Wendy in my car are not the same. In my study she is demure, obedient and not particularly observant. In my car she becomes a little hooligan with a disdainful growl at those of her kind who are unfortunate enough to be compelled to pad it in the mud. I have observed that usually Wendy is unobservant, but in my car she acquired the visual organs of an eagle and the sensitivity of a microphone and can see and hear a horse (literally *bête noire* to her) a mile away. This is curious, because on her walks she passes a horse with a contemptuous sniff as being unworthy of notice. But in the car she shrieks out her superiority over the equine slowness of her pet aversion as we flash by and leave Dobbin wondering what all the commotion is about. Yes, I think the secret is a sense of superiority—a Triton of a flying Wendy among the minnows who are not able to propel themselves by mechanical means.'

Ernest Thomson Seton, the distinguished artist-naturalist: 'All sentient beings love the sensation of rapid motion, and the more so when that is secured with little or no effort on their behalf. I believe that all animals would learn to enjoy the swift transit of a car ride when their fear of its strangeness was overcome.'

Mr. Jorian E. F. Jenks: 'If our terrier (one of the old Jack Russell strain) is missing, the first place we go to is the garage. Lately I have been doing some rabbit-fencing, and since all the horses are busy, have taken the material in the car each morning, parking close to the job. Although rabbits are one of the dog's great interests, and the locality is full of them, she remains in the car all day, descending only at long intervals to see how we are getting on.'

Miss Ruth Bickersteth, who has always had a Jack Russell: 'One of them used to suffer from sickness when not allowed to have its head out of the window of a car or railway carriage. Another Jack Russell is always sick in a small boat, but—and it had done a good deal of voyaging—never in a steamer. The keen enjoyment of travel by car and rail is due to going somewhere, companionship in adventure, anticipation of further excitements, and all the time interesting new smells and the sight of other animals and a feeling of superiority over them; it is surely having nothing interesting to smell or look at makes a dog bored and sick at sea.'

L.J.: 'My Airedale's intense preoccupation with cars somewhat shocked me. I preferred to think of dogs as the best type of Countryman, pottering round hedgerows and rabbit-burrows, alert to each rural sound and smell, and when driven to the side of the road, growling that the country wasn't what it was. But Peter would leap on the rack of the

115

chauffeur's motor bicycle with all the frivolous alacrity of a flapper and balance himself on it at quite a high speed. On one occasion when the chauffeur invited me to test the cycle's speed in the trailer, Peter wrestled his way in too and as we touched 90 miles, and I prayed that if death came it might be swift, he howled with delight, his whiskers streaming, his body taut—turned before my eyes into a complete road-hog.'

Mr. F. G. Forshaw, writing as the owner of a kennel, tells of experimenting with two dogs—an English setter and an eight-year old airedale. 'Both have travelled far and often in a car, and being housed in hotel stables are friendly and used to meeting people, in fact the airedale is allowed complete liberty. A friend of mine was keen to have this airedale and suggested that he could take the dog from us at any time, owing to the dog's love for a car. On being invited to the front seat the dog accepted with alacrity, sat there with great contentment and was obviously very pleased. But when the car began to move he became frenzied, almost breaking the window to get out. Here seems to be a case in which a dog, fond enough of a car to sit in one while stationary (a thing he often does), was only interested in being driven by the person he was fond of. It is worth while noting that this same dog always stands on the seat, head out of window, showing more than the usual signs of complete enjoyment. Now as to the setter. He will jump into any car at every opportunity, but he also refuses to accompany anyone he is not well acquainted with. There is, however, a difference. This setter always curls up and goes to sleep immediately the car starts to move and continues to sleep until he realizes the car has stopped, when he at once sits up and takes notice. In this case it is difficult to say why the dog likes to be in a car, and whether he is pleased or not. I have several other setters, all used to cars and eager to go for a ride but with one exception they all curl up and sleep.'

Mr. Sydney H. Ottley: 'We have at home a mongrel (exhibiting strong signs of a not distant greyhound ancestry) which has withstood all my efforts to persuade him to join us even for the shortest run.'

116

WHY SHOULD I WALK?

TWO MORE DOG STUDIES

Mr. William Rose Burns: 'In India I had a Manchester terrier devoted to motoring. One day at Karachi when I had climbed into an aeroplane, the pup came too. Her excitement communicated by heart-beats was intense. After a safe landing joyful ecstasies continued.'

Mr. A. W. Horabin (*Western Australia*): 'Some of the car-riding dogs here are in a class of their own. They ride standing on the running board of the car. On most cars there is quite a big space where the running board joins the front mudguard, and you will often see farmers driving about with the sheep-dog standing there. I suppose it requires a little training, because I have only seen farmers' dogs do it and never town dogs. Also I have only seen one dog which lies down. Most of them stand, and when there are two dogs, one each side, the effect is quite smart, like the footmen on the royal coach. They seem to be able to balance wonderfully. I have seen then travel like this at a speed of 30 m.p.h. on rough roads.'

Mr. J. de G. Delmege (*Kenya*): 'As a district officer in a native protectorate my duties involved much travelling, both by car and lorry, and I found my terriers equally fond of either. My impression always has been that one of the chief reasons for the attraction is the fear of being left behind, that ever present bugbear of a dog's existence. Once aboard they felt themselves secure. Of course there were individual idiosyncrasies. Binkie, a pseudo-scottie, was a car snob. If nothing better offered he would sit himself in my assistant's little air-cooled Rover 8, but when my 17 h.p. Overland appeared would promptly change over. This was not mere loyalty, for when another friend, superior in rank and emoluments came on the scene with a palatial Cubitt de luxe model, Binkie scampered over and ensconced himself on the front seat. Wilberforce, a rough haired fox terrier, was a doggy motor maniac; he adored a car just as much when standing idle, and his joy was to be well under the engine where oil and grease could get soaked into his coat. For journeys the running board was his chosen seat.'

ø

'T'awd man deed,' said the ancient, 'when our fowerteen acre was wheat time afore last.'

About Making Your Own Boat
by Sir Richard Acland, M.P.

THE trouble about boats is that they are expensive to buy, difficult to make, difficult to carry about, and you don't knew where to keep them. My brother and I have made several boats which can be carried on the back, or two can go at the back of a small car. They are very safe for children to paddle on a pond. They are wonderfully stable down rapids on the flooded Exe, and with a little skill they can be sailed successfully on lake and sea. Also in breakers you can surf-ride in them, and withal we are only very moderate carpenters.

FRAMEWORK. Take a sound deal plank, 9ft. by 1ft. 2ins. by 1in., and cut shaded portion in diagram 1 9ft. by 1ft. 2ins. by 1in. The top is most economically cut with bow saw but is an appalling labour. You now want three ribs. The middle rib is drawn in the second diagram. The shaded part is of course a halved joint. The other ribs are exactly the same except that instead of 1ft. read 9ins. from the ribs to the keel. Now take three-ply. If you use ordinary three-ply you will have to varnish with the utmost care, and even then you will run the risk, if the water gets in, of the three-ply peeling up. On the whole you had better buy second quality '$\frac{1}{8}$in. waterproof three-ply' from Tuckers' Creek Mill Works, Crayford, Kent.* You require four pieces to cover the bottom. To find the shape roughly, take a huge piece of stiffish paper, drawing-pin it to the middle rib and work away with scissors. Repeat in wood. You need long wedge-shaped pieces along the keel between the ribs on which to screw the bottom. If you procure 'Seamflex' from Alfred Jeffreys, Marsh Gate, Stratford, a close fit is not necessary. The four pieces for the side are worked in the same way with, again, long wedges at bow and stern. Now, where the sides touch the bottom, you need 32 rhombus-shaped pieces of wood to take a screw from side and bottom. Now go over all the cracks with 'Seamflex', and then with 'Terrofix' (thin), also from Jeffreys, glue on long strips of chair webbing along all the joins. The floors you will be able to devise, but

---

*Some years hence, alas !

118

every half inch lower is useful.

RUDDER. You will be able to devise a rudder with a cross

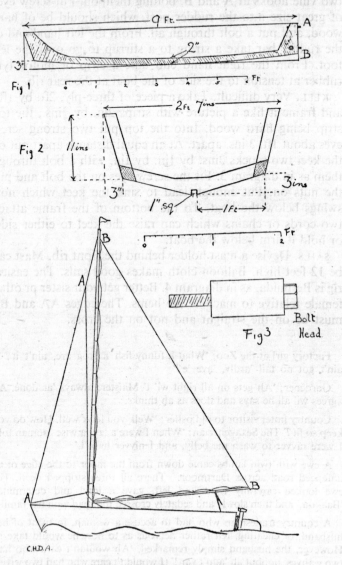

Fig 1

Fig 2

Fig 3

Bolt Head.

C.H.D.A.

WORKING PLANS FOR THE BOAT

bar as in a racing eight. To fix it on, with a large brace drill cut the circle shown in black in the first diagram, and put in two vine hooks at A and B, bolting them on. Put screw eyes of great size into the rudder post, which should be of hard wood, and put a bolt through all. From the left hand end of the rudder bar take a string to a stirrup to go over the left foot. From the right hand end take a strip of motor tyre rubber at tension to the side of the boat at the rear rib.

KEEL. Very difficult. Take a piece of three-ply, 2ft. by 1ft., and frame it like a picture with strips 2in. by $\frac{3}{4}$ins., the top strip being hard wood. Into the top put two strong screw eyes about 1ft. 3 ins. apart. At an equal distance apart put on the keel two blocks 3ins. by 1in. by 1in. with a bolt through them as in diagram 3. Fit the screw eyes on the bolt and put the nuts on. Put enough lead to sink the keel which now swings below the boat. To the bottom of the frame attack two cords or chains which can raise the keel to either side, or hold it firm below the boat.

SAILS. Devise a mast holder behind the front rib. Mast can be 12 feet high. Balloon cloth makes good sails. The easiest rig is Bermuda, as in diagram 4. Better get your sister or other female relative to machine the hems. The edges AA and BB must be on the straight and not on the cross.

✑

Factory girl at the Zoo: 'What a funny fish a frog are, ain't it? It ain't got no tail 'ardly, 'ave 'e?'

Gardener: 'Ah gets on all right wi' t' Maister; always 'as done. Ah agrees wi' all he says and does as ah thinks.'

Country hotel visitor to old ostler: 'Well, you look well. How do you keep so fit?' The Sexagenarian: 'When I were a lad, a wise 'ooman told I were nivver to wash me belly, and I nivver hasn't.'

A ewe with twin lambs came down from the moor to the edge of an unfenced road across Dartmoor. There all three stopped dead. The ewe looked carefully right and left, gave a loud and determined 'Baa-a-a,' and then slowly and sedately crossed the road with her family.

A country tradesman who had to accuse a woman, in front of her husband, of cheating, felt rather nervous as to how he would take it. However, the husband simply remarked, 'Ah wouldn't care who had two wahves, nobbut ah 'adn't yan!' (I wouldn't care who had two wives, if only I hadn't one.)

Concerning Authors' Cottages

1—H. E. Bates

I REALLY believe we had been in unfruitful communication with almost every house agent in the south of England. Yet all we wanted was a country cottage, with decent water to drink, reasonable sanitation, and above all a garden, a bit of untouched earth if possible. Nothing elaborate or pretentious. Above all, nothing arty. We were not looking for Tudor manor houses with black yew hedges and old vineries, not because we didn't like these things but because I was a writer and therefore couldn't afford them. I wanted a modest, solid, quiet place in which to live and work and grow flowers.

After two years of search it began to look as if we had asked for a French chateau or a Spanish castle. Every cottage in England seemed to be either sordid or arty. We visited many, knocking our heads against beams, sniffing cesspools, and getting generally depressed. 'And why the country?' said my friends. 'In the summer, well, yes. But the winter!' Everything was against us.

But in February 1931 our luck changed, for we came across a Quaker who had some ideas of preserving the countryside and its buildings, and in a casual sort of way he told us that he had amused himself by making a 'bungalow' out of a cowhouse and had further ideas of making a cottage out of an old granary. Did that interest us? It did, but we were dubious. We inspected, as the house agents say. It was February, it had rained for two days, and the granary stood exactly in the centre of an old farmyard. It was like a derelict ship standing in a sea of mud. It was indeed a sort of ark, the granary itself actually being perched up on two stout stone walls, in order to be high and dry, leaving a sort of half-open cartshed beneath. The cart-shed was full of what Kentish folk call an old clutter of stuff: cart wheels, beams, buckets, rat-eaten

---

The skilful author of novels which have an immense public in the United States and in this country, he is also one of the very best short story writers, and an interesting man to talk with. The name of his cottage—in Kent—is The Granary. He is chairman of his parish council and cares about rural problems. Indeed we once talked of the possibility of his becoming my colleague on the *Countryman*, but finally agreed that the constraint of a regular job might endanger his imaginative work

sacks, sheets of corrugated iron. The wind had the true cart-shed iciness. We went upstairs gladly. It was pitch dark, there was a smell of mouldy corn, the wind lifted the roof a bit mournfully. We went downstairs gladly. Really, it wasn't very hopeful. But finally we stood away from the place. And instantly I liked it. It was so square and solid and honest. Its grey stones and chestnut-red tiles were beautifully mottled with bright yellow lichen. It was finely fashioned. Every stone was as sound as when built, the roof came down with the typical Kentish double slope, and above all it faced south and away from the road. I saw myself looking out of the windows across the wide field bordered by oaks and horse chestnuts. I measured the thickness of the walls—eighteen inches. I wondered how much land went with the place? Could I have an acre? What sort of soil was it? What sort of soil! Later I was to trench down to a depth of four feet without discovering anything but the lightest and loveliest loam that ever any gardener hoped to see.

We admitted it had possibilities. The granary was L-shaped and it would be enough to occupy only the base of the L at first. So we had tentative plans prepared, reckoned the cost, and discovered that for the price of a jerry-built, semi-detached monstrosity in a surburban street we could have the cottage we had so vainly been seeking, a place of solid and beautiful workmanship, dry as a granary must be, and planned inside to suit every one of our fads and fancies.

By Easter we had made our decision and work was in progress. Always remembering that we could one day use the remainder of the L, we planned six good rooms: downstairs a kitchen, a study for myself with east and south windows, and a dining-sitting room 22 feet long, with 18 feet of window space and an open-hearth fireplace. This room, with its light, its winter warmth and summer coolness, its smooth old pine beams stretching the full length of it, its simple fireplace of warm red brick, has been a joy to us and to all who have seen it. Upstairs we had three bedrooms, all with south-facing dormer windows, and a north bathroom and lavatory. Since the lavatory is of supreme importance, we decided on septic-tank drainage, which functions perfectly. The floors and doors are of polished deal, the doors having simple wooden latches. The floors, being also of great importance, were laid in eighteen inches of concrete. And now the second flood might come and we should sit warm and dry.

The house was finished in a little over six months, a beautiful, neat, snug place that looked as though it had never been a farm-building. And, indeed, it seems odd and half impossible that I am sitting warm and comfortable on a spot where the wind once howled bitterly through the wheels of dung carts and that my books should sit under the beams where birds nested. I do not know how old the place is, only that I have lately come across a beam with 1779 carved upon it, but its history is full of delightful incongruities. Grain was once stored here, and the rats as old men have told me, came in plagues; and now a baby has been born here and a novel written and Mozart's music sings through the place as often as the wind once did. Yet it has nothing arty-and-crafty about it and as long as I live in it never will have. It is a place for work and living. Grain and words, bread and books—they have always gone together, as any author will tell you. It isn't so long, indeed, since we found some pale yellow grains of wheat still lodged in the crack of an elm-beam under my book-shelves.

The garden needs an article, indeed a whole series of articles, to itself. Meconopsis Baileyi and all kinds of alpines now blossom where there were once forests of prize docks; roses flourish on what was once an old cart track; and to-day, which is May Day, what was once the farmyard is a blaze of purple and white and lavender and rose and gold.

2—St. John Ervine

I LIVE in the country because I like living in the country. The thrill of being one of eight million pasty-faced persons who are crowded into the smallest space that will hold eight million pasty-faced persons is one that I have never been able to experience. If I were a dictator I should go about with

---

Was there ever a prettier swordsman with any foe than this Northern Ireland novelist-playwright-biographer-journalist-controversialist, a visit from whom is always a refreshment? Who has not listened to or read his work? He lost a leg in the first Great War.

a knacker's hammer and knock down two-thirds of the houses in London and I should not greatly break my heart if the inhabitants of them were buried in the ruins. I should do still better, I think, if I were to knock down three-thirds of them . . . I lived in London for the better part of twenty-seven years, and I can claim, therefore, to have some knowledge of life in that wen. There are a few parts of it where I would be willing, if heavily bribed, to live again, but the largest part of London is an offence to the eye and sometimes an offence to the nose. I hate the sight of all those smug streets, stretching dully into the distance, as I hate the agitated way in which everybody moves about. There they go, hurrying like hell nowhere! . . . And rending the air with their din as they hurry. The legend that one is at the centre of things in London is one of those astonishing legends which delude the silly and amuse the intelligent. How many of the eight million persons in London are at the centre of things? Not enough, I believe, to populate a large village. And what, pray, is the centre of things? To the Bright Young Things, if any of that malodorous lot are left alive, it is, I suppose, a club in which I would not be found alive or dead. To politicians, it is either the House of Commons and the Carlton Club or the National Liberal Club or the Reform Club. To actors and dramatists, the West End theatres. And so on. But only a very few persons are able to obtain admission to these centres of things, and even they look bored. I see more bored men and women in the streets in one day than I see in my neighbourhood in one year, although I daresay there are bored people here, bored because they have private means and no work. London is a headachy place, stuffy and noisy but the country is enlivening, freshly-aired every minute of the day and has only those noises that are pleasant to hear. Nerve-racked townsmen, overwrought by the sound of their resonant streets, come into the country and have the audacity to say that they cannot bear its noise, although their ear-drums have almost been split and their nerves torn to shreds by city sounds. Country noises are good noises, natural noises, evenly distributed and made comfortable to the ear by the space in which they can vibrate.

In addition to their audacity in complaining of the sounds of the country, these people litter our lanes and fields and foreshore with their refuse. Their dreadful droppings are all over the place. The coast of England in the summer is one enormous dust-bin, a great garbage heap, and no townsman is happy until he has added his bottle to the pile, especially if the bottle be broken. As I drove through the New Forest a few weeks ago, my companion said to me, in disgust, 'It's beginning to look like Long Island!' 'You mean Coney Island', I replied. The place is befouled with hikers' and motorists' garbage, and to satisfy the requirements of these defilers of the earth, a shanty-town of road-houses and bed-and-breakfast houses and petrol pumps and other eyesores has sprung up to make beauty hideous. The fools who own these shanty-town buildings do not realize that they are actively engaged in ruining the very thing which enables them to make a living, namely, the loveliness of their country.

I like the country because, except when townspeople are about it, it contains no clutter; because one can have solitude in it; because one can live near to growing things and enjoy the blessings of fresh fruit and fresh vegetables and not be dependent on stale stuff and things out of tins; because one can have a sense of community; because one can still live like a human being and not like an overworked machine; and finally because, as I said at the start, I like living in the country.

3—R. H. Mottram

'THE cottage was a thatched one . . .', says the old rhyme. Well, mine isn't. It is of rough-cast walls and red Norfolk tiles. It does not try to be picturesque half as hard as it tries to be useful. We built it ourselves when we were tired of living in a very inadequate house in a row in the suburbs. We are still in the suburbs because we prefer the efficient services of a county borough like Norwich. But the

---

I last met the writer, looking fit and well, at the luncheon to Dr. L. P. Jacks, for forty years editor of the *Hibbert Journal*. How many fine novels and other books has not Mottram written since his *Spanish Farm*?

country comes right up to our hedge, and rabbits and hedge-hogs, woodpeckers and finches come through into our garden, as well we know when the first eats off young cabbage plants, the second goes to sleep in the rat-trap and won't get out unassisted, and the others make free with our trees.

We have just upon an acre, and when you take out the house, some flower-beds, a drying-green and a portion let off, we have room to grow practically all the vegetables we can eat, and have fifty trees, of which thirty are apple and the rest plum, pear, fig, walnut, quince and medlar. The apples last well into the winter, potatoes into the spring, celery, leeks, greens and roots see us round until rhubarb is ready and sea-kale, and it is time to think about lettuce.

We have an attic room for books, a cellar for storing, a garden house for children, a shed for oddments, and a little plantation of elms for poles. What more can anyone want?

Very unremarkable? Certainly it is. The townsman of the twentieth century trying to solve his problems is no heroic figure. We came here with small children and the first necessities were, we felt, trustworthy drains, water, light and supplies. That is why we stayed within three miles of the centre of Norwich. Desire for some degree of privacy led us to build in a small cul-de-sac, some hundreds of yards off the main road, on the crest of a little bank that the old builder shook his head over. "You'll grow nothing on that old sandhill," he said. He was wrong. We grow a good deal. Also ten years of progress have made us glad we chose the spot. The now deafening and dangerous road traffic is invisible and hardly audible to us. And when new streets are laid out we cannot be overlooked. We have room for a junior cricket pitch, in a net, and the little plantation of elms we have never wished away. What games have not been played there! But the old builder was partly right. Certain things will not grow. The slope is too well drained. Pears and plums come with difficulty, cherries are of no size; and, of the soft fruit, while gooseberries are sturdy, we lose some currant bushes every year. American black-berries like it, of course, and our paths are always dry. My grandfather left the land a hundred and fifty years ago. I have gone back to it as near as ever I desire to be.

4—*T. F. Powys*

I DO not know that I have seen a cottage so much like a doll's house as ours. An ugly one, too. But here in this haunted village, where even a hedgehog has his fancies a little ugliness may often hide more comfort than displeasure. I hate the dainty cottage of modern nicety; the build of ours is far more to my mind. One is supposed to sigh, as though one should worship, when the door is opened and one beholds a jade carving. I would prefer to see a black bottle, that a poor man may at least become better acquainted with.

Only see our cottage as it is, my dear friends. A doll's house made of bricks that once were red, and now by the damp sea mists have lost their colour; martins' nests under the eaves, in which the birds twitter at night as if they tell God's secrets. A half acre of grassy garden, the sound of trains when the wind is in the north, and the buzzing of inquisitive gnats is all we have to boast of.

Anyone can look into our garden; we do not hide ourselves behind bullrushes. But no one cares to, for there are no sweets to see. Though a week or two ago, and for three days too, there was something even in our garden to look at. For a long while we did not plant our flower knot that we made a year or two ago. But after a thunderstorm when there was water to be had my wife planted a splendid geranium. I helped, too, and Susan, who is not yet two years old, watched, but in a reflective manner that boded no good. The next day this same Susan came with me to admire our new plant that already had a lovely red blossom.

It was Sylvia Townsend Warner who took me to see one of our most original writers, and this year he wrote to me from his home in Dorset with his accustomed verve and originality. So many confuse the four brothers of the remarkable Powys family that it is of interest to bring together their signatures, see next page.

Theodore Francis Powys, is the author of *Fables, The House with the Echo, The Dew Pond, Mr. Weston's Good Wine. Soliloquies of a Hermit, Innocent Birds, Mr. Tasker's Gods, Mockery Gap, Mark Only, Black Bryony, The Left Leg, Hester Dominy, Abraham Men, Kindness in a Corner, The White Paternoster, The Only Penitent, When Thou Wast Naked, Unclay, The Two Thieves, God's Eyes a-Twinkle, Make Thyself Merry,* and *Goat Green.*

John Cowper Powys of *Wolf Solent, In Defence of Sensuality. A Glastonbury Romance, Wood and Stone, Rodmore, Ducdame, Wolfsbane, Mandragora, Samphire, The Complex Vision, The Religion of a Sceptic, Visions and Revisions, Suspended Judgments, The Meaning of Culture, Mortal Strife,* and *The Art of Growing Old.*

Llewelyn Powys who died a few years ago in Switzerland, wrote *Confessions of Two Brothers, Ebony and Ivory, Thirteen Worthies, Black Laughter, Skin for Skin, The Verdict of Bridlegoose, Henry Hudson, The Cradle of God, The Pathetic Fallacy, Apples be Ripe, Impassioned Clay,* and *Earth Memories.*

A. R. Powys, C.B.E., was the Secretary of the Society for the Protection of Ancient Buildings, 'Anti-Scrape.'

The plot had been Susan's playground, where she could dig with her little wooden spade, casting the dust of the earth into her hair with unlimited satisfaction. She stood with me and looked.

On the third day Susan approached the bed alone, as if she had a serious task to do, which indeed she had, for seizing the stem of the geranium she immediately pulled it up.

It is best to be born a nettle when a baby is about, or something at least in which it can take no sort of interest.

When the geranium was gone, our garden, I thought, was more at its ease, for to appear dull and untidy is an act of policy in these ungentle times. We are so very ordinary and common here, that even the bees look a little ashamed of their company when they take a sip of honey from the white clover.

Of course we are proud of our weeping ash, but we dare not hope that our weeping ash is proud of us. Though I think the pile of faggots that we have in the back garden really consider us as people of imagination because we have prepared for a cold winter, when I shall chop the firewood and wonder why I can never remember good poetry as I used to do.

If you look for sweet williams beside our door, you will

Theodore F. Powys

Llewelyn Powys

A. R. Powys

John Cowper Powys

only find bindweed, and in the garden you will only see hay-cocks where there should be potatoes.

When the grass is cut I make the haycocks, and can hide behind one of them so that I am not noticed from the road. But all things tend to their end, and even the finest haycock will settle at last into the earth. So that when November comes a little heap of sodden grass is all that remains. I suppose I ought to be more tidy, but one is as one is made to be.

A home is sweet to childhood, and sweet to age. I like to see the same fields each day. Even the very plainness of our cottage attracts me the more to it. I do not care to roam as I used to do over the far hills. My horizon is closing in. I now find myself more pleasantly diverted sitting at my ease under the ash tree than stepping briskly in a wanton manner over the high downs. The tide is at the ebb and I draw to home. Gentle Pan is my guide and comforter, for this god can pipe and dance as well in our little corner as upon a mount in Samos. I have more pleasure carrying water to the stupid hens and to bold cock Richard than I used to have in viewing the West Bay and the Solent from our highest hill.

5—Basil de Sélincourt

WHY do I live in the country? As I have lived in it and in one spot for some thirty-five years, there are readers, no doubt, who will expect me to assert that it is the only proper place for a man to live in, and invite them to emulate my noble example. But, after all, I am writing in the main for other countrymen, and shall not be believed unless I make a genuine confession. I have no right or title to live in the country at all. I fell in love with the country in my early youth, and after a five years' engagement came in to a little money, just enough to enable me to marry the country—in fact to build a cottage on a bare field. But you know what

De Sélincourt is my neighbour at Kingham, with which Idbury is connected by one of the oldest roads in the kingdom. In recent years his successful fruit and vegetable growing has diminished the amount of his delicate writing. We served on our local rural district council together. His first wife was the lamented Anne Douglas Sedgwick.

that famous advice to those about to marry was? I had it
from several of my most trusted friends, and, in spite of a long
life of conjugal fidelity, I repeat it now to all who may be
wishing and wondering. To marry the country is far worse
than marrying a husband, or even than marrying a wife. I
hope you never heard that ribald *poilu* song about the man
who tired of his lady-love; and all he did to her; with the
refrain: *Mais elle est revenu-ë, le lendemain matin*—Well,
nothing was ever heard or thought of that comes back as the
country does. Its hold is pitiless. If you possibly can, steer
clear. Unless utter compulsion has fallen upon you, stick to
mankind.

I am supposing that you are, as I am, one of those unfortunate and inferior beings who must choose between the
country and the town. I have been credibly informed that a
complete existence involves two establishments, and that
neither town nor country can be fully seen and enjoyed except
by bigamists. To qualify for this happiest solution, I, personally, should need to add an 0 to my income on the right hand
side; but really I do not see how, even when the millennium
arrives (which some still think so near), we can all of us
expect to be countryfolk; for though, no doubt, there would
then be money enough, there would not be country enough to
go round. Perhaps that is why I am specially anxious that you,
dear City reader, unless you are absolutely bent on joining us,
should remain where you are.

For, in the course of a chequered career, one point of
vision has always been clear to me. The charm of the country
is that *you* are not there: *Dort wo du nicht bist*, as another
great song puts it; though it ill befits a sinner like myself to
say so. A settler, worse still a 'literary' settler, an idealist, in
short an impostor,—anyhow I know I cannot live in the
country without, by the mere fact of my inharmonious
presence, spoiling the picture: all the more, since the kind of
country I chiefly care for is country wild and free. People
seem satisfied as a rule if the sky is free over their heads; but
I am not satisfied unless I feel some freedom also in the earth
around me; and to build a house and go in and out and about
it without smirching the earth, to sink into the landscape and

become one with it, is the sort of thing that only a nesting bird knows how to do. Rural England, you may tell me, was everywhere tamed long ago. But that only means that to beauty of nature it added beauty of art, another and a subtler difficulty for you to cope with; and the mere fact that, with your car or if it be only with the motor bus, the country is at your mercy now, defenceless against you, where distance protected it when I was young, makes the difficult critical.

For of all hateful things hatefullest to me is that Laodicean mixture of fields and houses, houses spattered over fields, with bushes and fences and here and there a pillar-box, by which I more and more see our country eaten up—fly-blown with it, teeming. *Guarda e passa!* I look away; I hurry by; but it is interminable! And what of England's age-old individual stamp (each county different) and of her strong rôle in the world to be? Can she not yet surmount this slavering, subsidized suburbanism?

However there is still some 'country' left. What pleasure is there in living in it? In that silence, that solitude, a sustaining assurance visits me that the elements, earth, water, air, are overflowing man, not man the elements. Earth itself becomes a partner in the changing seasons, I feel the weather coming up out of the ground. Nor is all well unless my neighbour animals are at their ease. When the brown owl hoots from my gable, when the partridge brings her brood to the back door, when I find a leveret under a cabbage leaf, or see a snake wind casually across the lawn, then I say, like Mr. W. H. Davies, that if these can find peace in my garden, I can too.

6—J. A. Spender

FOR about eighteen years I lived entirely in London with only such escape into the country as was provided by friends who had houses in the country near London. Then to my London house I added rooms in a farmhouse in

---

Spender was the editor of the green *Westminster Gazette* on which I served with him for years, the biographer of Asquith and Campbell Bannerman, and the author of books which picture faithfully the political life of his time. A stout, informed and judicious exponent of the principles of the old Liberal Party, he had the distinction of being read by almost as many Conservatives as Liberals. His life has been well written by the editor of the *Spectator*, who contrives to find time to be an M.P.

the Thames valley for a refuge at the week-end. This lasted me for ten years longer, and I have the most grateful memory of the excellent cooking and perfect service provided by the farmer's wife and her daughter. A charming little garden which we were allowed to call our own added to the pleasure.

Then at the end of ten years we decided to make our home in the country and be content with a small flat in London, reversing the usual order and having, so to speak, our house in the country and our cottage in London. After four years we dropped the flat in London, in order to have a bigger house and, above all, a bigger garden in the country. An eight-acre garden (including three ponds and a little wood) in the heart of Kent seemed very near Paradise, and so it was for twelve years.

But taxation and advancing years don't go well with big gardens and greenhouses, and the time came to reconsider ourselves. Back to London? Never for one moment. Our retreat is a hill-top, 650 feet up, with a four-square view over the Home Counties which I think must be unsurpassed, a rather green house with a little observatory on top which gives it the look of a pagoda in the distance, and an acre of garden in the loveliest setting of orchards and woods breaking steeply down the hillsides; an enchanting pink and white dream in blossom time.

The young should not live in the country unless their life is there; the old who have lived in London should be near enough to be able to drive there and be back by midnight— easy enough with a small and trusty car. The advantages of being where I am seem to me overwhelming. I have fresh air, silence, the daily pleasure of stepping out on to a lawn instead of into a street, friendly and interesting neighbours who take me into their confidence about their farming and their fruit-growing, walks in all directions through woods and fields, sketching-ground at my door, freedom from the innumerable small distractions which fret and worry the town-dweller and dissipate his strength. But to enlarge on this theme would be boring to the countryman and, as experience has taught me, unconvincing to the townsman. We have all our tastes and they vary with the years.

DUCKLINGS

SHRIKE AND SQUIRREL LARDERS

SEA KALE

7—H. M. Tomlinson

TULK'S HILL is above the Chesil Beach, about midway between Portland and Bridport. Behind it a superior landmark rises to 600 feet, the highest point of that stretch of coast, and deeply scored by earthworks, as the more conspicuous promontories of Dorset usually are. Who Tulk was I do not know, but a local ancient pretended to recognize two round barrows on the summit of the hill as the graves of Mr. and Mrs. Tulk. By all the signs, this countryside was populous when men were working flints, but to-day you have a chance to surprise roe-deer, if you know where to look for them. We have watched a family of them, of an afternoon, up by the barrows. I have been told that this bit of the county was well cultivated fifty years ago, but great areas of it to-day would convince even a townsman that furze, thistle and rag-wort may not be the best testimonials to the wisdom of Whitehall. Though I do not complain about them. In fact, it was the suggestion of the wild which first attracted us to the spot.

We got to know it some years ago, while renting one of the cottages of the Old Coastguard Station, a few miles from Abbotsbury. When that station was sold, the owner of a neighbouring estate, Labour-in-Vain, a friend of ours, was good enough to offer us a patch of his land, if we cared to build. At the time this was no more than a pleasant dream. Presently, though, it occurred to us that our own place on a coast so attractive but with hardly any habitations might be no worse than shares in a derelict rubber-plantation or a salted gold mine, and anyhow might be the equivalent of an insurance policy. It might have advantages not to be got out of other investments. (And certain disadvantages, we had to learn, with what may develop out of assessment.)

A civil engineer, with attractive ideas in the designing of cottages, did the job. It was essential, as the little house must sit on a bare hillside, about 200 feet above the sea, that it

---

Which of us has not been at sea and ashore with the author of so many outstanding books about voyaging and voyagers? He was a colleague of H. W. Massingham on the old *Nation*, and now lives in Dorset.

should resemble a natural outcrop, from a distance, as near as a building may. We wished to add a trifle to the hill, not a gratuitous decoration. It is built of brick and local stone (forest marble of the Jurassic) and is thatched with reed. Its walls were treated with liquid cement, for it faces south-west, where the gales come from. Its windows look out across Lyme Bay with nothing between us and the Bermudas except the occasional trail of a steamer's smoke; though we rarely see farther than the Start, which bears a trifle to the north about thirty miles away. It looks into the eye of the usual wind, but there is never a trace of damp, though we have known heavy weather drive the spindthrift so far inland that it has killed much of the foliage, bringing a look of autumn weeks too soon, several hundred feet above our roof.

No dust and no damp. The interior walls were left rough-plastered. The fireplaces are for logs, and need no coaxing, and make no smother, however the wind may blow. We were afraid at first that the place would give a lot of work before it was home-like when entered for the summer term, but we have found that its design and construction keep the contents much as we leave them; except once, when an unlucky Little Owl fell down a chimney, and was not careful before it died. There is a thatched porch, with seats of elm at its sides, and it was a fancy of the more youthful enthusiasts to hang on a bracket there the bell of the barque *Victor*, of Liverpool, with the usual lanyard to its clapper, instead of a door knocker. A real masthead light guides wayfarers across the fields, at night. By day, from that porch, we can see the coast from Lyme Regis (and often from Beer in Devon) to the light-house on Portland Bill. In 'The Dynasts' that broad sea is Deadman's Bay.

The trouble was the garden. I may say that, to begin with, the garden had to be terraced and paved, which came to real sums of money, beyond the original count. This should not have startled anyone except a townsman, seeing what the gradient is like, and the tough earth. But the ground is not so tough as the rabbits. They are worse than any gradient. Will sunk wire-netting keep them out? It will not. Our tentative plantings have had a desolate time of it, but we rush in the reserves, when the front ranks fall. Altogether it is good fun. At least, the cottage has taught us that the land is a problem, older than history, and that only those whose hands are habitually stained by it know anything about it worth attention.

8—Hugh Walpole

I BOUGHT my cottage, Brackenburn, in a very risky way. I had wanted, ever since I spent my first Cumberland summer at Gosforth between Wastwater and Seascale, to make my home in Cumberland. I was aged ten then. This desire, seems to me now my perpetual Christmas Stocking.

Anyway, ten years ago, I searched the Lake District for a house. There were few vacant and all were either too big or too ugly, I had set the car's nose towards Edinburgh when someone told me that there was a cottage for sale looking on to Derwentwater. Once again I went round the lake (I'd been round it three times already). This time I caught the 'For Sale' board, and, mounting the garden steps, I saw the view of the lake. A lady came out of the cottage window as they do in the fairy-stories. I said 'How much?' She said 'So much'. I said 'No, so much', and bought it there and then. I hadn't even seen the inside of the cottage. I asked nothing about drains or water-supply. But it was all right. It was, with one exception, the best thing I ever did on my life.

It's a good ordinary little cottage. The rooms are small and overfilled with books and pictures. At least they'd say so now, when one bust by Dobson and a steel armchair are enough for any room. It is very brightly coloured inside. I like my Elizabethan needlework that hangs over the fireplace. I have some Tang horses and a good glowing rug with purple flowers. I have the works of Sheridan Le Fanu and Dorothy Sayers in the spare-room and watercolours by Charles Holmes of this Cumberland country in the dining-room, a dog, a set of chessmen and Charles II's copy of Chapman's Homer.

From the early days of the *Countryman* I had cordial letters from the kind-hearted Sir Hugh, who, though he wrote among all his other works *A Prayer for My Son*, died a bachelor. He was himself a Bishop's son.

I suppose the garden isn't much. It is only an acre in extent, but there are two streams that run through it from the top of Catbells, two bee-hives, a pool under the trees by the lawn, a little wood, a rock-garden and a great many flowers. The flowers grow in rather tangled confusion, but that's because Charlie, the gardener (whose wife is the most famous bee authority in Cumberland) likes it that way. Hemmed in by flowers you look out to the lake, to Blencathra, to Skiddaw. I say that is lucky for any man. Vegetables won't grow there, or they grow at the wrong time. There is only a cabbage when cabbages are dreadfully common in Keswick. There are wood-pigeons, brown squirrels, hedgehogs, and very fat thrushes. Also many robins.

A fine thing is the library. It is at the far end of the lawn away from the cottage. Originally there was one long room looking over the lake and on to this I have built another as high as the tops of the trees. This has a grand view, sun on every side; and the two rooms hold altogether about eight thousand books.

This top room is the centre of the world for me. China and Peru, Russia and America can do what they please. No newspaper ever enters it and no one who wants an autograph either. Is that selfish? I don't suppose so, because I am com-pelled, often, to step outside. But it's a *good* room. Altogether I'm lucky in this cottage.

9—Sylvia Townsend Warner

'I HAVE a country cottage,' may mean the possession of anything from a bungalow to a small manor house, from a semi-detached villa to a reed-thatched, old-oaked architect's fancy, plumbed within and half-timbered without. My cottage has four rooms, and would let, unfurnished, at the usual local rental of 2s. to 2s. 6d. a week. It is neither picturesque nor convenient. But it is freehold, and stands in a small garden, and its price was £90 only.

When I bought it its water-supply consisted of a water-butt and an understanding that the tenant might fetch water from a well farther up the road. Fortunately, its back kitchen, being a lean-to, had a roof sufficiently lofty to allow of a small tank being fitted indoors, collecting the rain water off the slate roof.

To this I added a small sink, draining into a sump in the garden; and while heaven permits (and in this convenient climate heaven generally does) this allows me a water supply for kitchen purposes. Only those who have had to carry water into the house and out again can appreciate the beatitude of a tap and a run-away.

I have, when I choose, constant hot water also, for the lofty back kitchen had a copper in it. There is a general idea that a copper is useful only on washing day or for boiling Christmas puddings. This is a great mistake. A copper is most valuable in solving two great problems of village living: how to have enough hot water, and how to dispose of rubbish. To work well, it must be kindled like a fire; with sticks, cinders, and enough coal to raise the water almost to boiling point. After this, and fifteen to twenty minutes should be long enough, it can be fed with the surprising quantity of papery rubbish which accumulates in any present-day household; and with a little more attention, and a few handfuls of cinders, the water will remain hot all day. A copper will burn almost anything, it will even calcine tins; but it is a waste to feed it with vegetable rubbish, which can be rendered into garden manure.

Like most village people I cook on oil, with a twelve-gallon oil-drum replenished by the monthly van. As the copper is one mainstay, the stock-pot is another. With a stock-pot I can snap my fingers at tinned soups and meat extracts. At its richest, it gives me a consommée; at its most exhausted, the basis of a mulligatawny. And in its way it is as useful as the copper at engulfing fragments. But, people say, a stock-pot, unless constantly reboiled, is apt to go sour. It will, if, when taken from the fire, the lid is left on and the steam allowed to drip back; it may, if vegetables are put with the bones and meat trimmings. But it is not necessary to add vegetables; a bouquet of herbs will give it an aroma, and if vegetable stock be needed, it is far better made of vegetables alone.

After buying her stock-pot (and let it be of stout aluminium, not the traditional iron tank so unwieldy and slow to boil) the cottage cook will be well advised to stock a herb-bed, the nearer the kitchen door the better. It should contain at least a dozen herbs: sage, green and purple, mint, marjoram, tansy, chives, parsley, thyme, common and lemon-scented, tarragon, hyssop, basil, savory, southernwood, rosemary and balm. Nasturtium leaves and seeds are admirable in their season, fennel is liked by many, and there may be a use for rue, though I must say I have not found it. Having grown these herbs, and they will all grow as obligingly as weeds, she must study their flavours, learn to compound them, and learn, above all, not to use too many of them at once. Such combinations as chives and nasturtiums, tansy and balm, thyme and southernwood, are as exquisite as the usual mess of mixed herbs is dreary.

From the kitchen door it should be easy to keep an eye on the garden to avoid that wasteful tragedy, the too-well-matured vegetable. A broad bean kept till its green jerkin has turned to a fawn spongebag is a broad bean misunderstood. Bullet-like peas, long, tough, hairy runner beans, harvest-festival marrows—those who live in towns or placate a gardener must put up with these; but the cottage cook, if she grows her own vegetables, need not submit to such odious longevities. She must pounce on the innocents; nature will always see to it that there are enough sexagenarians.

*

'Ah, 'tis a baad pain, Miss, a very baad pain; I wouldn't wish it to an iron gate.'

From a parish council minute book. 'Mr. —— thanked the council for appointing him as their clerk and he could only express what he felt by saying that he repeated almost the same as the chairman had already said.'

The church cleaner: 'The biggest fright I ever 'ad was when I were doin' the church one evenin', and it were gettin' dark, but I went on because I wanted to get finished. I heard a noise like someone a-draggin' a chain round the aisles. I couldn't see nuthin', and I went out of that church as quick as lightenin'. Then I says to myself, "Don't you be so foolish," and I went back to see, and it were Master Jervis's old goat a-trailin' of his chain round and round.'

A Garden from the Wild
by Eric Parker

O N a day in May, 1910, I stood in a clearing, about 450 feet above sea level, in a larch wood on the side of a hill in Surrey. We had bought twelve acres of woodland, larch and hazel, and we were to build our house where I stood.

The larches were between 15 feet and 20 feet high, and covered about 10 acres: the hazel was a strip of coppice along the southern boundary of the plot. Between the larch and hazel, running east and west, was a woodland ride, with six oaks standing along its bank. This ride was joined by another, running south and north along the western boundary of our twelve-acre plot. Along this ride, on a high bank which formed a sort of rough terrace, stood eight more oaks, and these two lines of oak, with the green rides running under them, seemed to form the natural boundaries on two sides of what should be our flower garden.

Our next task was to grub trees. The architect—my friend the late Ernest Newton, R.A.—chose the situation for the house, a nearly flat space in the larch, from which the side of the hill sloped away north, west, south-west, and south; and on this space, cleared of trees, he built a long rambling house filled with sunlight. He also had the task of planning terraces of bargate stone with flower beds, on the south, west and north of the house: on the east was to be the forecourt; and for the rest, we were to plan the garden as we pleased.

We began by grubbing larches, at 2d. a tree, over a large space in front of the house to the south, to form a lawn. We grubbed others on the west, to form another lawn leading to the western ride, and we grubbed all the hazel, except for an outside line which made a natural hedge between our plot and the road. With the open space thus gained we laid out an acre of kitchen garden and sowed down an acre with grass, on

Editor, first of the *County Gentleman*, (to which, on leaving Fleet Street, I contributed for some years 'The Diary of a Journalist Turned Countryman') and then of the *Field*, and is the author of many pleasing books of instruction on bird life and a variety of rural subjects. He has been a contributor to almost every number of the *Countryman*. He lives near Hambledon, and his books about cricket are well known. He has also written *Eton in the Eighties*.

139

the edge of which we planted groups of apple trees. Between this grassy orchard and the kitchen garden we made a long herbaceous border.

This was the main outline of the garden until the War. But during the three years which came before 1914 we were busy planting, and gradually grubbing more larch. We planted spruce among the larches to the north and north-west, for windscreens, and we grubbed larches to make views from the terraces round the house. And these views, indeed, formed the main attraction of the garden. To the north-west we looked out on the whole line of the Hog's Back; to the west, to Crooksbury Hill, crowned with pine, and the levels of Hampshire; to the south-west, Hindhead, and to the south, Blackdown; to the north, east and south-east all was woodland.

We were able before the War came, to plant the beginnings of a heather garden, on the east side of the lawn among the larches, and on the west and south-west, belts and clumps of lilac, laburnum, hawthorn, cherry, prunus, rhododendron, azalea and other flowering shrubs. Behind these were the children's gardens, with belts of sweetbriar. It all took time. Then, during the War, although I was away, we were able to buy some other ground outside our twelve acres, and the real business of garden making began afresh.

Our main plan was to trench new ground to which to transfer the kitchen garden. Also in a wood in the new ground was a bargate stone quarry, so that at last a rock garden became a possibility. From 1919 onwards, therefore, we were occupied with unending new work. In turn we made a grass tennis court (since discarded by the family for a hard court farther away): a lily-pond garden, paved with stone and edged with yew, in which I amused myself with topiary (peacocks, ships, fleur-de-lis, a dolphin); a flight of broad steps, from near the south-west corner of the house terrace, bordered by azaleas and other shrubs, and leading down to a rock garden with strings of ponds running through it; belts of which uriana roses and flowering trees and shrubs, among them Eucryphias now 20 feet high, halesias, camellias, and two sorts of Grevilleas, one of them, *rosamarinifolia*, now more than 50 feet in circumference; all these steps and belts and spaces of rock garden, with a succession of grass terraces running east and west, being gathered up to the south corner of our original flower garden, into a stone-paved circle in the centre of which stands a bird-bath.

To the rock garden we added year by year, and cut through a bank on the edge of it and grubbed hazel beyond, so as to be able to look from gentians and phloxes and the deep blue of Lithospermum across a slope of primroses to the pale distance, like a horizon of sea, of the Hog's Back. We made a new orchard, through which run two lines of espaliers, by borders which hold in succession crocuses, crown imperials, hyacinths, tulips and irises. In the spring of 1933 we made a formal, stone-paved rose garden, between the green terrace of the old tennis court and the daffodils of the orchard, and in the centre we placed a pond with a fountain—a little leaden statue of a boy and a snake, after Verrocchio.

And last autumn I added something more. We used to argue, she and I, as to what was best to be done with our original piece of sown grass with its few apple trees. I wanted to make it all into orchard, she wanted it to remain a sort of child's playground. So last autumn I decided that it should be the best child's playground anywhere to be seen: so I planted daffodils and apple trees all round its edge, and in the middle of the field there is a mown space inviting children's cricket. As I write in May the apple blossom is coming out above the daffodils.

If yu du as we du yu oont du as yu du. (Norfolk vernacular.)

Mistress: 'The dentist will no doubt give you gas.' Maid: 'No, M'm, I think not, not gas; there's electric light in the town.'

'No, sir, no, she don't go to no place of worship, no she don't, not Mrs. White don't, not if I know anything of it.'

Border farm servant seeing a man carelessly twisting straw ropes that bind down the ricks: 'I once saw a man making them from sea sand and barley chaff.'

The old woman at the Ulster frontier was asked if she had anything to declare. Nothing at all. But what was in the bottle? Oh, only holy water, holy water from Lourdes. The customs officer pulled the cork. 'Whisky it is,' said he. 'Glory be to God!' cried the offender; 'a miracle!'

Chairs, by *Professor A. E. Richardson*

THE chief feature of country-made furniture, whether executed in oak, beech, cherry or pear wood, is faithful adherence to the fashion of more finished town-made articles. The most imposing specimens of country-made chairs, after the fashion of Chippendale, fetch high prices. There is scope, however, for the collector who desires furniture of character among the masses of carpenter-made examples. The common chairs, for instance, that formerly graced the servants' hall at the Great House make excellent seats for everyday use. The ladder-back and rush-seated

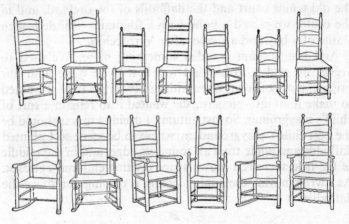

NOT BOUGHT UP IN OUR VILLAGE

American rush-bottomed chairs, all, with the exception of the third from the end in the bottom row counting from the left, dating from 1725 to 1825.

spindle chairs of Lancashire, Yorkshire, and Wales, illustrations of which may be seen in Morland's pictures, have a homely dignity which is pleasing. The collector should be on the look out for specimens of the type called Windsor chairs. These are genrally of beech. They range from those with straight top rails and cabriole legs of Hogarth's time to those

Professor Richardson, R.A., F.R.I.B.A., has a noteworthy collection of eighteenth century furniture and odds and ends—it has been visited by Queen Mary—and has been known to rig out a dinner party of friends in the clothes and wigs of the period.

with vase-shaped splats and the later Windsor types of 1840–50. Even to-day plain chairs of this type form part of the modern output at High Wycombe and can be purchased at prices ranging from five to eight shillings. Old Windsor chairs fetch from twenty-five to thirty shillings apiece. Armchairs of similar character range from four to ten pounds. The name Windsor chair was derived, it is said, from the fact that George the Third took a fancy to a high-backed armchair while he was resting in a cottage near Windsor. It is said that Farmer George ordered some to be made for his use at the Castle. Collectors should remember that every county in England evolved cottage and farmhouse furniture of a regional character. True, the general characteristics of eighteenth-century furniture were derived from the London makers, but the old instinct for craftmanship operated.

Tramping On The Cheap
by an Artist

WHEN travelling I avoid hotels and public-houses, mainly for reasons of economy though there are some country innkeepers whose price for food and lodging seem quite inadequate to leave them any profit. Three-and-six I have been charged in Lincolnshire for a supper of bread and cheese, apple-pie and a pint of porter, an excellent bed and breakfast. But quite half of the village landlords to whom one applies will have nothing to do with casual comers who arrive late, and say either 'Full up' or 'Don't put up strangers here'. In a private lodging-house or temperance hotel one will get beef-steak and strong tea for supper, an airless bedroom, and breakfast in company with a suffocating paraffin stove; and then be offered the visitors' book, in which to write, 'Home from home'. But the worst thing about inns is that one can never get away soon enough in the morning. My own plan is to travel by bicycle, starting as soon as may be after daybreak, and not beginning to look for lodgings until dusk. A strong carrier on the back holds the

The writer (in 1931) was the late Thomas Hennell whose posthumous *Countryman at Work* with a memoir by H. J. Massingham has been lately published. He was a devoted student of rural arts and crafts, and an engaging character.

tools of my trade, together with tooth brush, razor and such extra clothes as may be needed, a wholemeal loaf, butter and cheese, and often a pot of honey, which (as David found when pursuing the Philistines) is a reviving food. I don't believe in carrying things on one's back; it is unnecessarily tiring, especially in the rain. For sleeping out, I tried carrying a tent, of the two-poled ex-Army kind, called a 'one-man bivy'. But this made a rather awkward load. After that I bought a grey Army blanket for 4s. 6d. but it was inadequate when the nights were cold, and so I used another one inside it. These went quite well on the carrier with the other luggage, and I usually slept in barns and sheds. The floor of a waggon lined with straw is a particularly comfortable bed. It is draught-proof, and has the advantage of being out of reach of rats and other animals. Not all barns are so comfortable, nor so well provided with hay or straw, as one might be inclined to imagine. One may have to be content with a collection of musty sacks, or a few inches of hay on a substratum of cobbled floor. Once, at a barn where they had been threshing, there was no choice but to sleep on a surface composed of the tied-up mouths of sacks of grain, which were piled two sacks deep over the whole floor of the barn. I may have been un-lucky but I have found the shelters which farmers provide to house their fruit pickers or extra harvesters wretched, with the wind lifting and drumming the corrugated iron roof. Oast-houses are nearly always well-built and comfortable; so are mills, though they may be dusty. To sleep in cow-houses is said to be particularly wholesome. The romantic pleasure of sleeping under haystacks is usually attended with severe cramps. But, given a fairly good night, nothing is more delicious than to wake up among the fields and trees, in the twilight of a mild mid-summer dawn. I have said nothing of those lodgings which, out of the kindness of their hearts, householders sometimes give to benighted travellers. Some-times these are much better than sleeping out; occasionally they are worse. My contention is that travelling is interesting in proportion as it is cheap. Also it is necessary to have some sort of objective. If not particularly interested in something or in everything, stop at home.

144

'Old England'

y Sir John Buchan-Hepburn

He got his name of Nutter because his mother had been gathering nuts in the wood behind the village when he was born, and they were both brought home in a wheelbarrow. When I first knew him he was seventy, and he might have been a Saxon serf.

He stood about five feet four, but was so broad that he looked less, and his arms were so long that they looked out of proportion to the rest of his body. This gave him a look of great strength.

He had been married three times, and was seventy-five when his last child was born. How many children he had by the three marriages I could never make out. Every time I went to his cottage there seemed to be another one. I suspect that Nutter himself was hazy on the matter; but there must have been at least twenty.

He was a rabbit-trapper. Each winter he rented several hundred acres of downland; but though rabbiting was his trade there was nothing he could not turn his hand to in farm work, and anything he undertook he did well. Once he did some fencing for me, and I helped him. One bit of chestnut fencing we put up did not please him, and he took it down three times until he was satisfied.

He could only just read and write, but about money matters he was scrupulous.

Between the parson and himself there was a feud. Often Nutter was home only on Sunday, and there were then lots of odd jobs for him, among them killing his pig. His cottage was close to the church and his killing always seemed to happen during the morning service. The vicar went to see him about it. Nutter retorted that the pig was his own and what time he killed it was entirely his affair. Did he tell the vicar what to preach about? No, he minded his own business. The vicar could do the same. And Nutter continued to kill his pig on a Sunday morning to the accompaniment of the Church bells.

145

The Sins of Rachel Stickney

IN the autumn of 1799 a farm of 800 acres, known as Ridg
mont, in 'the seigniory of Holderness', in the East Riding o
Yorkshire, was in the occupation of a thirty-five-years-ol
Quaker called William Stickney. It had been let to his fathe
and grandfather before him, and no lease had ever been exe
cuted, a fact honourable alike to the Quaker tenants and thei
Roman Catholic landlord. When the Stickneys first had th
holding, 300 acres of it were under water and 200 acres unde
gorse, but the land was now in a high state of cultivatio
William Stickney, who had his family taught Latin by th
rector, could trace his descent from 1520, and, as his portra
shows, was a man of some presence and distinction. He was
farmer of originality enough to have written a pamphlet i
defence of rooks, to have had his name given to a new grass
and, long before Sir Oliver Lodge, Mr. Newman and Mr
Priestley, to have strung wires over crops in an attempt t
electrify them. He had married a Richardson of Clevelan
('Records of a Quaker family, the Richardsons of Cleve
land') and they had among their children a daughter name
Rachel, who on September 19th of the year of which we writ
was just ten years old. On that date she began to write in
small book of hand-made paper, with interleaved blotting pape
and a marbled paper cover, the 'Memuranduns' which follow:

This book is for Rachel Stickney to make memuranduns o
her faults in

9th mo 19 I have greaved my mother today with not comin
when colled on i have again grieved my mother with tellin
her she said wrong and being angry With sister H

21 I tallked too much to my Mother when she was talking t
me

22 & 23 got those two days over tolarably

24 I said to my mother I am sure thou says very wrong

25 I was rather too pevish when I first got up but was carefu
the remainder of the day

26 nothing materal accured this day

27 I have not got the day over without greeving my mothe

came to be rather greaved at me for giving too much way to anger

28 Too pevish again this morning but I hope I shall take more care

29 I only gave my mother cause to Blame me twice today and I hope it was not for very great faults the First was being rather unlling to give my Br a little of something I had and the second was being too much deposed to stay in the kitchen

30 This Day only one thing happened To be noticed and that was being sadly Petted about a sore finger

10 mo 1 and 2 these too days got over nicely for nothing accurred that I remember of

3 day nothing 4 I behaved very unbecomingly to my Mother in replying Impertinently to her when she told Me to light a candle and what was still Worse I blamed my mother for another For her manner of treating me instead of acknowledging myself to blame When she talked to me for what I had done

5th 6th 7th I dont remember that I did anything very materal tho I sometimes said more than I should have done in reply to my mother when she told me to do things

8th I dont know that my mother hath ever to be cross with me at all for witch I am glad.

9th 10th 11th nothing at all that I know of

12th I grieved my Mother very much with telling her that I thaught she had a Pleasure in wipping My Sister

13 14 nothing Material I have made no memorandums for 6 days So that I dont remember every Particular in which I have done Wrong however this I know that I have often greeved my Mother with arguing too much when She told me to do things and also With vindecating myself when She reproved me and my liking for the kitchen still continues too great but never the less I do hope I am rather better in all these respects

From her Sampler

21 This morning I was very naughty being unwilling to dress my Sister Hannah as mother desired and made a many word about it

22 I have not been very good tempered not sufficiently attentive to my mother orders I grieved her with going out without leave and dirting myself also with being Idle about getting to my sewing and still liking the kitcing too much

23 I grieved my Mother this Morning with being unwilling to wash myself as much as she thaught nessary and made a great deal to do about the cold of the water tho it had been in mothers room all night

2 of 11 mo It is such a long time since I have wrote anything down that I dont remember evey thing by far but I know that I have often grieved my Mother with not coming when called on and not doing as I was bid and staying too much in the kitching

6th 3 and 4 I dont remember any but on 3 day I behaved very imperteninntly to my Mother about something that I was going to have made

8th and 9th I grieved my Mother with not doing as I was bid and saying too much when my Mother told me to do a thing but I intend to do better

21th It is such a long time since I have made any memorandum that I dont remember every particular but I remember that I grieved my Mother with letting my Sister Sarah fall of the bed and pining my scirt up too high and talking unbecomingly to my Mother about it and not siting proprly in the meeting and staying too long in the kitchen

26th of 11 month 6 7 and first I dont remember anything but one second day behaved only very indifarantly speaking unbecumingly to my Mother and for writing badly and for not doing on a bit of paper first

27 and 28 I dondt remember anything but 29 I grieved my Mother with telling her that I thaught she was almost allways contrary to what I did on 3 day of 12 I yet have too great propensity to arguing and contending with my Mother and to spending too much of my time in the kitching

4 of 12 month to my great satisfaction I conducted myself this day so as that my mother told mee she was pleased to see me

OLD STYLE

SPRING IS HERE

get so much the better of my wrong propensities

5 day I believe not much accured this day tho I think I rather
relaxed my watch against a wrong deposition

5 day stayed too long in the kitchin when I should have got to
my books and feel I am again sliding into my old habits O
that I might be helped to continue my edevours to concur
them

17th of 12 month it is a week since I have made any
memurandoms in which time I doubt not but that I have
been guilty of many faults tho I hope upon the whole that I
have been nore careful than at some other times times but last
night I broked out unbecumingly in contention with my
Mother for wich I was sadly grieved at myself and I also
grieved my Mother this and several other morning in being
long of geting drest I have again grieved my Mother with
telling her a thing was ont when she said it was

19th I have grieved grieved my Mother several times yesterday and to day in contending with her When she told me to do
a thing and last night with likeng better to hiron in the new
room than in the siteng room with her being in an ill youmer
about it

20th of 12th month only one thing happened this day and that
was verery near letting my Sister Sarah fall and that was with
throughing her about in my harms

22 To my great shame I was very much out of temper with my
Mother about pining my great coat hood before I went to
meeting because it came too much over my face

23 I was shame fully out of temper with my Mother this
evening about going to bed at 8 oclock and this was not all
for I said several unbecuming things to her during the day
ah mee shal I never have to say better of myself I hoften think
I will try to mend but thorough unwachfulness the enemy
gets the better of me

24 of 12 month I grieved my Mother today wanting to do
more at something I was doing than she wanted me to and
being greved about it

It is four days since I have made any memeanduns in wich
time I doubt not but that I have been guilty of many faults

but I know that I have grieved my Mother several times with contening With her and not doing things when she bid me

31 I grieved my Mother today with being in an ill Humer about seking the thread paper but on 30th day I dont know of anything

7th of 1 month 1800 I have grieved my Mother very often with contending and arguing with her but on 7th day I grieved sadly I wanted to go into the blacksmiths shop a bout something and she would not let me and I contended with her about it

8th of 1st month 1800 I grieved my Mother today with contining and not doing things whes she bid mee

9th Jan grieved my Mother with not going to bed soon enough and staying too long in the kitching

10th I dont know of anything particular but on sixth day I grieved my Mother again with not going to bed soon enough and staying too long in the kitching and not making memurandun

1th day and 2nd day I dont remember of anything but on 3 day I grieved my Mother with santring about going to bed

4 day I grieved my Mr with not coming in to get my lessings but on 5ty 6th 7th and first I remember of anything

2 day I grieved my Mother with not coming in soon enough

3th day nothing

4 day I grieved my Mother with being in a passion because I hurt myself very much

5th day I grieved my Mother with not being willing to wash myself behaving unbecumingly about it

6th and 7th day I dont know of anything but on first day I grieved my Mother showing an unwillingness to doo things

2nd and 3 day I dont know of anything but on 4th day I grieved my Mother with wanting to make beds instead of coming into the sitingroom

5th day nothing but on 6th day I grieved my Mother because I got her a wrong cap and she told mee to go and get her another I said I did not like to go up and down stairs so often

first day I dont know of anything but on 2th day I grieved my mother with talking too much

3th day Nothing

150

4th 5th 6th 7th and first I dont know that ever my Mother spoke a cross word to me
2nd and 3rd day I wanted to do more in the kitching than my Mother thought suitable

5th day I grieved my Mother with
not being willing to wash myself
behaving unbecomingly about it
6th and 7th day I dont know of any
thing but on first day I grieved my
Mother showing my unwillingness
to doo things — 2d and 3 day I
dont know of any thing —
but on 4th day I grieved my Moth
with wanting to make beds instead
of coming into the setting room

4th day I grieved my Mother with being unwilling for my Sister D to iron and pull out cloaths and talking too much about it

3rd day and 4th day and 5 day I dont know of anything

6th day I grieved my Mother with contending about something and of 7 day I grieved her with not going to bed soon enough

3rd 4th 5th 6 7 12 I dont know of nany matereal except one knight I grieved my Mother with santring about going to bed and eating my potatoe in the kitching it is a week or more since I have made any memurandums so that I dont know evey particular but I know that I have grieved my Mother several times With not going to my books soon enough and not making memurandums as often as I should 7th and 1st I dont know of anything but on 2nd day I grieved my Mother with not letting my Sister Dorothy wash up all the teathings and taking them from her

3rd day I grieved my Moth with talking too much about dress talking to martha in an unbecumg manner and telling my Mother it was better to put the day of the weks than the day of the month

4th day I dond know of anything but on 5th day I grieved my Moth with being too much with nanny

6th and 7th day I dont know of anything but on 1st day I grieved my Mother with washing myself in the back kitching

2nd day nothing

The reader who has been touched by this record will like to know something of Rachel's later life. She was sent to a Quaker school, Tuke's school in York for which Lindley Murray wrote his grammar. There her bad handwriting grew fine and her spelling irreproachable. A marvellous neat geometry notebook of hers full of delicately drawn figures, and her much-written-in copy of 'The Minor's Pocket Book' survive. One of her sisters was Mrs. Ellis, author of 'The Women of England' and other books on which Thackeray had a friendly word in the 'Book of Snobs'. When Rachel grew up she married Jonathan Binns, a farmer, and on the '16th of 10th month 1808', when just over 19 she, wrote him a long and beautiful letter, in which she said:

'*I often my dearest J. B. feel very desirous that if we are ever united in the closest bands (for I trust our hearts are already so) we may prove a mutual help to each other in the important work of religion and that I may not be as a stumbling block in thy road to felicity but that we may walk together in the paths of virtue and enjoy hereafter the reward of a life well spent. I dont look for perfect happiness in this world but I think that a closer union would contribute more to the completion of what is generally allotted to mortals than anything which this world affords and I hope that I shall ever conduct myself in such a manner as to ensure thy love and esteem it shall ever be my constant aim to contribute as I possibly can to encrease thy share of happiness.*'

Alas, on November 23rd, 1817, Rachel died. She was only twenty-eight and she left six children, the eldest barely seven and the youngest fourteen days. Her husband survived her for more than half a century of faithful widowerhood. There lies before us the old-fashioned birth certificate of one of Rachel's children:

'*On the twenty-third day of the ninth month one thousand eight hundred and sixteen was born at Leach house in the township of Ellel in the parish of Cockersham in the county of Lancaster unto Jonathan Binns farmer and Rachel his wife a son who is named Jonathan George. We who were present at the said birth have subscribed our names as witnesses thereof. John Smith, surgeon. Mary Monks.*'

For permission to reprint the 'Memuranduns', and for the sight of all other memorials of Rachel I was indebted to the great kindness of the late George F. Binns, F.G.S., her grandson, who passed away at the age of eighty-six. In the saucer of the cup in which I drank tea with him he had placed one of Rachel's silver tea spoons, which bore her initials. After tea Mr. Binns showed me with reverent affection a lock of Rachel's hair, dark with a glint of gold and two strands of white. I also had the opportunity of reading five loving letters to Rachel from her mother: the disposition of Mrs. Stickney was not completely reflected in the piteous 'Memuranduns'. Rachel's father had died in 1848, and been buried where his forebears had been laid for two hundred years.

ø

Said toothless, good hearted, capable, old Mercy, who nursed the sick, laid out the dead, did a bit of upholstery and was in regular request as a midwife: 'Well, I brings most of 'em into the world and I touches them up to go out of it.'

Murder by a Mantis, by D. Marion

A MAY morning in a Kenya garden. 9 a.m. 'Memsahib. Come here. Hurry, Memsahib!' A little black fiend of a child, squatting on his heels, beckons to his mistress. He gesticulates wildly, pointing to a bush. Memsahib hastens to discover the cause of Jerogi's excitement. He shows her a tiny russet bird sitting rocking precariously, on a branch. 'Ah, the poor thing; it is starved', she says, and stretches out her arm to take it in her hand. Jerogi seizes her wrist. 'Hapana!' he exclaims. A leaf moves. A green twig shoots out and grabs the bird by the throat, and another clenches round its neck. Two tender green twigs, no, they are alive. They have crab-like pincers. Memsahib stares in astonishment. They are the gortesque forearms of a mantis—the leaf, its body! Wonderful camouflage. It is already too late to rescue the fluttering bird. Its tiny legs jerk out stiffly, then curl inwards. Jerogi breaks off the branch and holds it up for closer inspection. The mantis, intent on its meal is not disturbed. Peering close, comparing the leaves of the twig with the insects' folded wings, they are identical in size and shape, of the same shade and similarly veined. Even the body, scaled and concave underneath, is like an oversized leaf stalk.

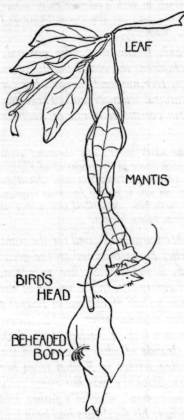

LEAF

MANTIS

BIRD'S HEAD

BEHEADED BODY

Memsahib attaches the branch from which the murderer hangs, suspended by its grass-stalk legs clasping its victim, to a creeper in order to watch developments. 9.30 The mantis has broken the skin of the bird's throat. It is eating and sucking furiously. The champ of its wasp-like jaws is audible. 9.45. Bird's head hanging by a shred. 10. Head severed. Body in one claw, head in the other. 10.30. Mantis intent on demolishing the head. 11. Beak and one eye are all that is left of head. Remaining eye being attacked. The mantis's body is assuming the proportions of a little barrel. 11.30. Beak, the sole surviving piece of the bird's head is on the ground. Mantis feasting on the trunk. 12. Mantis's body more distended. A crack is noticeable down either side; evidently it is capable of expansion. 12.15. Mantis eating with less enthusiasm. Its body is distended by means of quarter-inch lateral cracks, which disclose, taut rose-coloured skin. Rapid and laboured palpitations are apparent beneath the skin, indicating gross abdominal discomfort. 12.30. A deflated little bag of feather lies upon the ground. The mantis has disappeared.

The Country Bus, by Joyce M. Westrup

THE heavy bus
　　Swayed smoothly down the hill
　　Into the sun of an Autumn afternoon.
And all the tired eyes of the passengers
Blinked happily. The school children
Whistled together, high and sweet and shrill.
The bus was like a cage of sleepy birds
In a gold mist.
Suddenly the conductor
Knew it was so. A smile
Brightened his long sad face;
'Blimey!' he said,
'You're like a bloomin' lot o' little sparrers.'

Joyce Westrup was formerly on the staff of the *Countryman* with her husband, David Brontë Green, who has written *Country Neighbours* and *In the Wood and Other Stories*.

A Grave Digger's Diary, 1763-1831

*A neighbour of mine, Mrs. Marshall of Shenington, writes Miss M. K.
Ashby, was recently dusting a large old book when there fell out of it
a few yellowed papers covered with faded handwriting. The papers
proved to be this diary, intermittently kept but continuing over some
seventeen years, from 1814 to 1831*. The handwriting and orthography
are those of a person who seldom writes and never reads. In spite of
this I thought at first that the author must have been a vicar or curate,
for he was evidently an official of the church and had a deep interest in
the morals of his village. On September 15th, 1831, he buried an old
woman 97 years of age, but then he writes in 1830 that on St. Swithin's
Day when George IV was buried at ten at night, "i knold the bell 14
hours in the time." Though curates have a charm that sextons lack, I
was forced by the last and other entries to conclude that we were
handling the record not of a clergyman or even of a parish clerk but of
a gravedigger.*

EDWARD ARPIN I do remember in the year of 1763 that
Bread was sold at one shilling one penny the peck.

in the same year ann Silver come to keep my Fathers
house and she was with child and in august next she was
Brought abed of a male child and she had it named William
Silver, that had 4 eyes 2 in the face as others have 2 upon the
head

In the year of 1780 a peck loaf for 1s 2d in the year 1800 a
peck loaf for 6s 2d in the year 1801 a peck loaf is 6s 6d in
the year 1806 a peck loaf is 3s 6d In the year 1812 a peck
loaf is 6s 4d

Remarks

In the year 1800 August great thunder at Regement their
was hail stons Found Merurd 12 inches

and one Christmas day the Bird that is called Cuck-oo was
seen and heard to sing By manny Folks at Willsend

In the year 1801 near Stone-Stratford there was a hawe
Thorn Bush upon the Full Bloom January the 12 Northamton
News

In the year 1801 July there Fell in Iterley A hail Stone that
Wayed 16 pounds and a half Northampton News

---

*Several more sheets were found later and these form the opening of the Diary.

Feb 28 a Miss wooded the church Minestr Mr Timms Daughter was delivered of a fine Gearl that 6 fingers on each hand 6 toes one each foot

in the year 1813 John Miller of Filmersham made an ende of Wheat seeding January the 3

October 3th I and my famley had green pease Both Blue and Prounefirs for dinner

Oct th 20 1813 I had 3 pounds wight in money for helping caring the Raimens of Mr John Greey to the Church of Felmersham

Decmbr th 10 1813 A peck Loaf was 36 ditto 1738

Janry th 7 A peck Loaf 3–9 1814

Out of 26 Famlys thiris 10 widows in the parish of Felmersham

Nanns Susanah Lee Eliz Church Sarah Drage Mary Brown Mary Dotson Mary Groves Ann Brooks Sarah Broatfield Ann Hickman Sarah Arpin it never was known in the oldist

Mutton one shilling and tow pence a pound

In the year 1814 January the 6 A snow fell and Lay untill the 3 of April

the 19 of April they Sold onions 4 pence each

the 28 of April i had some Boild Butter milk for my ddener

In this parish of Felmersham there is But 38 houses and their is ten old Maids and eleven widows December 17

1815—January the 3 A peck loaf 3s 4d Mutton is $9\frac{1}{2}$ a pound

Febry the 19 Ann Baker was Ravish'd By Robert Smith

April the 18 A flock of Wild geese was seen it never was seen in the oldest Age

1816—January the 1 A peck loaf was 2s 10d

May the 22 A peck loaf was 4s 3d

August 27 I went Weeding oats

Septr the 1 I went into my Month to harvist it was never so leate in the oldest Age

Septr the 18 I am Beetwen sixty and seventy year old and i thresh't 9 duzzon of Wheate Sheaves for 3 Bushel of wheat

November the 7 I whent A gleaning Beans and it snow'd the 8th we got harvist home but Their is a great Maney Beans and Oats to com home in the parish

A peck loaf is 4s 7d Wheat is 5 shillings a Bushell

November the 16 Joseph Swannell At Hardwick made on end of caring (carrying) Beans and Oats

December the 21 We had harvist home at Ensbury St. noos Felmersham Parish land lett in the year 1764 for 14 shillings the Acer 1816 at 14 shillings a Rood 1 Rood to the Church 2 Acres to the Poor men 3 Acres to 12 widdows

1817—Mrs Swannell of Odell after beining in Larber from december 1816 the 26 to January 1817 the 11 was delivered of her 15th Child Elizear is her name

A peck loaf is 5s 2d

June the 30 A peck loaf 6s 8d

September the 19 A peck loaf is 5s 8d

1818—February the 16 Begin to cutt stone

May the 20 the Begin to bild Felmersham New Bridge

June the 13 turnd the First Arch of the Bridge

June the 16 the Begin to make a new Bake house for Mr Brown

June 27 they turnd the 2 Arch

Mr Payen Begins harvest July the 23

A peck loaf was 4s 4d

August the 3 turnd 3th Arch

August the 14 Edmond Lodlow had his First harvist Supper After Buyin Williams hannoh Land

August the 22 turnd the 4 Arch of the Bridge

June the 6 Thos Eyals of Carlton went over the Bridge with a cart

Octr the 6 turnd the 5 Arch of the Bridge

November the 14 Finished the Bridge

Novr the 14 i had a Cowcumber Growd in my Gardin Mesured 5 inches Round as good as if it had been in the middle of Summer and the vine growd upon Goltey ground it never was known in the oldist Age hear Before

November the 29 i had sum kiddney Beans for my Dinner fresh got off the vins such thing was Never known in the oldist Age

December Smmell Swannell the 3 son of Will Swannel Mixt his Wheat among his Barley for the hogs Charls Neal

158

had it Ground

1819—January the 5 Richard Wills the Parish Clerk is 68 years was married to M Ann Arch she is 26 years old

Charles Bonnor of this town was Married to his foath wife in the sixth year he had three in the Forthteenth Munths

January the 27 A Great Flight of doves went to Rodwell Chappell Between 6 and 7 oclock at night

Feb 24 part of the First And last Arch Fell Down

Octr 14 They turnd the second Arch that Fell down

Octr the 25 it snowed 3 hours

A peck Loaf is 3s 6d

Novr the 5 i got a Cowcumber 7 inches round

1820—After 1 years and 19 weeks Labour the Fineched the Broken Bridge July 8

Octr 1820 Will Winsall was married to Diana Nutchins he was 65 she 62 years

1821—A peck loaf is 3s 0d

November the 17 I hear William Norman say he should like to go to heaven And sit upon a white horse And ride about heaven

Decr 3 Bread is 2s 10d A peck

Decmr 23 i went to get primroses upon the full Blow A clove pink Also upon the full Blow on Christmas day 25 which had never seen the sun for 2 months more over We have such A great water that All the Arches of the Bridge was all coverd with water

1822—January 2 A peck loaf 2s 8d

January the 6 it was Froast and snow it Rain the 9 and 11 and one the 16 the Dust Blowd about on the 17 Day Froast an snow

February the 4 William Swannell Begin to sow Lamonse Wheat

William Eddin of Odell to his wife the next morning at 3 oclock had a child

William Drage Felmersham the same ditto

William Solsbury Milton his was Born in 3 hours time

Novm. Edward Arpin Bought Mutton at 3 pence a pound

Decembr 10th Thomas Barker 72 years of age went away For Debauchery With Mary Ann Drage 14 years of age

1823—January 26 Thomas Barker com home again

Thomas Barker went away again Febr 4 Muton 4 pence a pound

March 1 Thomas Barker come home again Mutton was 6 pound

October the 31 it was the Greatst Flood that ever was known it Drove the walls down from the Bridge

Bread was 2s 6d a peck Mutton is 6 pound

1824—John Brooke was Sent Away transported For 7 years Beyond the seas

In the Month of March was found A stone coffin with a Body in it

Bread was 3s 0d a peck loaf

August 10 Radwell Feast Tusday morn in the hour of two i heard 3 Battels Fought Bettween A man and his wife Before she would hould her peace the Blows was as if the was Rending of wood that was Dickins Prigmore and his Wife But she was in fault

the Next day the bould (bowled) for tea And suggar Bread and Butter and snuff

Thursday Joseph Swannells Hay cock on Fire

On Sunday Next we had a mob of 30 of our men Rison (risen) upon the irish men all our Men had Bludgins in their hands But our Farmers Joseph Payen Samuel Swannell William Swannell Joseph Swannell Made pease

Septr 15 Charls Bonnors Wife Kicit (kicked) the the skin of all down his shinns the Blood ran and his stockin stuck all the next day

A new house Bulte at Rodwell Moore End A new Gearley Bulte at Sharn Brok And opned Octr the 3

1825

Jany 24 John Hannah Jintell Man Born [gentleman born] come to work on the rood for his living Bread 3s 6d a peck loaf

Febry 10 Robert Costin and James Hulet sent prison for sheep stealin

Feb 13 Joseph Payens Barn at Hardwick was set willfully on Fire

Feb 18 Benjamin Parsons sent to Goal Beatin Joseph Wills

one of the watches at the above fire

March 22 James Pain went away for stealin flower from Willaim Brooks

March the 11 Robert Costin and James Hulett was condde'd to Be hanged But was Reprev'd But was transported For life

March 16 George Costin Dickins Prigmore was sent to the Goal for setin fire to Mr pains Barn at Hardwick and Sheap stealin

April Hugh Applejohn give Ann Prigmore 1s

March 17 Francis Hulett was sent to Goal for the fire and sheep stealin

April 25 James hulet and Robert Costin was sent Beyond the Seas for sheep stealing

April 15 Hugh Applejohn had Ann Prigmore into his own room and give her one shilling

July the 15 George Costin and Francis Hulet was conmed to be hanged But was transported for Life Dickins Prigmore turnd Kings Evend

Oct. 11 a flood

Octr 21 snow and very could

Oct 20 Gott a cowcumber Mesured 9 inches and a quarter Round

1826

Feb we had 15 Floods Salt is one penney apr Pound Bread is 3 shilling a peack Loafe

One Monday 27 A Great fire Brok out at Kempstone 40 houses Burnt

March 9 a Flood out we had 14 Floods this Winter Bread 3s 9d peck Loaf

We have had A peacin cold Spring

In July A Great Tempeast Burnt farm and wheat hovel at Harold

Very Forward harvist Mr Chapman Gott harvist home at Oakley the 29 day of July

A great tempest July 31 thrown down Rushdon spire and shiverd all the whole Church so that the Esty Mation of damage is to Be Fore 4000 pounds to repair it again

Robert Hulett at Oakley Gott Harvist home August 5 and

his pease and Beans was Lite and he sode 3 Bushels of salt upon his Benans to keep the straw for his kittel to eat it was never known in the old Age

Samuel Swannell this last seedin sod 20 Bushells of salt upon 2 lands of Barley and its not better but rather worse

Ann Dolton was Drunk and found in Humphrey Payen straw hovel her daughter Elizabeth was drunk and satt upon Marrioats stiale [stile]

Felmersham Church the tower has been new timberd and thier was a Brace put up in the tower to supporte the old timber The Portch which is Built new From the Ground Oct 7.

Octr 22 it thunderd Most part of the day

the Revd. Henery Davice Ward Prech'd his First searmon at Pavinham Chappel of East Decm 24 at Felmersham Mother Church one Christmas Day

1827

June 12 was Found the part of the in side of some woman in the well against Thomas Greeves house it was bound up into a napken

July 28 Willaim Edmund Low and Edward Arpin Clerk paid the poor in the Church porch it was never known in the oldist Age before

16 of July the Begin to Bulde the work house

James Buit went away Oct '28

A peck loaf is 2s 10d pence

August 21 Samuel Swannell sent a wagin Load of new wheat to Stoke mills it Never was knowed so soon in the oldest age

1828

June 23 William Brezzer had his Neck [broke] and Jams how sett it again

We had amids Floods 23 days it was never knowd in the oldis Aage

Bread was 2s 8d peck loaf

Octr 2 A great Flood peck loaf 4s

Octr 20 A great Froast an ice Bread is 3s 10d A peck

Novm 12 Robert toll sent Gaol for stealing An Apple tree from William dennis

Novm 18 Robert Smith for Robbin parrsions hen ruste

1829

Jany 15 Revd Henery Davice Ward Married

Bread 3s 8d peck loaf

Will Dix cald a fool But gott girl with Child and he (gave) her 1s. 6d. to be aste at Church when she was sworn her Child to Daniel howe

John Turner to North America

29 June 39 men women and children set off to go to Boston in Massachusetts in the united States of North America

Sept 21 My daughter Hagar in her 49 years was Married to William Leighton Aged in his 81 he is 32 years oldist

Bread 3 shillings a peck

Octr 7 it snowd an raind (in 1829) 89 days and very cold

1830

January 10 Joseph Swannell set sail to the West Indes

Nov 25 it snowed very cold and the snow was upon the ground the 12d of March

May 8 John Hannah Charles Bonom sailed to West Indeas

King George 4 died June 26 he was Buried on St. Swithins Day at ten at night. And i knold the bell 14 hours in the time.

1831

Jany 11 Mr H Ward Apointed Justice of the peace, Rabert truit the First as went to him

Jany 24 Thos Poolys widow a great Decentor was put to Bed of a girl unknown whos

Feb 8 A very great Flood and 2 Bakers went with a cart and Bread to Mitton End and man a blacksmith name Pruddon to Bletsoe to work untill night and he went to Milton to come home with the 2 Bakers and the all come together and come down the Flood to Rodwell Bridge Foot and the over turned the cart Smith got out of the cart to Swim over But he has not Found yet. The 2 Bakers got out. the horse and car was By water sent into perrys Meadow it was never knowd in the oldist Aage

[*This is still talked of in Felmersham.*]

Sept 15 I Berried an old woman 87 years of Age Catherint tite.

163

THE GAINSBOROUGH PICTURE

The appearance of the 'Grave-Digger's Diary' brought many expressions of appreciation. A poet said that it would be his lifelong regret that he had never thought how much he 'should like to go to heaven And sit upon a white horse And ride about heaven', like the William Norman of the Diary. The poet does not know whether he most admires the man who had such a glorious Blake-like thought or the Diarist who recognized in this a sublime aspiration.

Other readers had the helpful impulse of trying to find out something about the Diarist; but though there are survivors of some of the families mentioned in the Diary, the Grave Digger himself seems to have left neither descendants nor memories. He writes himself down Edward Arpin, which, judging by the varieties of spelling of other names in the Diary, was just as likely to have been spelt Harpin or Orpin. This name brought to Mr. C. D. Linnell, of Pavenham (until 1858 forming one parish with Felmersham) the recollection that the 'Parish Clerk' of Gainsborough's famous picture at the Tate Gallery was named Edward Orpin! But this Edward Orpin was parish Clerk not at Felmersham but at Bradford-on-Avon, Wilts., where the portrait was painted in 1769. Mr. Linnell writes: 'The Orpin coincidence is truly remarkable but I cannot think that they were the same people. Our Orpin, I find, was baptized at Pavenham in 1756 and was Parish Clerk of Felmersham from 1824 to 1834. The Felmersham Orpin was thus only 13 years old when the picture was painted. May it be that he was a relative of Gainsborough's Parish Clerk? Four miles from Felmersham, at Harrold, there is a resident of the name of Orpin, but neither his grandfather nor greatgrandfather had any connection with Felmersham. The problem of how the Diary got from Felmersham to Warwickshire is still unsolved.'

Why did Orpin write his Diary? Mr. Linnell advances the ingenious theory that he was stimulated by the achievement of the vicar of the neighbouring parish of Shevington, the Rev. J. Orlebar Marsh (1766-1832), who lived at Felmersham, officiated there at funerals and weddings, and wrote notes on the natural history and remarkable occurrences of the district. Several collections of his MSS. are in the British Museum.

❦

Farm-worker, overheard in conversation with another farm-worker about gardening, refers to a third farm-worker's garden which is overgrown with weeds: 'I wonder who gets old Joe's shootin' this year.'

A sheep belonging to a Quaker farmer fell into a ditch on a Sunday when the farmer was wearing his better clothes. He succeeded in getting it out, muddying himself the while; but it slipped back again. He got it out a second time, and got muddier still; once more it slipped back. He made a third attempt, dirtying himself still further—when it managed to slide back yet again. Then the Quaker cried, ' "Damn thee", as the Church people say!'—(The story is sent by a Quaker reader.)

The Wrong Kind of Pruning
by Raymond Bush

WHEREVER I go I see apples, strong and stout in the branch, putting out fresh heavy growth each year, and wilfully prevented from forming fruit buds. Always understood that new growths should be cut back to about two inches, did you? Well this tree is a clear case of wilful murder by secateurs. A strong-growing tree simply must not be treated like this. Growth above ground is an indication of vigour of root system. If your tree persists in growing shoots a yard or more long, leave them unpruned for a year or two, reducing the jungle luxuriance by the removal of a whole limb if need be. Then, when your fruit buds have formed, proceed judiciously with gentle thinning. Now that old tree there is in need of invigoration, and you may well take out a third of the main branches and reduce the spurs by half on what you have left. You must learn to consider apple trees as individuals needing different treatment in order to get the best results out of them. If you had bought one-year old trees you could have shaped them to what you wished. It is quite simple; you get just a single straight shoot about four feet high as a one-year old. Plant it and cut it off at about knee high if you want a bush tree. The top three or four buds will break in the spring as shoots, but it is a mistake to let the top three do so. Take a sharp knife, make your knee-high cut come out just above a bud, leave that bud there but remove the one below it, leave the next and remove the one below that one. Then when your tree is grown up it will have branches springing from the stem at good intervals, and no crotched trunk. Three leading branches are quite enough for, to increase them, all you need to do is to choose two side buds adjoining on the shoot, and cut off above the top one. Your three branches will then be six in the following summer and twelve in the summer after that if you want them. Yes, I see you cut the feathers or side shoots away all down the trunk of

The genial author of the *Countryman's* outstanding 'Fruitgrower's Diary' and of those admirable books, *Fruit Growing, Frost and the Fruit Grower, Fruit Salad* and *The Harvest and Storage of Fruit*. He had his schooling at Rugby, and adds to his practical experience of fruit-growing, knowledge acquired by continual touring of the country.

those few trees over there. It was a mistake, for, in the early years, short leaf-carrying shoots serve to feed the trunk of the young tree.

A Summer-House in a Tree
by Lieut.-Col. C. H. Buck

DURING my childhood at Newport in Essex, there was, at an inn in that village, a small house in an old elm, where travellers enjoyed having tea. Our own summer-house was constructed in an old tree, with wide-spreading branches, ten feet up, and was about ten feet square. Ever since those early days I have had a fondness for this kind of building and in India made one in a tree on the top of the Salt Range in the Punjab and another between two trees over a tiny gorge at Dharmsala in the Himalayas. At the age of ten I was sent to a school near Huntingdon where I spent much of my spare time up trees. In a far corner of the playing grounds there were three elms which made a most excellent 'ship'. They were named by me the main, fore and mizzen and possessed their 'yards' and 'tops', a 'bowsprit' and various other parts of a full-rigged sailing vessel. I am informed, by a friend of his boyhood, that Sir James Barrie played pirates with him and other children in a tree-house and wrote stories for the games; also that 'Peter Pan' had its origin in one of these. In 1932 I constructed a summer-house up an oak at the edge of my little garden in Hampshire. Its floor is thirty feet up. It has a floor-space of nine feet by eight and is provided with a watertight roof and a lift for taking up the tea-things. There is seating accommodation for nine persons, with room for three chairs. It is necessary to select a tree which is not brittle like an elm or fast-growing like a syca-more. An oak is the best. Above all, it must be remembered the the upper half of the building, including the roof, should only be fixed to the main stem and not to branches liable to bend and wrench it apart.

Colonel Buck died a few years ago but Mrs. Buck writes that the summer house is still in 'excellent condition and

166

a joy to children young and old'. Shortly before writing, several children had been to tea in it. 'We have had as many as fourteen children sharing the seats and taking up a few stools. I have told the children that if the summer house could speak it would have tales to tell as most of it was made from the packing cases of a General who had been all over India, China, Egypt and the Middle East.

Trespasser Catching, *by A. G. Street*

I SAID to myself that I should prosecute any trespasser I caught that afternoon. First came two women. They left the road and walked up the field towards me. They were each carrying their tea in a shiny black leather bag. They were dressed in black, and each was approximately fourteen stone. Both were getting puffed with the uphill walk. As they were passing me I addressed the nearer. 'Are you aware that you are trespassing and also doing damage?' 'Law!' she said, putting down her bag. 'Be us?' 'Yes,' I said, 'you should keep to the highway.' 'Yerr that, Betsy?' she said to her companion, 'My! Look at un. All gritty and stwony. Think of my pore wold feet. You should keep thicky road in better fettle, Sir so as we could walk on un.' 'The road is not my liability. I must ask you for your names and addresses.' 'Betsy, we be vor it. Sir, bain't you Maister Eldridge?' 'If you must know, yes. Now will you give me your—' 'John Eldridge, Master Jacky, doan't you remember Charlotte? I've bathed 'ee many a time. You be growed into a fine chap. Lord! I can mind you a cryin' for the sponge.' It was indeed true. I could dimly trace in this huge woman the nurse-girl of my child-

---

The *Countryman* published some of Street's earliest work. Indeed this sketch appeared before the first of his widely popular books, *Farmer's Glory*. There must be now almost a dozen and a half of them. Street, who is also known as a broadcaster, farms in Wiltshire, where his father was a farmer before him. A curious fact is the similarity of his handwriting with that of Adrian Bell, who has written so many stories on rural subjects.

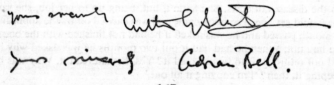

hood. We chatted amicably for a while and I explained that I had a lot of trouble with people trespassing and was trying to stop it. 'That be all right, Sir,' she said, and as she went on her way, 'us won't do it no more. I be reel glad to a seed 'ee.'

I looked down the field. Children, in the charge of a girl of about thirteen, were straggling up the hill all over the field as if it were a public recreation ground. As they came near I called them and asked for their names and addresses. They all wept. I began to feel a brute. However, it must be done, I thought, and turned to the biggest girl. 'Now then, it's no use crying—your names?' 'Mine be Mary Luther, he in the short knicks be—' Here she took to sobbing. It was hopeless. 'Oh, get along', I said, 'and in future keep to the roads.'

They straggled away and I noticed a man coming up the field, stopping every now and again to admire the view. 'Right,' said I, 'I'll have one more shot.' When he came opposite me he stopped. 'Isn't it a perfectly topping day, Sir,' he said, beaming at me. 'It is,' I said; 'but why do you walk on my field instead of the highway?' 'Well,' he said; 'look at the highway. This is much nicer for walking.' 'Yes,' said I; 'but you realise that you are trespassing, I suppose?' 'Trespassing,' he said, 'why this field is grass. I would never think of walking on a field which had a crop.' 'My dear Sir,' I said; 'I have gone to considerable expense to lay this field down to grass.' 'But I don't understand. Everyone walks on grass. Grass isn't a crop.' 'Oh isn't it. Grass is the most valuable crop the British farmer tries to grow.' 'You know that's awfully interesting. I've often wondered why there was so much grass land. I never thought grass had a value except for hay.'

∅

Rural policeman committee man to a suggestion that there should be nigger minstrels, 'That'll make 'em clean their teeth.'

A youth at a farmhouse asked the village librarian if she had a book on the diseases of cows. She hadn't, but, being up to her job, she said she would get one. The book came and was carried off by the applicant. A month passed and he was asked if he had not finished with the book. He had not. When he had had it out two months he was asked why he did not return it. Had he not read it? Yes, he had read it. Why was he keeping it, then? 'I'm copying it all out.'

Is London or the Country Better for Brain Work?

WHEN the headmaster of Westminster school said, 'In order to live your life well, play in the country, but work in the town; it is in the great vitality of the great town's life that the individual is stimulated and compelled to think,' the *Countryman* communicated with a number of distinguished men and women. Did they think that their best work was done in the town or in the country? The replies were as follows:

ARNOLD BENNETT.—It makes no difference to me where I work.

HILAIRE BELLOC.—It never made any difference to me! So little that I can't remember what was written in town and what in country.

G. K. CHESTERTON.—I do not consider I have ever done any good work, but I prefer much living in the country.

NOEL COWARD.—I prefer writing in the country owing to the greater quiet.

CLEMENCE DANE.—Sometimes I work better in town, sometimes in the country, it depends entirely on circumstances. I love the town, but to live in I'd choose the country. Town stimulus is artificial. One works well in a town because one gets the chance of meeting all sorts of exciting people, of going to theatres, concerts, galleries and so on. That is to say, one is taking mental cocktails all day long; but the end of a month of mental cocktails is complete physical exhaustion! Now the country gives one food and drink for the spirit, and never tires one out. It is not a play place, but a home. Perhaps one does not always work so quickly at 'home' because outdoor life is always taking one away from the writing desk, but I am sure in the end that the *quality* of the work done improves. That's my own experience, and though I don't want to lay down any law for other people, and I don't want to be ungrateful to town, if I had to give up one or other altogether it wouldn't be the country!

JOHN DRINKWATER.—I cannot just now give you my

reasons, but with the most humble respect I think the Head-master of Westminster is all wrong.

ST. JOHN ERVINE.—I find myself able to work equally well in town or country, provided, of course, that I can secure myself from interruption. The trouble is that in town, because of the telephone, an author finds increasing difficulty in keeping himself free from interruptions that are sometimes impertinent. People who would not dream of interrupting a man's work by making their trivial requests in person have no compunction at all about doing so by telephone. That is the reason why many writers decline to publish their telephone numbers in the Directory. They wish to save themselves at least from interruption by total strangers. But it is their damnable friends who are the worst. Many of these, knowing that a writer is generally working at home in the morning, purposely telephone their small social requests to him at that time, and seem to imagine that their interruptions are of no consequence. I think the ideal way of living is to have some contact with a town, but to have one's main life in the country, where there is a great sense of neighbourliness and a deeper knowledge of life. See page 123.

HAVELOCK ELLIS.—There is no general rule, and I know that a distinguished philosopher of the last century (Shad-worth Hodgson) preferred to isolate himself for intellectual work in rooms just off Regent Street. But, for my part, I have always chosen, so far as possible, to be in the country—moreover, in the open air—for intellectual work. From time to time I enjoy cities and the privileges they offer, but I am most compelled to think when most by myself.[1]

JOHN GALSWORTHY.—I can work in quiet parts of a town nearly as well as in the country; but I should say that about two-thirds of my work for the last thirty years has been done in the country and probably the most sustained and strenuous efforts have been made there.

ALDOUS HUXLEY.—I do not agree with the Headmaster

[1] When I met Havelock Ellis he was living in Brixton, but happily he was able to spend much of his time in the country. He sent me encouraging messages when I was editing, first the *New East* which I founded in Tokyo, and then the *Countryman*, which I set going and edited in the Cotswolds. When he came to see me it was in keeping with his liking for a quiet life, to request that no one should be asked to meet him. How far we have travelled since the period in which he was prosecuted in respect of books which are now taken as a matter of course. I remember that it was only in Japan that I was able to get volumes I lacked.

of Westminster. My own practice is to work in the country and take holidays—or rather work less and less seriously—in the town. The Headmaster of Westminster seems to imagine that noise and hustle are synonymous with vitality. I should have thought that a very superficial observation of men and societies was sufficient to expose this fallacy. The noise and agitation of modern cities are, for the great majority of people, impediments to serious inward living of good spiritual quality. And the ready-made amusements of modern cities—from the picture paper to the cinema, from dancing to listening in—are merely substitutes for thought and excuses for laziness. They generate a terrible boredom; that is why the modern city dweller can never stop hustling or jazzing. Like the water beetle, if he stood still for a moment, he would sink. What the Headmaster of Westminster calls 'the great vitality of the great town' seems to me to bear a close resemblance to the great vitality of a dead frog's leg when an electric current is passed through it. The most highly galvanized corpse-cities are, of course, to be found in America. For the Headmaster of Westminster, Los Angeles and Chicago must be earthly paradises and New York the New Jerusalem.

SIR W. ARBUTHNOT LANE.—I fear I require the stimulus and rush of London to do any work I wish to do. The necessity of having to complete one thing when you have already too much on hand makes one put a lot of energy into doing it which one could not arouse without the stimulus of urgency and the requirement of doing some work in a certain time. When one is on a holiday it is difficult to concentrate. At all events, it is my experience. I like to play hard and to work hard. I love the country for a time, but my heart is in the rush and bustle of London. I quite agree with the Headmaster of Westminster School.

E. V. LUCAS.—My experience has been that in town as it offers fewer distractions, I can work with more steadiness: in the country, when the sun shines, the competition is too disturbing.[1]

SIR OLIVER LODGE.—Now that I live in the country and do

---

[1] His visit to Idbury was memorable. The other time I met him was when, as his guest, with, I think, Lord Gorell and the editor of *Punch*, I was for the only time in my life, at a night club.

my work there, I find an occasional visit to London stimulating and perhaps even necessary. Friendly intercourse with other minds is a great help. One learns sometimes at firsthand what is going on in laboratories; and if one remained in the country, all the year round, one might be liable to vegetate. I find however that for actual production and quiet thought, life in the country is best. In town one gets stimulus, but not much time for digestion. Food for thought one can get anywhere. It is easier in the country to interleave work with exercise. Exercise in London, though necessary is hardly agreeable. And there are apt to be too many distractions to continuous work.[1]

ROSE MACAULAY.—I should think whether work was better done in town or country would depend on the nature of the work.

J. RAMSAY MACDONALD.—My experience is not quite that of the Headmaster of Wesminster. If I had to choose between the town and the country as a place for working I should unhesitatingly say that I can not only produce more in the latter but that the quality of the work is much better. I think, however, the real fact that a change from one to the other is necessary, as one's mind requires the rest that comes from variety. To do all your play in the country and all your work in the town seems to me to be a bad rule.[2]

JOHN MASEFIELD.—I do all my work in the country out of doors, when possible.[3]

A. A. MILNE.—I find it easier to settle down to work in London, for the reason that in the country there are so many better things to do; but when once I have settled down, I can work equally well, or badly, anywhere.[4]

GEORGE MOORE.—I should like everybody to remember, the Headmaster of Westminster School not excepted, that people taken up from the country to be educated in the towns never return to the country.

---

[1] I saw his method for dispersing London fog, and he talked about the electrical encouragement of cropping.
[2] One of his last messages to me was from the other side of the Atlantic. He had discovered a copy of the *Countryman* in Labrador.
[3] The Poet Laureate kindly wrote of the *Countryman*, 'I prefer it to any other periodical'!
[4] Did anyone ever get a letter from him which was not amusing? Adults have enjoyed his plays. Children have risen up to call him blessed.

R. H. MOTTRAM.—The question you ask me is a stumper. I'm blessed if I know. What is an author's work? Writing with a pen, sopping up impressions, interviewing publishers? All of them, of course. Some are necessarily done in the country, sometimes, others, otherwise, at other times. I believe the town and the country to be mutually dependent, indispensable to each other. At the moment, being over-towned, you have my good wishes in redressing the balance. Once redressed, stop! Heaven defend us from a peasant population like France, Russia or the States! Probably our island individualism will wreck it anyhow. (See page 125.)

C. E. MONTAGUE.—My Fourth Form master at school had a thunderous way of saying, 'Go down two places for making a rash generalization,' and I should like to say it as thunder-ously to any one who says that mankind at large can work better in a town than in the country. I dare say *some* men do so, as *some* ship-boys may sleep better 'on the high and giddy mast' than in bed; but many ship-boys certainly prefer their beds and many busy people positively thrive on depri-vation of the stimulus of motor horns, street cries, tramcar gongs, etc., while they are working. As to my own work I do it, so far as I know, equally ill in town and country. As to my betters in our trade I fancy that

> All places that the eye of Heaven doth visit
> Are to the wise man ports and happy havens

and that Thoreau would have written all right in Fleet Street, and Dr. Johnson in Arcady, whatever either of them says. I fear that to you, a hundred-per-cent, countryman, this may seem but a shauchlin' testimony, but the plaguy habit of *halbheit* or anti-sweepingness, or untrenchancy, grows on me apace, so that I can't take bell and book and candle in hand to give either town or country a whole-hearted damning. (See page 176.)

H. W. NEVINSON.—It is hard to say. I suppose my best work has been done in wars and revolutions and other dis-turbances, for instance, in Ireland, and that has been chiefly by telegraph or by hurried letters, and entirely in the country, except during Russian revolutions in Moscow and old St. Petersburg, or in Dublin. My books, however, and my essays ('middle') for the 'Nation' under Massingham were written in London, and I think I write that kind of deliberate stuff best in a large city. For two reasons: (1) I find a mental stimulus in mixing with journalists and writers like myself, and in discussing the latest questions with them; and (2) I am so happy and interested in the country that it seems a waste of time and opportunity to sit still and write when Nature is carrying on her primeval course, and men and women around me are doing work that is obviously so much more genuine and beneficial than any writing of mine can possible be. Besides, curiosity and the love of beauty are always tempting me out, and I cannot stay brooding over books and papers—'for fear of growing double,' as Wordsworth said.[1]

LORD OLIVIER.—I do not feel sure that I rightly interpret the mind of the Headmaster of Westminster School in the advice which he gave his boys. Speculating on the probable careers of his scholars, it occurs to me that some of them will be soldiers, who will probably have to do their work in the country, wherever their depôt may be, and will very likely go to town for amusement. Their sports and exercise will no doubt take them to the country like other people. Sailors have to do their work on board ship or at naval stations; the advice can hardly have been addressed to them. Clergymen and doctors have to do their work wherever it is set them. Few town clergy have time to play in the country. public schoolmasters both work and play predominantly in moderate-sized towns with rural facilities. Professional and business men have to work where they meet their colleagues and clients. Landed gentry, agents and farmers have the privilege both to work and play in the country. Speaking generally, the only people who have much choice in the matter are people with unearned incomes and means of mobility. The only working class to which the advice appears to me to be of optional application is that of literary men or philosophers, who may be presumed to be referred to as needing to 'be

---

[1] Nevinson was one of the bravest men I have known, valiant not only in his writing but in action in London Streets and in Africa. A few moments before he died he climbed to the top of Idbury Manor, with his wife Evelyn Sharp, and wrote his name on the wall. His books in which there is good writing and stimulating reading, include *In the Dark Backward, Running Accompaniment, Changes and Chances, Visions and Memories, Words and Deeds* and *The English.*

'stimulated and compelled to *think*.' If that is the correct interpretation, I should dissent from the Headmaster's proposition. A journalist or a reporter must of course do his work in Fleet Street. He needs no advice to play, when he can, in the country. But so far as any form of original art or profitable thinking is concerned I should myself be disposed to advise precisely the contrary. For creative literary or artistic work I am convinced that the workshop had better be in the country. Even factory employers at Letchworth report that their workers do much better there than in London Access to books or other technical requisites must of course be assumed. So far as my own activities even in practical administrative matters have been concerned, I have always found my few valuable inspirations come to me either riding before breakfast or on country walks or doing manual work out-of-doors. An office or a study is better in rural than in city surroundings. Quite apart from these (possibly personal) idiosyncrasies I believe it to be common experience that what the Headmaster speaks of as 'the great vitality of the great town's life' is merely distracting and dissipating of anything but superficial and imitative and gregarious activities. It is stimulating, like a mustard plaster, and brings the blood from the brain and heart to the skin, producing a misleading illusion of health and vitality. On careful reflection I think it would be agreed that most of the work that is best done in the town is either work that it is a pity should be being done at all or work devoted to neutralizing the diseases of a city civilization, whether moral or physical.[1]

SIR BERNARD PARTRIDGE of *Punch*.—I have practically no experience of work in the country.

T. F. POWYS.—The words of the Headmaster of Westminster are not wise ones. All my work has been done in the country. But I don't go and play in the towns

MAY SINCLAIR.—I work well in London, but I prefer the country because of the quiet and good air. The country is best for actual work and London for stimulus.

---

[1] As Sydney Olivier, one of the early Fabians. He was successively Secretary of the Board of Agriculture (as it was then), Governor of Jamaica and Secretary for India. A neighbour in Oxfordshire, I recall some bracing talk with him. *The Memoirs of an Original Character*, by his wife, with recollections by Bernard Shaw, is informing and entertaining.

SIDNEY WEBB.—I am a Londoner by birth, so that I am neither impartial nor likely to convince the country dweller. But surely the question is one of habit and disposition, opportunities and duties? My own suggestion is London for intellectual stimulus, for facilities of investigation, and for extended education. On the other hand, the country for quiet study, for writing and for convalescence and rest—and for old age! Other towns for nothing at all.[1]

HUMBERT WOLFE.—I think it is true to say that the vast majority of my verse has been written in towns. I am, however, far from clear whether the environment in which work is performed is of great importance. The importance is rather in the impressions which have been received and are later translated, and as regards these, I have of course, like all other sentient people, been profoundly affected by the English and the Swiss countryside.

VIRGINIA WOOLF.—Speaking very roughly I think the country is best for reading and London best for writing. I can give no reason, and it may be merely a superstition on my part.

C. P. SCOTT.[2]—You ask me to say why I prefer to live in town. I don't. I live as far out of town as my occupation will allow me, and I thank Heaven every day for a bicycle which enables me to get out a little farther. No man in his senses, would, as a matter of taste prefer to live in Manchester rather then in the Cotswolds. I can imagine an Athenian preferring to live in Athens rather than in Bœotia, but then Manchester is not exactly a modern Athens. Really, of

---

[1] Afterwards Lord Passfield, but his wife remained Mrs. Webb. The two of them must have written together—so that they themselves hardly knew where one left off and the other began—more than a score of books. 'Our views', as they were accustomed to call them, were the basis of much of the social legislation of later Liberalism and of Socialism. A visit to them made a writer gird up his loins in discussion. For an unsympathetic picture see *The New Macchiavelli:* for the truth about their prowess, disinterestedness and kindness, Bernard Shaw and everybody who really knew them, and *Our Partnership.*

[2] The famous editor of the *Manchester Guardian*, from which I received, in my teens, my first payment from a newspaper—2s. 9d. His principles—'comment is free, facts are sacred', 'journalism is an instrument of civilisation'—are effectively set forth by J. L. Hammond in *C. P. Scott of the 'Manchester Guardian'* and by several colleagues in *C. P. Scott 1846–1932.* From the year in which he acquired the *Guardian,* 1907, until his death, he 'never drew a salary exceeding £2,500, devoting all his profits to strengthening and improving the paper'. When once he came to see me at Idbury—I had not the honour of being related to him—he apologized—it was a coldish Spring day and he was in his eighties—for wearing an overcoat, a light dust one. His bust is one of Epstein's most successful works. His rarely endowed son-in-law, C. E. Montague, writes on page 173. His own books include *A Hind Let Loose, Rough Justice* and *Fiery Particles.* His widow has been a colleague of mine on the Oxfordshire Bench.

course, it isn't a matter of taste; it's a matter of destiny. Those of us whose life is concerned with a town ought not to fly away from it; the only question is whether we ought not to live right in the heart of it so as to get the full savour of it and to feel the full pulse of its life. It's a mistake to run twenty miles away into some little pocket of population which is cut off from the great town and yet has none of the real flavour of the country. This is to break up society into fragments and to renounce most of the responsibilities and a good many of the satisfactions of the citizen. That is what has happened to a disastrous extent in Manchester, where, but for the University and the tie of lectures, we should have but little of a stable, cultivated society life. It has happened to a like extent in Liverpool and Birmingham and, in consequence of that, there seems in those places to be somewhat more of civic pride. The advent of the motor has added to the centrifugal tendency and it looks as if soon suburbia and beyond will swallow us nearly all.

Jarge Has a Tooth Out

'I ALLUS say as we wanted a tuth drawer hereabouts', said Jarge as he spat a mouthful of blood down the surgery sink. 'Old Dr. Peacock what was here afore you come, he were a master, though he got mighty tremblified 'cause he worn't no teetotaller. They did used to say o' him as he pulled as many teeth in twenty years as 'ud fill a well. See that place? he done that. An' there worn't no numbin' then, like you young doctors does now; we just had to set through it. One night I had the tughache cruel "Sit you down in that chair", the old feller says, "and hold tight o' the seat wi' both hands". And then he laid hold o' the tuth wi' his nippers. He had his knee in my stummick, and the sweat stood on my face like dew. An' when he'd done I felt the place wi' my finger, and, blame me if he ha'n't pulled out the wrong 'un. But I'll tell 'ee what, master, you young doctors, wi' your numbin', don't hurt us in the teeth like the old 'uns, but you hurt us a sight more in the pocket, and you can't numb that'.

The 'Primitive', by M. K. Ashby

I was walking one Sunday past the little 'Primitive' chapel in our village with my nephew of four and a half. A hymn was in progress. The blare and bray of harmonium and voices were intolerable. I had an impulse to lift the child in my arms and run, for I knew by the turn of his small head that questions and comment were coming. He had asked me a day or two before whether 'that' was 'a house'? I had said 'No', it was a 'sort of church'. 'What', said he now, 'what *are* they doing in there?' and, keeping to my plan of giving honest but minimum and un-explanatory answers, I said, 'They are singing a hymn'. John looked for guidance about this 'music'. I could not bear that he should associate such a sound with religion. For him to suppose it to be a key to the spiritual world would be calamitous. I waited for his next word, and he said, 'Ah, well, perhaps they're *learning* to sing, Auntie'. Out of the mouth of that babe had come wisdom, and we got past the chapel and its song without either falling into contempt or superiority.

Some weeks later I met a rural sociologist who talked of all that Methodism had meant in village history. It had supported the spirit of the labourers through their worst times. It had maintained civilization against poverty—not against the bondage of a single generation—that would have been easy— but against the dire privation of three. It had held together, upon a simple level, genuine social centres, full of life and energy and brotherliness. Then we fell to discussing whether the smaller chapels were still in any way vital to village life, but neither of us knew, for we had not entered one for many a year.

A few Sundays ago I was passing our little chapel again. Once more there was singing, but I heard only the last word of the hymn. Someone opened the door at that moment and went in. I saw that the little room was nearly full, and, feeling the occasion was therefore not too intimate for an outsider's presence to be welcome, I went in and sat down on the back bench.

All were settling themselves in their places as snugly as bare deal permits, and gradually all eyes were alight, and balanced, as it were, on the figure in the pulpit. A tall, bowed labourer, with a handsome, gentle face, screwed up little blue eyes, and fallen cheeks, stood there, and with large, stiff hands and slow movements opened the great Bible.

This is what I heard from him. I shall not attempt to reproduce the preacher's precise language, his grammar or his vowel sounds. There were unfamiliar and even difficult constructions. Some of the pronunciations were the same as we believe to have been the use of Shakespeare. Sometimes obvious difficulty and lack of confidence resulted in expressions not classic on any showing.

'It is harvest time but I won't talk to you about harvest. We've had a bad season and if we are not so foolish as the papers make us out, and don't get bitter and faithless and despairing because our acres haven't done well, we're glad to stop thinking of the stooks that are out in the rain. I'm going to talk about grass. Aye, grass. Here's my text: just, "The grass of the field." "If God so clothe the grass of the field...." You know how that text finishes but there's no need to go further. God cared for grass so as to clothe it wi' beauty and adorn it wi' flowers.

'The pity of it is that the Bible wasn't written in a beautiful, grassy country, not, as I gather. Perhaps it wouldn't ha' done for Christ to ha' walked too often up little Nettleford Hill or along Kennel. He'd not perhaps ha' thought we needed saving and he'd have given us, it might be, only a lovely nature worship, and that, my friends, is not enough. But it does me good to think of Christ looking round on our ground, up to the beechwood and down to Shotwell Brook. Beauty he loved, an' I don't doubt it lightened his sufferin'. There's no daisies in the Bible, nor no celandines, not even in the Psalms. And yet it's a sight most freshening to the mind in Spring to look down the fields in this and the next parish and see the daisies on the crowns of the old plough-ridges, and the celandines in the vales! They wouldn't be there if we was to drain better; but thank God many an accident brings beauty, and out of ruinous farming comes the shining gold of celandines. But that's going back to the Spring of the year, which with

179

Autumn on us I shouldn't.

'Only I love to compare the seasons. The softness of this September mixes well in the mind with the blustering winds of March. And the smell of the walnut hoods challenges a body.[1]

'But I'm forgetting. I'm talking o' grass. Of all the natural gifts of God I thought of grass to talk about. Grass is always with us. It never fails us, even in the farming sense. It clothes the whole world as with a cloak. It feeds the beasts and they feed us. Permanent grass is a rest for the thoughts; I lay me down in green pastures. The green colour o' grass rests the eye, the neverfailingness of it rests the anxious mind; and the feel of it is rest for the body in summer season.

'The Bible says of the spring grass, "The tender grass showeth itself." Tender—that's the word. Tender green to the rejoicing eye: tender to the young calves just turned out. The tender grass.

'There's one text that don't seem to speak well o' grass. "The grass withereth." If anything withered as sweet as grass, 'twould be a beauteous world. There's more than farmers loves the smell o' July hay. And the grass that withers standing makes a fine music in the wind, though it takes a fine ear to hear it. And have y' ever seen the red sunset reflected on a million shinin' dry bents in autumn? It's a sight I can't talk about: but you may look for it in August when the sun's rays come level wi' the ground out of a red sunset. I mind I see it every night o' that week when the War was breaking out. I noticed many a thing that week as I shall never forget. A man's eyes and ears are sharp when a shadow's creeping over his peace and his wealth.

'Aye, and that reminds me, grass robs death of its terrors, for who but feels soothed at the thought of the green grass waving over a body that has been hurt too often, and hungered, and been brought to tears with weariness, and that's laden with hard and painful memories that the mind and the will would fain throw off? When I was young my thoughts would be too much for me, and I'd long to be beneath the daisies; not up in Heaven. The tired part of a man can't stand the thought of Heaven; for that you want newness of

[1] Hood, the green shell in which the walnut lies.

YOUNG BRACKEN UNCURLING

spirit. But God in his mercy lets us throw off exhaustion and leave it kindly buried beneath the grinsid (greensward).

'There's lots more I could say about grass, but I wot it would all come to the same. What I really want to say is— look around you at the common mercies of the Lord. There's clouds and trees. You'll find some fine words in the Bible about trees. There's bread; and cattle; and I'm savin' up a sermon for you about little childer'—all things that be around us now and always. Now let us thank the Lord for his mercies.'

And then we sang:

> Count your blessings,
> Name them one by one,
> And—it will surprise you—
> What the Lord—hath—done.

⌀

What it Means to Milk

TAKE a low three-legged stool in the left hand and a pail half full of water in the right hand. Sit on the stool and hold the pail between the knees. Take a small rubber ball in each hand, and, with the first finger and thumb pressed tightly together, squeeze each ball alternately with the free fingers against the palm of the hand. Do this for a minute (sixty seconds). Then travel forward on your stool a few inches, resettle your pail between the knees, and squeeze the balls again for a minute. Travel forward again in this half-sitting posture and repeat until you have travelled four or five feet and squeezed the balls for ten minutes altogether. Try it with a full pail of water. Get someone to give you a slight push backwards, and see what happens. Then, in your imagination add to this the discomfort of flies biting your legs, arms and nose, Do you like the idea of this twice a day, seven days a week?—H.W.

⌀

Landlord to old countryman who lived on his estate, in a two-roomed cottage, alone with a billy-goat, 'Isn't there rather a smell?' Countryman, 'Bless you, sir, billy's larnt to put up with that.'

A Diary of Tom Tits

Here is a record, made in Gloucestershire, of what happened in and about a nest box, put up on April 24, to which two tits came constantly to look between April 25 and 28:

APRIL 28. Tits started to scoop out nest box. Hen flew out with beakfuls of sawdust, perched on apple twig and spat it out; then bits of bark.

29. Still busy getting out sawdust. Cock-bird excited, singing and flying to and fro. Later in day, they started getting a few bents and feathers.

30. Busy building. Hen frequently to and fro with straw and bits. Later moss. Busiest time seemed to be from 7 to 12. Cock still flew up and down chirping and elated; quieter during the afternoon; excited and sang from 4 to about 5.30; quieter onwards.

MAY 1. Hen worked from 7 to 9.30. Chiefly straws and moss. Saw one feather taken in. Cock-bird calmer—flies with his mate but does not carry nest materials. He was to and fro, eating the coconut. Hen busy building 10 to 11.45. Then a lull till 1. Busy till 2.30. Lull. Fetching straws from 4. Cock-bird looked in the box. I saw a feather taken in, but chiefly straw. At 5 both flew away and did not appear again.

2. Arrived in apple tree 6.28 a.m. Cock fed on coconut, hen on the old tree. Both flew off but back again, evidently feeding all the time. Hen entered box at 6.37, evidently arranged nest and both flew off again, returning at 7.50, hen with nesting material—looked like short bents. Longer away when finding nest materials. Cock appeared to express satisfaction when hen returned with nest materials. A lull in building between 9 and 10. Then flew off for materials—she goes in three different directions for them. Cock perches on the edge of box and peeps into nest. Hen returns with feathers. He goes into nest first. She waits on a twig with feather in her mouth and then flies into nest too. 11.30 to 12. a lull. 1.10 back with straws and then 1.45 with wool. Away all afternoon till about 4—only built a little more and left between 6 and 7.

3. Cock-bird awoke me 6.45 chirping and excited. Hen busy building—fetching wool; longer away in search of it.

182

Busy off and on all day. Brought feathers. Don't take long to arrange.

4. Building at 6.45. Cock-bird still feeds on coconut. Less excited. 8 to 8.15 feeding on the old tree—washed and plumed themselves, then off. Hen back with large beakfuls of cow hair. Went into nest and was some time arranging it. Always takes a good look round before entering nest; darts about from branch to branch when other birds are about and does not fly in till all clear. Played about on the tree and flirted with each other, cleaned their feathers and did not do much building 11 to 12. Cock excited later; seemed to have lost her. Then she appeared on the tree and they flew off together. Saw her go into the nest at 1.30, had a look round and then off again. Did not do much building. He lost her again, and was calling and calling, and then flew off to find her.

5. Awakened by cock-bird chirping and excited. Hen flew in and out of nest. Then both away till 10.30. He fed on coconut; she very pleased with her nest. Flew in and out chirping—up and down on perch bowing and fluttering her wings. He came down to perch and looked into nest. Returned every now and then during the day. No building.

6. Birds quiet at 6.30. Cock to and fro to the coconut—did not see hen. Was she laying? Saw her go in and look at nest between 10 and 11. Then away. Do not appear to live in nest at night.

7. Awoke to chorus of birds at 5 but no sign of the tits. He came on to coconut for his usual eed at 6.45. No sign of either of them later on. 10.15 both appeared, she with a mouth full of dried grass. Flew into nest with it and out again —saw no more building, and birds only came and looked round to see all was well and then off. Cock-bird looked into nest from perch but did not go inside. Both away at 7.30 for good.

8. Birds to and fro all day. He feeds on coconut. Hen peeps in the nest every now and then.

9. Saw birds kissing touching beaks. Wash and dress themselves in the damson tree. I fancy she lays early. To and fro as usual during the day.

10. Did not see birds about so much. He was fussing

between 6 and 7 a.m. and calling round. Then she appeared.

11. Cock-bird chirping away at 6.55 a.m. Both appeared at 7, and she in and out of nest and then off again 9. To and fro all day.

12. Both about early, he very chirpy. Then flew away. He appeared between 7 and 8 with what looked like a grub in his mouth. Flew into the nest and then away—back with another —conclude he fed her and that she had started to sit.

13. Cock busy, bringing food between 6 and 8.30. Flew in the nest and out again quickly. Then she flew off 6.40, and both away together—did not see when she returned. He fed her with green caterpillars at 12.30 and during the day off and on.

14. Cock busy feeding her at 7 when I looked out and onwards. Chirps to her to say 'I'm coming', takes a good look round to see all safe before flying in and out again. She came off 7.40 to meet him on the tree. Took the green caterpillar from him, sitting on the bough by his side—a pretty incident. Both flew off. Did not notice when she returned. He was busy feeding her during the morning. Saw her fly back into the nest —evidently been out for an airing. He brought her another green caterpillar. She flew off and on twice within an hour. He seems to disappear in an evening. Where does he go?

15. Cock busy feeding her with caterpillar chiefly. Every now and then a fat white grub. Quick in finding these. Flies off in three different directions for them. She flew off at 8.15. In at 8.31, he escorting her to the nest, both with grubs in their mouths. He flew out again—less feeding between 10 and 11. Busy again, feeding her with little white grubs when I looked out at 3.55, chirping as he landed in apple tree and then popped into nest with food, to give two or three grubs, then a caterpillar. Always lets her know he is coming.

16. She flew into the nest at 6.35 a.m., he in with her and then off again. Busy feeding her, with intervals of rest. She flew off for a short airing at 12.30.

17. He busy feeding her at 6.25. Then both flew away together. She back into the nest in three minutes with a large thing in her mouth. Looked too big for a grub. Flew in and out twice between 10.20 and 10.35. In finally with a cater-

184

pillar in her mouth. Evidently took a big store in with her. He continued to bring her food.

18. Showery and cold. Saw her fly off at 7.20. He busy as usual with his food for her. Saw her fly off again at 9.45 and back in at 9.50. He followed and went in for a minute or two. Busy feeding her from 10.30 to 11.45, when there seemed a lull. On again afterwards. Saw her fly off to him on the branch near by nest box at 3.47. He gave her his morsel and they flew off together. She back again at 3.55. He returned at 4.15 with a grub. Called to her, she flew out to eat it then both flew away. She back at 4.22. No sign of cock-bird after 7.30. What does become of him?

19. Saw hen fly off at 11 and 2.45. Feeding went on as usual all day. Seems to end about 8 p.m. No sign of birds after then.

20. Same as usual.

21. No feeding going on when I looked out at 5, but hard at it at 7.15. He flew on to perch with a caterpillar. She popped out on the edge of nest box and took it from him. Then flew off at 4. Again later, he flew back with a grub, rested as usual on the tree bough, chirping for three minutes, then turned his back on the nest, still with grub. Finally she flew out, took the grub and then they both flew away together. Feeding ended before 8 and all was quiet.

22. When I looked out at 6.30 a pair of starlings sat on the perch and looked into the nest. She seemed to scold and fight them from inside, as starlings were also scolding from the perch. I frightened them away. He busy bringing bits from 7 onwards.

23. The same.

24. He chirping away and bringing her food. Saw her at 9.55 doing her toilet on apple bough, then back into nest. Saw him arrive with grub 1.15. Usual call note till she appeared and took it. Much as usual all day. He flew into nest with caterpillar about 7.20. Stayed in long time. 9 to 10.11 both in and out. He seemed pleased. She sat preening herself as if pleased too. Both in and out of nest. Much the same as usual till about 5. She then appeared to be sitting and he feeding her not so long as usual. More pauses. He flew in again at 8 with grub and away. She flew out in the meantime; he back

with grub, looked in nest, found she was not there, so flew off with grub in his beak. This is the fourteenth day from when I thought she had started to sit.

26. Feeding going on as usual when I looked out at 7, though he was not quite so busy. Longer pauses. Can't make out what is going on for he seems less fussy, does not call out before he enters nest, stays longer in nest When bringing in grubs. All quiet after 8 p.m.

27. Saw him fly into tree with caterpillar. Sat calling to her and preening his feathers but she did not budge. So he flew in with his food. Saw her fly off later for a few minutes. A sparrow chased her and she flew back into nest, then turned on the sparrow as the sparrow sat on the perch looking in with his feathers ruffled. She drove him off. Cock busy feeding as usual but kept on later, between 8 and 8.30, after a lull. Why? Because it was a lovely hot day.

28. He busy feeding when I looked out at 7. Later she flew off. Then he appeared twice, while she was away, with grubs, went into nest and remained some time inside. Evidently there are young ones. He seems quieter and does not call out before going into the nest box.

29. Both were sitting on a branch and making love to each other. He then flew into nest with his grub and stayed in a minute or two. She flew off and then back into nest. Both busy feeding all day till 7.45, grubs and caterpillars.

30. Both busy all day feeding.

31. Feeding went on till 9 p.m. Beaks seemed full of tiny caterpillars.

JUNE 1. Cock still does most of the feeding, she off every now and then. He quicker and more fussy and chirping.

2. Both birds busy feeding when I looked out early. Going off in different directions, first one then the other. He sat with his beak full of caterpillars chirping to her in the nest. Then she flew off and in he went. Remains longer in the nest now and brings larger beakfuls.

3. Nothing doing at 7 and 7.30, but busy feeding at 8.

4. All going on as usual. No signs of the young ones yet.

6. Looked out at 5.10 and they were both to and fro with food and so on most of the day.

186

7. No signs of birds between 6 a.m. and 7. A wet early morning, so conclude they are not up so early.

8. All going on the same. He arrives with his food and she is inside. He sits fluttering his wings on the perch and calling her till she flies off. Then he pops in and out again.

9. No sign of young birds. Parents busy feeding all day.

10. Birds busy all day. Seemed rather excited later on—chirping and fluttering on and off perch, as if calling the young ones to come out. Parents flirted on a bough together and beak touched beak. 9.10 p.m. feeding still going on.

11. Between 5 and 6 feeding was in full swing. Heard young birds chirping.

12. Cock-bird came and fed on coconut two or three times between 6 a.m. and 7. Not done so for weeks. Busy feeding and to and fro all day.

13. Both birds chirping and fussing, and to and from perch by nestbox on to tree bough with caterpillars, looking into nest and popping back again, still holding food and evidently trying to persuade young to come out. Finally, old birds popped into nest and fed them. All this at 11.20. Sun shining brightly. Feeding went on all day.

14. Awoke on hearing a chirping of old birds incessantly between 6 and 7. A dull morning after soaking wet night. Looked out and no sign of birds, but chirping still going on. Then one of the old birds appeared with caterpillar, to and fro from tree and perch, looking into nest, and then flew away, and I never saw nor heard them again after 7, so young must have flown very early.

Later on both parents, with several young ones, appeared to feed on the lichens and on the old apple tree.

To summarise: April 28, started to get nest ready; May 4, finished building; May 12 to 28, hatching; June 14, flew.—*B.S.*

✍

The ploughman who looked over the hedge wished he'd a-known a nest of young goldfinches was in the plum-tree, because he'd a-'ad 'em. Goldfinches that has nesteses in a plum-tree sings very well, but them as is hatched on the bough of elm or oak ain't no good at all and best left alone. But you get one as nesteses on an apple bough—them is very good. And them as nesteses in an elder-bush is best of 'em all.

187

The Last of Our Grand Jury

by One Who Was Summoned

BY VIRTUE of a Precept to me for this purpose directed, I summon you to appear at the next General Quarter Sessions of the Peace for the County of Dalehillshire, at the Shire Hall, DALEHILL, in the said County, on WEDNESDAY, on the 6th day of JANUARY 1926, at a quarter past Ten o'clock in the morning precisely, then and there to serve on the GRAND Jury. Hereof fail not.

Given under the Seal of my Office this 23rd day of December, in the year of our Lord One thousand nine hundred and twenty-five.

ALPHA BETA GAMMER,

Sheriff of Dalehillshire.

So ran the missive which reached me on Christmas Eve along with others, more welcome. But being sound in wind and limb there was nothing for it but to make a note of the date in my new diary, and to resolve to extract what comfort I could from the knowledge that I was about to to my duty as a citizen.

Our Shire Hall has its counterpart in many other centres of local administration. Substantially built, it is separated from the road by a fore-court and it is flanked and supported by a garden of smooth lawns and fine trees. To the passers by it presents an appearance of antiquity combined with some claim to architectural quality, both of which are found to be spurious by those compelled by duty or misfortune to make its closer acquaintance. Still, the Shire Hall has a certain dignity of its own, enhanced no doubt by its association with the administration of justice.

I was directed to a doorway, at the top of a staircase which ran all round the large central hall, and found myself in a gallery, in the company of about twenty-five other unfortunates, of whom two were ladies, looking down into the Court. Below us, on the left, was the Bench, where the county magistrates were already assembled, discussing no

---

Grand Juries were abolished in 1933. This account was written by Dr. C. S. Orwin, formerly director of the Agricultural Economics Research Institute, Oxford University, and author of *The Tenure of Agricultural Land* and *The Future of Farming*—in which the case for the eventual nationalisation of the land is clearly stated—*Speed the Plough, Country Planning* and other books as well as treatises on farm costs and accounting. He lives in a remarkable old house in Berkshire, is a keen gardener and a good neighbour.

188

doubt, the cases upon which they were to adjudicate—or (is it possible?) the six-mile point with the Dale Foxhounds yesterday. Below the Bench were the desk and the person of the Clerk of the Peace, and the remainder of the Court was partitioned off to provide accommodation for the Petty Jury, the prisoners they were to try, the men of law who were to prosecute or defend these, and representatives of the Press and the Public.

Almost immediately the magistrates took their seats on the Bench, that is to say, all but three of them who remained standing somewhat self-consciously in the background. One of the seated then rose and begged to propose that Mr. Delta Omegger be re-elected Chairman of Quarter Sessions; he told his colleagues (we knew he would, before he said it) that he had never served under a better Chairman, nor one who filled the office with greater courtesy and dignity. Thereupon, one of the standing disengaged himself from the other two, and after thanking the Bench for the honour conferred upon him by their choice, took the Chair; we inferred, naturally and correctly that he was Mr. Omegger. Another of the seated now arose, and proposed that Mr. Sigmer and Mr. Torr be re-elected Vice-Chairman, and, with obvious relief, the two still remaining standing hurried forward and seated themselves on either side of the Chairman.

It was now our turn to take the stage, and the Clerk of the Peace, a nice old gentleman in a nasty old wig, told us to answer to our names. Twenty-five were called and twenty-four responded; a functionary known as the Bailiff was instructed to call the name of the absentee outside the Court, and three times a name which sounded like Stopnot was called loudly 'off'. But Mr. Stopnot failed to materialise, and without further ado the Chairman announced that he was fined twenty pounds. That left us of the Grand Jury with a complement of twenty-four, and the Clerk, having asked one of our number to be Foreman (there was nothing to indicate how the selection was made), proceeded to swear us in. We swore in fours, in alphabetical order, and as only twenty-three jurymen were required for the panel a gentleman whose surname began with a W was released from service, and made haste to leave the Court. The rest of us followed him with envious glances, and, for the only time in my life, I wished that my patronymic had been Zacharias.

The Chairman now intervened and, remarking that perhaps some of us might be making a first appearance proceeded to instruct us in our duty. We learned that it was not our job to decide whether any prisoner was guilty; we were not to hear, nor even to see the prisoners. All we had to do was to hear the witnesses for the prosecution, and to decide whether their evidence was sufficient to warrant putting the prisoners on trial by the Petty Jury and the Magistrates in Quarter Sessions. With that we were ordered to retire from the Court and proceed with our work as thus defined.

Accordingly, the next few minutes found us in a large room seated round a horse-shoe table, of which our Foreman's chair constituted the 'clip'. A double row of chairs between the heels of the horse-shoe were arranged to accommodate the witnesses who were to testify to us.

The Bailiff then proceeded to summon those concerned with the first case into our presence, and to administer the oath to them. Some comic relief was provided when it was discovered that two of the Grand Jury had got into the wrong room on leaving the Court, and had just sworn to tell the truth as witnesses in the first case! Their position having been rectified the case proceeded, and a solicitor's clerk from a Midland town gave evidence as to the embezzlement of petty sums, extending over a longish period, by another clerk in the same employ. A policeman gave evidence of the arrest of the prisoner, and within a few minutes of the opening of the case we found a True Bill.

The next case was one against three tramps who were charged with 'breaking and entering a living van and stealing a safety razor, a box of pills, and 1s. 1d. in money, the property of Henry George Oldham'. This, too, was a straight-forward case; three tramps had come upon a road contractor's van by the roadside, which had been locked up and left while its occupants adjourned to the village nearby. They broke the lock and annexed the articles enumerated in the charge. The principal witness against them, the owner of the pills, was very deaf, and his infirmity was the occasion of one or two amusing examples of cross-purpose dialogue, but we had no difficulty in finding a True Bill against each of the three prisoners. They were all young men, and some of us thought that the case might well have been dealt with summarily at the Petty Sessions.

At this point, two of our number were instructed by the Foreman to proceed to the Court and to hand to the Clerk of the Peace the True Bills already found, the object being, of course, to enable the Magistrates and the Petty Jury to make a beginning of their work, the trial of the prisoners. Preceded by the Bailiff, these two repaired to the Gallery above the Court whereupon the Bailiff produced an enormous fishing-rod which had lain concealed along the floor. To the 'line' at the end of this rod the Bills were then tied, and one of the Jury men proceeded to make a cast over the Clerk of the Peace below. Rising at the bait like a trout at a mayfly this functionary detached the Bills, and the two Jurymen withdrew to rejoin their fellows.

The next case was that of a sailor charged with attempted suicide. The man had come home on leave, and shortly afterwards, his mother, hearing a slight report, had run into his room to find him with a small revolver in his hand and a flesh wound in his arm. The revolver, which was handed round for inspection, was hardly more than a toy, there was no evidence to show that the man had any suicidal tendency, and we gladly returned No True Bill against him.

The three remaining cases were simple, and we found True Bills against a young tailor for stealing two pounds in Treasury Notes from his employer; against two men, obviously tramps though they described themselves as 'labourers', who had broken into a grocers' warehouse and stolen five bottles of whiskey and some packets of cigarettes; and against a shoemaker charged with breaking and entering the local Conservative Club 'and therein stealing a cash-box and 2s. in money'. So we filed back into our gallery above the Court, the fishing-rod was again produced, and the Bailiff attached the Bills to the line. Our Foreman, (he was surely no fisherman!) 'rose' the Clerk of the Peace twice before delivering the bait into his clutches, and then the Chairman thanked us for the conscientious way in which we had performed our duty to the State and we emerged into the sunshine and the obscurity of private life once more.

Some say that the Grand Jury is a superfluous stage in the administration of justice—a fifth wheel to the coach. I cannot say. All I know is that the proceedings in which we had been involved seemed to me to contribute something to the dignity of the law (the fishing-rod notwithstanding), whilst costing the country nothing. As for ourselves, we had the satisfaction of knowing that we had saved a nerve-shattered sailor from the further ordeal of standing public trial for an act of foolishness which he had regretted long since, and by which no one but himself had suffered. *Fiat Justitia!*

At a Country Circus

by Elspet Keith Robertson Scott

THE country audience swayed and gurgled when one of the two clowns—in his seventies—cried 'Hurry up, Joe, I've got to get 'ome in time to milk the ducks'. A bar of evening sunlight played on the rapt faces of farm labourers, sprouting youths, women with and without babies —one infant in fleecy white hung its sleeping head over the arm of an entranced and unheeding young mother—pink-legged and pink-faced flappers, ecstatic schoolchildren and an old man in corduroys with the face of a Roman senator. The orchestra of four were in turn musicians, door-keepers, programme-sellers, horse-tenders, or humorists. One in a qualified dress suit (over tights) turned out to be the star acrobat. A plump and piebald mare pawed the ground in answers to his questions and then sustained him in his leaps as he whirled the ring in glory to be eclipsed by the more delicate balancing feats of a beauteous lady. In her gyrations she transcended the laws that govern common folk who drew deep breaths of wonder. Her cold scorn, as she acknowledged the Punchinello quips of the ancient clown were in the traditional manner. But her hair was shingled. Gone are the riding ladies with flying tresses. This was a modern. Her modest tights—tights once thought to be a dress of daring— were less revealing than the female bathing suit of to-day. This lady had sat at the entrance, gathering in the sixpences and shillings; for she was the box office as well as the 'draw', and her pale, disciplined face wore the same intentness of expression as when later on I caught sight of her in her caravan bending over the sausages for the ring-master's supper. For the rest, the tradition was complete—horses, ponies, monkeys, dogs and men, and an urbane elephant that poised its tonnage with admirable precision on a very small tub, smiled with big disdain as it responded by genu- flexions to the clown's funnyisms, and did clever things lazily with its trunk. Our perilous plank seats were hard, but it was a shillingsworth. A circus is still the perfect enter- tainment for a rural audience. Far enough from any big town, not even wireless has stolen its glamour. Who can replace the clown? He held his hearers with the jokes of our great-grandfathers, tumbled when he should, rated the other clown at the right moment, and with unceasing patter covered all thin places in the performance. On the bills, all the enter- tainers, except the clowns, had Italian or French names, but shared their Midlands or Cockney speech. Between two and three in the morning the artists were pulling down tents and stands, assembling their animals, and getting all in order for the road. One night's performance is all that a little market town is worth. Soon the old clown would be telling clown No. 2 how he had been in the army. 'You, in the army?' 'Yes, I was in the Guards.' 'The Guards! You in the Life Guards?' 'No, silly, not the *Life* Guards—the *Black*guards!' And the accompanying slapping and punching of the tumbling jesters will warm the hearts of another tentful of rural people. There is no need to quote the late Lord Salisbury!

ø

The stone that is fit for the wall will not be left on the road.

In her outer suburb the householder had been accustomed to buy horse manure from a small boy at fourpence a pailful. The other day he mentioned that the price was sixpence. 'Yer see, Sir,' he said, 'my bruvver pinched the brush an' this 'ere's 'and-picked.'

'Bundling', by Joseph Davies

'I do not know whether this is modern laxity of morals or a survival of an old custom. She expressed no shame at having received the young men through her bedroom window by the use of a farm ladder'.—From a recent deliverance by a Judge at Assizes.

MODERN custom seems to approve of three stages of courtship: the stage when the couple begin to 'walk out'; the stage when 'everything is settled' and they visit each other's people, and so forth; and the stage when they are formally declared 'engaged'. The stages in old Wales were: 'love-making in the straw'; 'love-making by the fireside'; and 'love-making in bed'—that is, 'bundling'.

The courtship would often start with the couple meeting at a fair and the boy asking the girl if he might treat her for the day. If she was not of his acquaintance, however, he would arrange for one of his friends—usually a married man or woman—to 'fetch' her. Sometimes, if a girl was better looking than the average, there would be half a dozen 'fetchers' using their persuasive powers on behalf of as many boys. On the other hand, if a girl fancied a boy of her acquaintance, she was entitled to suggest that he should treat her. If she fancied a boy she did not know, one of her friends went to work. And whereas to-day a girl with a shiny nose is ridiculed, up to half a century ago the more shine a girl had on her face the prettier people thought her. In fact, on the morning of the fair the girls used to rub butter on their skins until they shone 'like Bristol bacon'.

After this meeting and treating, the couple would enter upon the first regular stage of their courtship. There would probably be a long walk to the girl's home, over dark and rough roads; but there would be no 'house' for the boy yet. He would leave the girl at the yard gate. Before parting arrangements would be made for him to visit her on a certain date. On the appointed night he would tap at the window, and if the girl had not in the meantime changed her mind, she would answer. Then they would go over to the nearby barn or byre where there was hay or straw. The usual time for this 'lovemaking in the straw' was from about nine o'clock until midnight, once a week only. Every district had its own traditional courting night. Widowers had a time of their own.

After a few weeks at this stage the young man would be 'promoted' and the second phase would be reached, 'love-making by the fireside'. The people of the house would usually be at the bottom of this promotion. A hint would be dropped to the girl—whether she was daughter or servant made no difference—that she could have her boy in the kitchen on their usual 'night', the young chap departing early enough to get home by daybreak. It was a rule that no member of the family should interfere with the courting couple; and something nice would usually be set aside for the boy to eat before his departure—butter-milk cakes or a dish of baked rice, always something different from everyday food. Sometimes victuals rather than girl might be the attraction.

After a short period came the third stage of love-making, 'bundling' or 'love making in bed'. As a rule, bundling couples were of the same status as our present day 'engaged' couples; there was a definite understanding between them concerning marriage. True, every bundling couple did not eventually wed, any more than every engaged couple does. But a courtship that had entered into this phase usually ended in marriage, and commonly a happy marriage. Girls when approaching the bundling stage were provided by their mothers with a special garment. This 'courting-stocking' was a cross between a Christmas stocking and pyjamas, of a size ample for both legs, and coming up to the waist. Such stockings were usually handed down from mother to daughter as heirlooms, and were used in Wales up to, say, sixty years ago. The young fellows of those past days would think nothing of walking fifteen miles each way to visit their sweethearts. Those owning, or able to commandeer, a donkey, would venture twenty miles afield; only the 'high class' would travel on horseback. Any fellow who tapped at a girl's window after midnight was regarded as of doubtful intentions, and would get no response. For the honest young fellow, after a preliminary parley through the window, the girl would come down and unbar the door, unless the door had been left open by arrangement. But even if the door had been left open, a preliminary chat at the window was required. Usually the farm ladder was brought into use. It was considered a mean trick to play on a girl to hide or lock up the home ladder; but when this was done—sometimes for fun, most times from jealousy—love found a way. Even as late as fifteen years ago, to the writer's personal knowledge, a fellow going courting would think nothing of carrying his own, or a borrowed, ladder six miles or more each way.

Should the girl have changed her mind after reaching the bundling stage, 'breaking it off' would be a simple matter. The rule was that if there was no response to the window tapping the boy was not wanted any more. The persistent lover might spend an hour at the window, even singing and reciting appropriate verses as well as making rosy promises, but if there was no answer from within, he would understand and would creep home. As a disappointed lover he would be said to have received the 'quiver'; and as soon as news of his dismissal by the girl became public property, his friends would present him with a 'white staff', a stick three feet long, usually hazel or willow, with bark peeled off. Girls would give the cold shoulder to anyone who had had the 'white staff.'

Bundling was by no means secret. The lovers were as proud of it as present day couples are of their engagement. Though the custom is now on the verge of disappearance it is not because of any change in the moral outlook and decidedly not as the result of external moral pressure. Changes in conditions of life are the reason. Where it lingers still the main differences are that the donkey has yielded to the bicycle, and 'love-making in the straw' has given way to walking-out, social gatherings, and the usual accompanying home. Mortal enemies to the fireside and bundling tradition are the coming of parlours, bus routes, more facilities for for social enjoyment, more freedom of movement, shorter working hours—and the glamour of the engagement ring.

☙

Worldly Scots farmer in bad harvest weather, to unco-guid neighbour, 'And are ye never worried aboot yer crops in this-like weather, Sandy?' 'Na that, ma frien',' he replied, 'I juist trust in Providence,' 'Umph!' said the worldly one. 'A gey lazy way o' farmin' that.'

How to Tame Wild Birds

by E. W. Hendy

THE best way to tame birds is to keep a bird-table, or tables. It is unnecessary, so far as the bodily welfare of the birds is concerned to feed them except in cold weather. But if you supply food for them all the year round they become accustomed to human presence, and, as Lord Grey has pointed out, realize that in a certain area—that is, on and near the bird-table—they are safe.

Tame robins have become proverbial: I have known many; but during the summer of 1930 they mysteriously deserted our board and our garden. It was the chaffinches that were tamest. Whenever the weather allowed we took our meals on a flagged space bounding the south side of our house, and, as we ate, the chaffinches walked round our feet, under the table, and devoured the morsels we gave them; occasionally they perched on the table. Pied wagtails and greenfinches sometimes came with the chaffinches, but they never ventured so near.

It was an interesting experience to look down from above upon a 'wild' bird at a distance of only a foot or two. From this vantage you can see every separate feather on the blue head and russet mantle of a cock chaffinch: you can watch him turning the hemp seed with his tongue as he holds it between his horny mandibles, and hear it crack. You may note, too, that his long middle toe is slightly turned inwards, to get a good grip.

Soon we began to recognize the differences in the individualities of our guests. The most trustful was a cock whose white wingbar was almost obscured by the greyish wing-coverts. He was the father of a family and brought two of his infants with him. It was ridiculous to see these fluffy hunched-up bantlings swinging their heads and bodies from side to side as they squeaked for food, though at the same time they showed that they were perfectly capable of getting their

---

Author of *The Lure of Bird Watching*, *Wild Exmoor through the Year*, *Somerset Birds and other Folk*, and other books one reads with pleasure and profit.

197

own dinners by picking up crumbs almost at their father's feet, as he fed them. Another cock chaffinch looked very worn with family cares, and was constantly collecting food and flying off with it. He was almost as tame as the first chaffinch, but the others were more wary. All were extremely quarrelsome; in fact they seemed more nervous of each other's presence than of ours. The tamest of the chaffinches were all cocks; hens came too, but they were far shyer. This was unexpected: I think the explanation is that while the hens were incubating the cocks had fed daily and hourly at our bird-tables and had become inured to our proximity.

I never succeeded in inducing any of these chaffinches to feed from my hand, though I have in times past had several robins who would do so. The chaffinches became suspicious as soon as I held my fingers near the level of the flags on which the crumbs were spread, though they took food only a few inches distant from my finger ends. I was surprised to find that the fledging chaffinches showed the same suspicion. Was this wariness a piece of inherited instinct or did they learn discretion from their father's example? Such questions may seem trivial, but if we could interpret them correctly they might lead to the elucidation of some of the most secret mysteries of bird-behaviour. The border line between instinct and intelligence in birds and animals is a very tenuous one: it is only by careful observation of individuals that we can ever hope to discriminate; even the smallest incident properly understood may prove to be a clue of infinite importance.

No doubt some fortunate human beings are endowed with a certain magnetism which disarms the suspicions of wild birds. Many of us can remember, in one of the London Parks, the man on whose arms, head and shoulders the sparrows used to perch in numbers. I once knew a lady who could put her hand beneath a sitting robin and feel the warm eggs, and another whom a brown owl allowed to take a similar liberty. These privileges are not vouchsafed to all. But anyone who can remain quiet—and does not keep a cat—can teach wild birds to trust them. And they will thus learn more of their individualities than from any cage-bound captive. A tamed bird in the bush is its natural self.

The Rector's Grace

by W. M. Letts

Benedictus benedicat—
With full heart I say my grace,
For my kitchen garden grows
All I need in little space;
Onions, carrots for a stew,
Comely kale that holds the dew,
Fruit the blackbirds share by stealth;
And my orchard keeps me fed
Through the Winter by its wealth
Of fine apples gold and red.

Benedictus benedicat—
As I pace my pleasant garth
How I bless the skill that made
My sweet peas of every shade;
That contrived beside my path
Lavender that swarms with bees,
Blessed thistles, blue as spears,
Clove carnations such as these,
Woolly mullein, grey lambs' ears.
What a heavenly debt my phlox,
Red and purple, pink and white,
And my warrior hollyhocks,
Ten, eleven feet in height;
Here are dahlias hued like wine,
Pansies shaped to heart's desire,
While nasturtiums burn and shine
Like the Pentecostal fire.

Benedictus benedicat—
Rough my voice but I've a quire
Fit to join the angels' lutes;
Robins, thrushes, wrens aspire
In the Spring with blackbirds' flutes,
Chiff chaff, finch and willow wren,
While my glad heart chants Amen.

The Strange Story of the Auricula

by Professor Sir Rowland Biffen, F.R.S.

ATTEMPTS to trace the history and origin of our old-fashioned garden plants form one of the many pleasant byways of horticulture. It is a task which can keep one busy thoughout the year, for it involves a study of the literature of bygone centuries during the dead season, and the more practical work of cultivating every variety one can raise or acquire during the growing period.

I drifted by slow stages into a study of the auricula. 'Study' is perhaps a too high-sounding word to use for what came to be in reality a mere pottering with complex scientific problems which are to be solved with any approach to finality only by someone with the resources of a considerable research station at his disposal. However, the incompleteness of the following account of its results may be a meritorious feature, for it may lead some other gardener to carry the story still further.

The cultivation of the auricula has a long and, in some respects, well-documented history. It dates back in this country to at least 1597, when the first description of the plant was published in Gerard's classical 'Herball'. By then it was apparently widely grown on the Continent, and the tradition that it was introduced here by refugees from the Netherlands about the year 1575 may well be based on fact. It became an established garden plant rapidly, for in Sir Thomas Hanmer's 'Garden Book', printed in 1659, some forty named varieties are described.

Even at this early period the colour range was a wide one, for he mentions 'yellow, white, haire colour, orange, cherry, crimson, purple, violet, murrey, tawny, olive, cinnamon, ash, dun', and others. Other contemporary accounts add still further to this list. These descriptions can convey only a vague impression of the flowers of the seventeenth century, but fortunately the Dutch and Flemish artists of the period included many auriculas in the noble bunches of flowers they

Sir Rowland Biffen became Professor of Agricultural Botany at Cambridge in 1908 and has been Professor Emeritus since 1931.

delighted in painting. These show that the old-world varieties
were counterparts of those now grown in our borders under
the name of alpine auriculas, except for the fact that the
present-day varieties are decidely more rich and vivid in
colour. But, though the soft dove-grey, *café-au-lait* browns
and quiet purple tints are no longer to be found among the
plants raised from commercial seed, they occur still in many
of the plants in cottagers' gardens.

In addition to this long series of coloured forms, two distinct types—the double and the striped auricula—had come
into existence. The double, once a highly appreciated flower,
is no longer obtainable in commerce, but a few of its once
numerous varieties still find a place in amateurs' collections.
They lack so many of the characteristics of the present-day
flowers, however, that few florists now have any interest in
them. Further, if those I have grown are at all representative,
they have the distressing habit of throwing trusses of single
flowers as often as doubles. The striped forms, which, in their
day, were outstandingly popular and often extraordinarlily
expensive, have become scarcer still. In fact they are said to
be extinct. But I have been fortunate enough to raise a few,
and hope they may prove a nucleus for the recovery of the
race, for their gay colour-effects are a pleasing foil to the
quiet formality of the show auriculas.

It was only after some three centuries of cultivation that the
origin of these alpine auriculas was discovered. Then Kerner's
observations made it practically certain that the plants first
collected in the high Alps were natural hybrids between two
very unlike species, *Primula hirsuta* and *P. auricula*. The
former has rosy-pink flowers and bright green foliage, the
latter sweetly scented yellow flowers and, for the most part,
leaves with a silvery cast. This effect is due to the fact that the
green ground of the leaf is obscured to a variable extent by a
coating of microscopic glandular hairs—the 'meal' of the
florists. If slight, the leaf colour is a grey-green; if dense,
white. It may also be concentrated on edges of the leaves,
thus outlining them with an exquisite silver margin. Kerner's
views, much criticized at the time and then more or less
forgotten, are undoubtedly correct, though the full story is

more complex than could be foreseen in the days when plant breeding was a mystery rather than a somewhat bewildering science.

During the period 1650–1750 no changes are recorded in the make-up of the flower, and an observer might well have considered that it was more or less stabilized, and that further striking changes were unlikely. But about the end of it there occurred one of the most extraordinary developments known

Leafy mutations. Left: primitive green-edged auricula with massive green leaves instead of a coloured corolla. Centre: sepals replaced by typical foliage leaves, but an otherwise normal flower. Right: a double auricula resulting from the replacement of the sepals, petals and stamens by green leaves.

to florists, when a strange and totally distinct type of auricula came into existence. This had two outstanding character-istics: the edges of the flowers were green, grey or white, and in the centre of each was a zone of shining white meal—the 'paste'—a feature still unknown in any other flower. This sudden change (for no one can imagine that anyone thought of a flower with these characteristics and then set out to build it up by a process of selection) was the result of the replace-ment of the normal petals by structures which, even in micro-scopic details, are identical with the foliage leaves. The paste, too, is a leaf characteristic seen to perfection at the base of the leaves forming the calyx of the flower. The green, grey and white edges of the flowers thus represent the various stages of mealiness seen in the foliage of *P. auricula*.

The mutation started the auricula off on a new course of development. The presence of the paste, which added im-mensely to the attractiveness of this strange flower, had one disadvantage, for, solid as it appears to be, a single drop of rain ruins it. This led to the auricula becoming a pot plant and hence, almost inevitably, an exhibition plant. So rapidly did this phase of its culture extend that by 1798, in the interests of judges and exhibitors alike, florists found it necessary to determine the 'points' of flowers suitable for the show-bench, and a schedule of seventeen requirements was drawn up which, almost unchanged, still defines the perfect flower. By the beginning of the nineteenth century the edged auricula had become everyone's flower, and surviving nurserymen's catalogues show that hundreds of distinct varieties had been raised. Coloured plates of a large selection of these were published in 1828 in Sweet's 'Florist's Guide' and show that the flower, by then, had reached a stage of perfection equal to that of the present day.

These early years of the nineteenth century form a peculiarly interesting horticultural period. Gardeners were no longer content with the natural beauty of their flowers, and they sought a formality and refinement which, once seen is immediately appreciated, although it is difficult to describe. It is dependent on the combination of a complex of attributes such as the proportions of the various parts of the flower, the shape of its outline, its markings, its texture, and so on. The assembly of all these features constituted as difficult a breeding problem as one could ask for, and even nowadays it has to be admitted that the resulting production of the perfect flower is mostly a matter of chance. Still, it was tackled, and by none more thoroughly than the weavers and miners of Lancashire, who during the 1850's were producing flowers which, hearsay has it, were the finest ever raised.

There is nothing known so far as to the date when the two other sections into which auriculas are classified put in their first appearance. One of these, the 'fancy', is in reality an edged auricula in which the colour brought in by *Primula Hirsuta* has disappeared, leaving the flower a symphony in green and golden-yellow. Good and distinctive varieties are easily raised, but the group has never been so popular as the second, known as the 'selfs'. The sumptuous colouring of these selfs and the presence of a paste suggest that they are hybrids between alpine and edged varieties, and crosses between

203

these sections tend to confirm this view. But they also appear in families raised from self-fertilized seeds from both the grey- and white-edged plants, so that a multiple origin seems almost a certainty. The mixture of plants which result from further breeding experiments will almost certainly contain a few fit to be included in any amateur's collection.

THE DUCK THAT COULDN'T READ

The artist is E. G. Barlow, the cartoonist, who generously gives so much of his time to his Secretaryship of the National Society for the Abolition of Cruel Sports

My Strawberries from Seed

by Henry Wallace

GROWING strawberries from seed is really very simple. You plant the seed in flats as soon as the berries are ripe in June and then keep the soil moistened every day until the plants come up in about ten days or two weeks. The seeds that don't germinate then will usually not germinate until the next spring. When the weather is cool during June and early July a high percentage of the seeds will usually germinate, whereas when the weather is warm the percentage of germination is low.

In the fall I set the plants out in rows about four feet apart with the plants about six inches apart in the row. Because of the fact that every seedling is different and my purpose is to find something superior to that which we now have, I keep the runners pinched off so that I can have an opportunity to make a comparison between the different sorts for flavour and size of fruit. Sometimes the plants will produce a few fruits the first year after the seed is planted. A really abundant supply does not come, however, until the second year.

Those that show promise I allow to run so as to get a comparison on a larger scale. Thus far I haven't found any especially outstanding sort, but the whole project has been worth while because of the opportunity given for closer association with the soil, wind, sun and sky.

The most promising kinds I have found have contained blood of the sort that we call Premier or Howard 17. It has great vigour of plant growth and resistance to leaf-spot diseases. The drawback is that the flavour is not as good as it might be. Some of our best sorts in the United States have been obtained by crossing the Premier with the European variety Royal Sovereign, which improves the flavour.

Last year when I was in Soviet Asia I obtained seed of three different Russian varieties.

Formerly Vice-President of the United States: afterwards Secretary of Commerce and candidate for the Presidency. Author of 'Corn and Corn Growing', 'Correlation and Machine Calculation', 'Statesmanship and Religion', 'Whose Constitution?', 'Sixty Million Jobs', etc. A specialist in corn and poultry breeding.

205

[The following note is by M. B. Crane, whose work at the John Innes Horticultural Institution is well known: 'The so-called alpine perpetual-fruiting strawberries are frequently raised from seed in this country. Indeed the variety Baron Solemacher gives very uniform offspring when raised in this way. The general run of garden strawberries, such as Royal Sovereign, Sir Joseph Paxton, etc., are, however, invariably raised vegetatively, whether grown by amateurs in gardens or commercially in fields. The deliberate breeding of garden strawberries has been going on in this country for nearly a century and a half, but so far this has been carried out by comparatively few people and confined to raising seedlings and selecting the best. These are perpetuated vegetatively and given varietal names. Some breeders, however, know that from certain crosses a high proportion of good seedlings is obtained, and it should be possible to put this knowledge to practical account in this country as in U.S.A. The raising of strawberries from seed is just as easy here as in U.S.A. and they are often raised in the way described'.]

An Adder Bit Me, by *Phyllis Kelway*

HE was a beautifully marked adder with clear zigzag lines down his back. I had fed him on viviparous lizards and he was in fine fettle. The sun was shining. Adders—even tame adders—love basking, so I picked up the glass case to take it to the sun. It was an aquarium with a slate bottom and very heavy. I slipped. The adder landed neatly on my hand and fixed his fangs into my little finger. I felt the prick, and seeing the handsome head where it was, I had a feeling of immense repulsion; but the snake relinquished his hold without being asked to do so. Momentarily I was staggered. The household had always threatened that I would be bitten; but he had been so tame. Even now, it was an accident—not his fault.

I put the finger to my mouth and sucked. Perhaps I sucked

The daughter of the well-known flower specialist. I knew Phyllis when she was a little girl. Always interested in wild creatures she became the author of engaging books of natural history.

desperately, for in my childhood we had lost a collie dog through an adder bite, and other animals too. I sucked and spat out what I imagined to be the poison.

I tried to analyse my sensations but felt nothing beyond a slight dizziness which was probably fright. Still sucking, I ran for the house. In the bathroom I examined the finger. The punctures were tiny, as though I had pricked myself in two places with a needle. Practically no blood was visible, and the finger was exactly the same size that it had been for the past ten years. I bathed the injured part in disinfectant, and before doing so turned back my sleeve. I had a horrid shock. Above the wrist the arm was inflamed; red and swollen. It was red right up to my shoulder. I set off running again, this time for the doctor. Fortunately, I had petrol for the car, so no time was wasted. The doctor took one glance at the arm and said, 'Come along at once to the infirmary'. Complications then arose because my Alsatian would allow no one in the car without me, so the doctor drove one car while I drove the other, feeling bewildered but otherwise pretty good.

At the hospital we were a peepshow. The doctors had not seen an adder bite before. They came down from various parts of the building one after another. We were all laughing a lot as though I had just slipped on a banana skin, but I was very tired. I told them to take notes, but no one did so. The nurses put extra rugs over me. A doctor kept looking at my arm and saying in a low tone, 'It's no worse'. Someone was telephoning for anti-venom serum. There was none in the neighbourhood. None could be obtained until next day, so I had plenty of time to die. I was frightened, but seeing that the doctors were alarmed too, I was foolish: I said I felt 'quite all right'. But they gave me black coffee all that day and quantities of brandy. One doctor said it was lucky the adder had had so little poison. I said nothing because I knew how I had sucked.

The poison worked for ten days. Bumps came up in my back and on my shoulder. My pulse went dead slow. I felt faint and tired. After ten days I was better.

⌀

Lecturer (urban) at women's institute, 'Then you turn on the hot tap—' [*loud laughter*].

The Plain Facts, by Dr. Joseph F. Duncan

THAT 'REVIVAL OF RURAL LIFE'. Doesn't it explain much that is lacking in our approach to rural social problems? Reviving rural life means attempting to restore something that has passed away, and that is typical of nearly all our thinking about the country—a sentimental melancholy because things will not remain as we imagine they used to be, and seldom were. We cannot revive, however much we may wish to do so; we have to recreate if we mean to preserve what is valuable in rural life. In Scotland where we had no villages, the unit was the parish, and it was a real social unit. There were the parish schools, many of them dating back to John Knox. There were the Parish Kirks, and even when the Disruption came, the Free Kirks duplicated the Parish Kirks. When the School Boards arrived, they were Parish Boards, and later we had Parish Councils. The Councils and Boards have gone; the Kirks and schools remain, but the parish is no longer a social unit. In spite of the attenuated population and the motor bus and wireless, we still think in terms of the parish and cling passionately to a sociological unit that has no longer any reality. The school is a good example of an outgrown mould into which we attempt to force the life of to-day. We are sentimental about the parish school and we talk about the tradition of the parish school, but we forget the conditions under which the school served the old community. It had a larger population to serve, and it was satisfied to push on the 'lad o' pairts' and did that well, but we did not keep all the children at school until they were fourteen. Nowadays the lad and the lass o' pairts pass on to the secondary school and the others are for the

Joseph Duncan, who was for many years secretary of the Scottish Farm Servants' Union and editor of an able *Farm Servant*, is one of the most respected of Scottish agricultural economists and has been a member of no end of Royal Commissions and committees of inquiry. He was recently given a Doctorate by Glasgow University.

With regard to what he says above on the Revival of Rural Life, he wrote to me some time later: 'Yet there does come an occasional gleam from a parish. In that part of Banffshire that eats into Aberdeenshire, a few miles from Turriff, there is a parish with 100 people, a school with 12 pupils, a girl teacher, and a W.E.A. class of 20 adults, a W.E.A. branch of 20 members, who made a voluntary contribution of £12 2 7½d to the funds of the Northern district of the W.E.A. If we could provide such a girl teacher in every parish, and we could keep the junior schools to not more than 12 scholars to a teacher, there is a lot to be said for one teacher schools. The rural problem is essentially the same as the urban problem in education, that we have to employ so many people as teachers who are not teachers, and that we do not give the few who are teachers a fair chance to teach.'

most part left to mark time in the later years of compulsory attendance because the small parish schools with one, two, or, in favoured circumstances, three teachers are not provided with the equipment and cannot specialize sufficiently to provide the variety of teaching necessary for the older pupils. If we would frankly discard the parishes and develop on wider areas, we could develop new rural schools which would give those pupils who are not setting out for an academic career an education which would have rural life as its outlook, a rural life that was wider than the parish. And what is true of school life is equally true of the cultural activities of adult life. We must widen our horizons if we are to meet modern needs.

THAT 'DECAY OF THE SCOTS TONGUE'. The truth is that Scots is little used nowadays except among the older people and in the more remote districts. It has been kept most alive in the North East, where one hears the old words used, but even there it is losing its grip. I do not see any way in which it can be kept alive if people don't feel it necessary. All these efforts to keep Gaelic from dying, to galvanise Irish into a semblance of life, and to make folks hot and bothered about the decay of Scots, leave me yawning. I speak Buchan with Buchan folk, and a mongrel Scots with older folk who will feel more at ease with me because I speak the vernacular. I find it much easier to speak English (or as near that as I can) to younger people, few of whom have any real understanding of Scots. Since the purpose of speech or writing is to make ourselves understood, the more we use a common language the less likelihood there is of misunderstanding. Those of us who know Scots are naturally sorry that it should disappear. We feel that the world will be a much poorer place because it will no longer use the words and accents which convey emotions to us no other words can do, but the folk who have never used these words lose nothing. They will miss much of the few good poets Scotland has produced as we miss much of Chaucer and Dunbar. But they will be no more able to help themselves than we are. A language must be a living thing of daily use; if it is not that, it becomes a cult and that mostly ends in cant. I doubt if the vernacular is suffering so much at the hands of the schools. They have Scots readers and Scots anthologies.

Tom Henderson has one just out which is going into the schools—'A Scots Garland'. You can hear the youngsters speaking Scots verse in the most melting accents—although few of them have any real understanding of the words. What is worth while in Scots verse will live until people can no longer read it and that is true of Chaucer and the earlier poets. The scholars will go on reviving it as long as it is worth while doing so and that is all the immortality we can hope for anything.

◊

Rabbits for Fun, *by Lady Lawrence*

As our rabbits were to be eaten, the unpleasant situation was faced by resolving to make pets of the parents only. The young were never to be named. This did not always prove easy for the baby rabbit, from the time it first ventures forth from the warm fur nest plucked from its mother's breast, to the emancipation of six weeks or so, is one of the most engaging of young animals. Baby rabbits run races like lambs. They play leap-frog. They jump perpendicularly into the air and jink right-about-turn before alighting. They sit up and demurely wash hands and faces. Put down a plate of mash. Instantly it is obliterated by a row of little backs, scuts, and sprawling hind legs in improbable attitudes.

They do, however, have their little idiosyncrasies. One will drink water till he swells visibly, and his little stomach gurgles like a cistern. Another refuses water all his life. One has a passion for the weed yarrow; his litter brother will pass it by. One is as bold as brass, holding on to your hand with two tiny forepaws to restrain you from taking away some titbit, while his brother may bolt into his box at your approach. Mercifully, at four months old or thereabouts, rabbits are not quite so endearing, and the conscientious rabbit-keeper who cleans out some sixty or seventy daily, who scours dishes, moves runs, makes hay, and breaks her back collecting weeds which are so much more appreciated than garden stuff, is able to steel her heart. To kill a rabbit is the swiftest thing.

To watch me trying to catch my rabbits is a source of

amusement to the family. One young rabbit screamed when I caught him—not to kill him—and did not cease till he was back in his run. He was being comfortably carried, not by his ears alone, which is extremely cruel. His screams of shrill rage were the screams of a child interfered with in its play. Rabbits should always be supported, and merely *steadied* by their ears. A rabbit suspended by its ears will lose consciousness in a comparatively short time.

The rabbits appear to be fond of each other. It is a pretty sight to watch them, when caught in a shower, rubbing down each other's backs with their tongues. The scoffer may say they are drinking the water drops, but my rabbits always have water. It is a pretty sight, too, to watch the sudden petrifying of ten youngsters at the stamp of a buck, particularly a 16-lb. Flemish Giant. The youngsters were as rabbits on a frieze—absolutely motionless, ears cocked, eyes unwinking. This position they held for nearly a minute, and then relaxed, but at each successive stamp they froze again.

A rabbit does not appear to have a very keen sense of smell. Drop a crust of bread in his pen and he is slow to find it. If, however, you give him a dish from which some other rabbit has fed, he notices it instantly, but instead of smelling he passes his throat over the dish from the chin downwards in a sort of caress. In the same way, if the buck escapes and makes his way to his ladies, he will stroke his throat again and again over the woodwork of their run; likewise a doe, on rejoining her young, if she has been separated from them for a while. The glandular system seems still in its infancy. Have the rabbit's under-jaw and throat secrets to reveal to the scientist?

Rabbits are naturally clean, and, like pigs—if they are given the chance—will keep one particular corner for their natural needs. Occasionally you will find one less fastidious, and it is interesting to note that such a doe will bring up her children to be equally careless.

In spite of their friendly ways when brought up together, rabbits have tempers. Watch a lady in kindle pick up her dish and dash it to the ground over and over again. She can be as temperamental as a cinema star.

As breeders seem so struck by the health and appearance

211

of my rabbits it may be of interest to say that I attribute this to perfect cleanliness, exercise, and a great variety of food. Put a heap of weeds in front of a rabbit. He will take first a mouthful of one, then a mouthful of another. Think of trying to feed a rabbit on cabbage leaves every day. After two years I have not had a single case of illness, or even indisposition. Perhaps I should say my rabbits are cross-bred, and the original parents were the best stock I could buy. My rabbits are all brought up out of doors, and play in the snow. From babyhood no check is put on wet greenstuff, and not one has turned a hair. (Frosted greenstuff, however, is avoided.) Their coats literally sparkle and their eyes are brilliant with health. With ample food and romping space, my rabbits' lives are merry if short.

*

The Old Parson

IN my boyhood we had no vestry, and so the vicar, except on communion Sundays, placed his hat and stick on the communion table, and, having unhung and donned his surplice, would proceed to the reading desk. An old clerk not only led the responses but gave out notices. 'Let us sing', he said, 'to the prize and glowry of God the —— psalm'. Once the number of his psalm was challenged from the gallery, 'It ain't the 76th; its the 72nd'. 'Well I could only see the "7" ' was the clerk's reply. Then the music struck up.—*W.J.L.*

*

On a visitor being scared by her bees, the old woman remarked, 'If ye're feared by a wheen bees, what'll you be in the swallings o' Jordan?'

Farm-worker to farmer's wife, after receiving and drinking a mug of beer, 'Well, I wull say as it's just raight.' Farmer's wife: 'Just right?' Farm-worker: 'Well, I says it's just raight becos if it'd bane ony better yo' would'na a' gen it mi and if it'd bane any worse I could'na 'a drunk it.'

Scene, a rabbit shoot. The end of a covert with the guns standing expectantly outside. A scared rabbit declines to bolt. Beater, seizing animal in his hand and flinging it over the fence: 'Get on now, caan't 'e and take an interest in the spoort; caan't 'e see the gentle voake be a waitin'?'

THE PLOUGHMAN'S ART

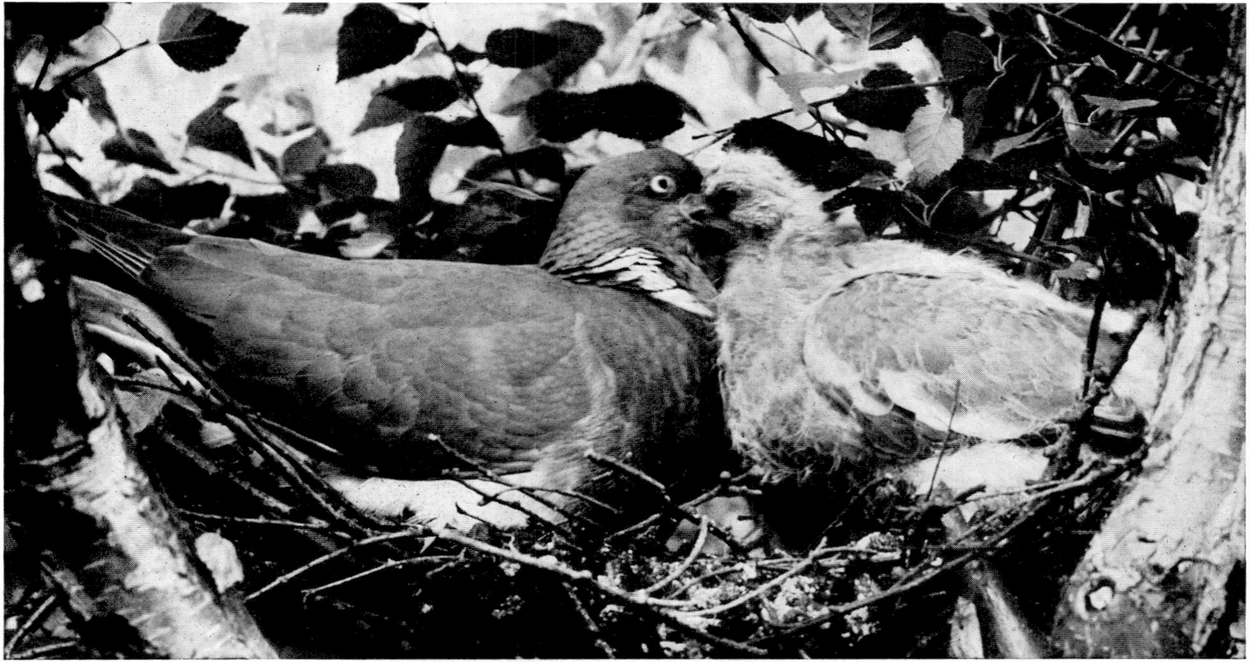

PIGEON'S MILK

Why do Weeping Trees Weep?

by a Director of Kew

How do pyramidal and weeping varieties like the Lombardy Poplar, Cypress Oak, Dawyck Beech and Irish Yew among the erect-growing sports, and weeping Ashes, Elms, Cherries and Beeches come about? These sporting varieties may arise sometimes as seedlings or a bud on a branch will sport and produce either an erect, fastigiate branch or a pendulous, weeping one. This may have occurred or been noticed only once, or it may appear now and again. If the sport or mutation is desirable it is propagated by nurserymen, either by means of cuttings, as in the Lombardy Poplar, or by grafting. The fastigiate and weeping trees have mostly been derived from an original sport.

In a few instances, such as the Cypress Oak, *Quercus pedunculata* var. *fastigiata*, wild specimens have been found fairly often in Northern Europe. The fastigiate form of the Common Juniper also occurs wild on the Continent. In other cases, no doubt, they may have occurred in the wild and passed unnoticed, for most of the weeping and pyramidal sports have been found in nurseries, whence they have been distributed as grafted individuals.

The Lombardy Poplar is almost certainly a sport or mutation and is of particular interest, since almost all the known trees are male and the few females recorded seem more likely to be hybrids between the Lombardy and Black Italian (*P. nigra*), then true female Lombardys.

In addition to the Lombardy Poplar being all of one sex, further support to the generally accepted view that it has been derived from a bud or branch mutation is afforded by a Lombardy Poplar in the Botanic Garden at Christchurch, New Zealand, which, when I was there some years ago, I noticed was bearing a branch which had reverted to the spreading character of the Black Italian. The reverting branch was very conspicuous half-way up the tall fastigiate tree.

Lombardy Poplars exist in two forms, one glabrous and

Sir Arthur Hill, F.R.S., who was Director of Kew when he wrote this article, died in 1941.

one pubescent, so it seems probable that they have arisen from glabrous and pubescent parent types of *P. nigra*. The pubescent variety is known as var. *plantierensis* and is said to have originated in the nursery of Simon-Louis at Plantières, near Metz. The glabrous one is var. *italica*. Many of the Lombardy Poplars in England are pubescent.

The Dawyck Beech, like the Cypress Oak, may as well be mistaken for a Lombardy Poplar at a little distance in winter-time. It is apparently a unique sport. The original tree is growing at Dawyck, near Peebles.

Other trees which have fastigiate varieties are the False Acacia, *Robinia*, the Norway Maple (raised at Plantieres in 1855), the Plane, Mountain Ash (raised at Dunganstown, Co. Wicklow), Birch, Hornbeam and Spanish Chestnut.

The Sycamore, Elm and Ash do not appear to have produced fastigiate sports, but the two latter have well-known weeping varieties. The Wych Elm, *Ulmus montana*, has two such weeping sports, the var. *Camperdownii*, originally found at Camperdown House, Dundee, and a variety *pendula*, which originated early in the nineteenth century at Perth. Our other British Elm, *U. nitens*, also has a var. *pendula*. Weeping forms do not appear to have occurred in Maples, Oaks, Spanish or Horse Chestnuts.

The fastigiate Irish Yew is interesting, since, in contradistinction to the Lombardy Poplar, all the trees are female. About the year 1780 two erect-growing trees were found by a farmer in the mountains of Fermanagh. One of these he gave to Florence Court, where it is still living. From this tree all the Irish Yews in cultivation have descended.

Another conifer which has produced both erect-growing and pendulous sports is the Common Larch, and I discovered two fastigiate trees a few years ago in one of the Forestry Commission's plantations in Wales.

Perhaps the most remarkable of all the pendulous trees is the var. *pendula* of *Sequoia gigantea*, which originated at Nantes in 1863. The tree has a tall erect leader and bears branches which hang down almost vertically, making the tree look like a slender spire.

Several other well-known types of sport occur among our

native trees, such as those with variegated, cut, curled or coloured leaves. Some, like the Copper Beech, may come true from seed, either wholly or partly, but more often, no doubt, they are propagated vegetatively.

❦

Sane Sanitation for Country People
by a Sanitary Inspector

THE only simple, cleanly and right sanitation in the country is the earth system, if it is applied with science and intelligence. The top spit of soil, especially old garden soil, is full of bacteria, many millions of them in as much soil as would cover a finger-nail. In the second spit of soil the bacteria are not so thick, and in each succeeding spit there are fewer and fewer. Soil bacteria consume waste products with amazing speed and success. The conditions for success are, in the first place, that only earth, and top-spit earth at that—assuredly not ashes—shall be used. The best plan is to fit at the back of the closet a hanging door by which the pail may be pushed in and pulled out. When the pail is pushed in it must have a shovelful of earth in it. Each person who uses the closet throws in a shovelful of top-spit earth from a box at seat-level, provided with a little kitchen fire-shovel. There should be a small trapdoor so that the soil box may be filled from the outside. Once a day, or as often as necessary, the pail is withdrawn and a reserve pail, which has been airing in an out-of-the-way corner, is slid in. The contents of the pails must be thrown down in a shed open to the air but not to the sunshine, which would be death to the bacteria. A little more soil may sometimes be advantageously thrown on the shed heap so that it shall not be wet and that the waste shall be fully covered. When the heap reaches a convenient size, another heap may be started. In a month or two heap number one will be found to consist of valuable fertiliser which can readily be used in the garden. The activity of the bacteria is shown, not only by the breaking down of the waste, but by the reduction of the paper to little eighth and sixteenth of an inch bits. We must not waste valuable fertiliser.

A Monumental Scandal

by Twelve Bishops

ON the deplorable invasion of the country churchyards by marble, the *Countryman* wrote that 'the Bishops who have neglected to remind the rural clergy of their duty, share the responsibility'. The following Bishops did not. (Some have now passed away.)

The man who would put hard polished marble in a Cotswold church or churchyard is aesthetically a barbarian and the incumbent who allows such a proceeding deserves a reprimand. No tabley can rightly be erected in a church without a faculty granted by the Chancellor of the diocese. In many dioceses there exists a committee of taste to advise the Chancellor.—*E. W. Birmingham.*

I wish that all country people could lay to heart your reminder as to the blot of a white marble tombstone in a country churchyard, especially in stone districts. In the words of a recent report of the Central Council for the Care of Churches, 'There is nothing more beautiful than an unspoiled English country churchyard, but unless some measures are taken to check the flow of staring and unsuitable memorials and to stimulate the proper use of flowers and shrubs, that beauty may soon become a thing of the past.'—*George Cicestr.*

There is need for a healthier public opinion in regard to the care of churchyards, and I sympathise with your view as to the incongruity of white marble monuments in districts where local materials are at hand which not only harmonise with their surroundings but also lend themselves most readily to local styles of craftmanship.—*Mervyn Coventry.*

Cold white marble is not the best medium for tombstones in churchyards.—*John Guildford.*

I am in hearty agreement with the concern of so many people to avoid Italian marble for tombstones and other monuments for the open air, and I shall always encourage the resort to native English stone.—*Albert Liverpool.*

The views expressed are from letters addressed to me.

216

I am in such entire agreement that now I print in the annual Diocesan Calendar what you will find upon the accompanying sheet. (See end of article.) What very often happens is that the mourners first communicate with the stonemason and do not apply to the clergyman until some unfortunate monument has been completed. One cannot be heartless and severe to those whose eyes are full of tears, or treat them in a strictly technical or disciplinary manner. What we really require to do is to win the hearts of the stonemasons. I have no cause at all for expecting that they would be unreasonable and merely obstructive, and when the right time comes I hope to approach them. I have heard that some of the marble monuments are actually worked in Italy. I do not know whether this is the case.—*B. Norvic.*

Marble is unsuitable for churchyards in the Cotswold district.—*Thomas Oxon.*

Glaringly out of place in a village church yard, white marble is to be deplored anywhere, and for the following reasons: (1) English stone, the natural outcrop of our island, harmonises with the local buildings, and is characteristic of English ways, outlook, and craftmanship. (2) English stone is far more durable under English weather, and keeps its original appearance untarnished much longer. I have it on the authority of a very experienced monumental mason whose work is all over this part of England, that marble cannot be, counted upon for more than twenty years, to look decent and in order. (3) The use of English stone means the use of English labour, and the retaining of English money in this country. (4) Since our monuments, at all events outside our buildings, for many centuries, were made of our stone, marble makes a glaring and disfiguring contrast in our churchyards. (5) Our English material—Cornish granite, Hopwood stone, Hamhill stone, and various local stones, are in my opinion, far more beautiful under English skies than the slowly discolouring Italian marble, and more restful to the eye. I am glad to say that there are many Incumbents and parish church councils in this county and diocese who will not allow marble in their churchyards, and I wish it were so all over England. With real thanks for your effort.—*Neville Portsmouth.*

I heartily sympathise. We are doing all in our power to keep it out of our country churchyards.—*W. G. St. Edm. & Ipswich.*

I am entirely in favour.—*Henry Southwark.*

I am quite heartily with you. Here, our old tradition is a beautiful slate monument. We have been campaigning for two or three years against the importation of foreign marble, and now I think we have got to the point at which there will be a definite black mark put against white marble monuments. Of late we have quietly secured that the monumental masons should be on our side, and there are some new regulations, issued by our Chancellor, on the advice of the Advisory Committee in the Diocese, designed to put great obstacles in the way of foreign marble coming into our churchyards; but without making its importation impossible by a faculty.—*Walterus Truron.*

Marble tombstones in stone districts are a great disfigurement. When I had charge of a country parish in Oxfordshire, I refused to allow marble in our lovely churchyard. Alas, a few specimens had crept in before. I hope that your efforts will be successful in raising public taste in this manner. The importance of preserving the beauty of our country churchyards which are so characteristic of the English landscape is very great—*James Wakefield.*

Only the other day I was commenting upon the incongruity of white marble tombstones in red sandstone districts. I should be willing to back up every effort to keep marble out of churchyards in the stone districts.—*Arthur Worcester.*

To a Bishop who says that ' he cannot see his way to taking any useful action' there may be commended the Bishop of Norwich's '*Notes as to the Use of Monuments, Tombstones, and Epitaphs*': 'No stone or monument can be set up, or inscription be placed, without the previous approval of the incumbent. The ordinary head and foot-stones and a kerb (without any knobs or decorations at the corners or elsewhere), enclosing the space where a body or bodies are interred, require no faculty; but when railings, altar-tombs, or monuments are desired a faculty must first be obtained. It is desirable that the stone chosen for monuments should be in harmony with the quiet beauty of the churchyard. If stone is not available, brick, slate, or *terra cotta* is to be preferred to shiny marble. Iron rusts unless continually repainted, and its use is not to be encouraged. English oak is to be preferred to soft woods. The lettering on a tombstone should be satisfying and beautiful, and a real work of art. Some words may be in larger letters than others but the mixing of various kinds of lettering ought to be avoided. Roman capital letters are best of all. Ornamental stops and meaningless ornaments should be avoided. The name of the mason should not be recorded. It is better that it should become known throught the quiet excellence and consequent admiration of his work than by any mention of it on the monument. Cases of artificial flowers and glass covers are much to be deprecated and they quickly come to look shabby and mean. Epitaphs are important and more care should be given to them. Mr. Vaisey's little book on the "Writing of Epitaphs", can be procured from S.P.C.K.'

'Till I Sin Ye'

TWENTY-FIVE years ago a man from a neighbouring village got into our carrier's cart, saying that he wanted to come to our village. On the way he got out and went into a house. The carrier waited for him; but, as the man stayed, at last went on without him. He calculated his passenger owed him sixpence and expected to be paid when next they met. Yesterday they met in a public-house and the passenger said, 'What do I owe you, Will, for that day as I got out at ——— and never paid ye? I 'ope you didn't think as I never meant to pay. I ben a-waitin' till I sin ye, and I sin ye along of other folk time an' again but I didn't like to gie it ti ye then'. And after a quarter of a century he handed over sixpence.—*A.K.M.*

It is good to know the truth and speak it, but it is better to know the truth and speak of palm trees.' (Arab proverb).

Casual labourer: 'Have you got a job for me, master?' Farmer: 'No. There's not work enough to go round among my men.' C.L.: 'What little I shall do won't make no difference.' F.: 'Come on, then, and get started.'

Cats that Swam and Cycled

by N. Teulon Porter

I HAVE had two cats who have led dogs' lives and were both of them constant and willing swimmers. They went for long walks in straight lines across country in a way which is more doglike than catlike. Dogs and wolves hunt as much in the open as in undergrowth, and are accustomed to hunting singly or in packs, running in straight lines, without possibility of refuge or cover, while cats skulk and stalk, and are never really quite at ease unless they are sitting under something, even if it is only a chair or a table. They make no prolonged physical efforts like dogs, though capable of enormous short lived energy output. Take a cat into the middle of a large meadow and she will wail and be filled with fear. If she can see even a rail fence and get under it she is comparatively relieved and will sit up and take stock quietly of the situation. So Tom, in my boyhood, and William twenty years later, lived more, I think, against their true nature by going long steady walks with me than by taking to the water. They were never so happy as when tramping, though they had always a tendency to make a gallop of the last twenty yards to reach any bit of cover or eminence they might see. A molehill was big enough to sit on a moment or a tuft of heather or rushes to crouch beside and regain that composure which I had not noticed they had missed until they regained it by some such means.

They both of them began life with me as kittens and were both short haired. Tom, the first, learned to swim by leaping short across the quiet pools of little mountain streams in his efforts to follow me on our walks. Having flopped in he swam out, and the third time, finding the stream was too broad to jump with ease, he yowled once or twice and then, excitedly and with shocking technique, swam across and was made

---

The author, formerly of Cambridge, now of Shaftesbury, and well known for his interest in the by-ways of sociology, was once called Toil-on Porter from the size of the burden he managed to carry on his back when cycling. As for his swimming cats, a correspondent saw a cat jump into a river from 65 to 40 yards wide and swim across easily, and some of us have watched the tiger, Diana, at the zoo, have her bath. A tiger has been seen lying in water up to the chin. A correspondent once observed a hedgehog swim across a stream.

much of at the other side. After that all hesitation seemed to go and he would always sooner swim than jump, except on very cold or windy days, when sometimes he would run two or three hundred yards along the river to find a good jumping-place sooner than swim, and then gallop after me shouting all the way. This fellow often, after having had to run very hard before he could catch me up, would make a running jump and climb up my stolid unheeding back as he caught me up, and spread himself over my shoulder and tap my ear violently with a soft paw as if correcting me for not waiting. After a hundred yards or two he would get down. He slept in a little wooden kennel nailed on the outside of the stable wall, and, I think, never saw the inside of a house. Often if I sat down beside the water, he would swim or wade about and even take trips of twenty yards or so to the far side, seeking fun and mischief. Neither of these cats ever learned to catch fish by clawing them out from the bank.

William was born in Cambridge and from a very early age rode on my shoulder wherever I went. He kept all my lectures with me and stayed absolutely still when he was on my shoulder, and I taught him not to accept advances from my bench neighbours. He went off shopping with me on my bicycle. He was hardly ever off my shoulder except at home over the fire. He always accompanied me on the river in canoes and punts, generally sitting on the prow—a very excited little figurehead—or, when we met other boats with dogs in them, very stern and still and forbidding. As no occasion arose for him to go into the water, as in Tom's case, I introduced him to it gently. First of all I took him in my hands quietly, with all his four legs hanging over, and lowered him so steadily into still water that finally he floated free of my hand with most of his back still dry and most of the air still in his fur underneath, and he forthwith swam. He climbed out on the bank near by looking very surprised but not at all frightened. Next time we did it, he made no more fuss than the first time, and it was not long before he took to the water for his own pleasure.

This cat went very many hundreds of miles with me on my pedal cycle through the wilder parts of England, riding like a limp sandbag on my shoulder and sleeping with me in my little tent every night. In hot weather he felt the heat very much, and, with open mouth and scarlet tongue flapping out, panted like a little motor car into my left ear. And then sometimes, when he saw water near by, he would make as if to get down, and I would stop awhile and let him swim.

On entering a wayside pub, he would go right through the house walking straight up on high legs in a way I have seen no other cat go. And so he would seek out any other cat or dog that might be there and straightway attack so impetuously that his antagonist never had a moment's time to collect itself for defence. This method seemed to be so demoralizing to both cats and dogs that I never saw a fight take place. The other fellow simply streaked off without asking any questions. Then William settled down beside me while I drank my beer until we both solemnly mounted our bicycle again and went on our way.

This was the cat who once, on the Lincolnshire Wolds, brought in to me, for my edification and praise, a shrew with a white throat—the shrew that caused 'Barbellion' of the British Museum such joy when I took it to him. William just put it on my face as I slept in the tent under the fence. And then it had to be caught again all the way down inside my pyjamas. When William slept I do not know. He seemed to be busy all night catching and bringing in to me unconsidered trifles.

Once he caused us both to be mobbed and arrested by a crazy rabble of German-spy hunters in the first week of the War. They had just looted a German pork butcher's shop, and then attacked me, for, as I heard one of them say: 'A man travelling with a cat on his shoulder must be a foreigner.' And, of course, a foreigner meant an enemy with such people in those gay days. We were escorted from the town by police in great state through a booing and sullen crowd until we had reached the quiet country once more and had a wash and brush up together.

*

Indian, lost at Stow-on-the-Wold, to native: 'Can you tell me where I am?' 'Yes, sir, you're in England.'

The Tolpuddle Martyrs
New Letters

There has come into the possession of the British Museum a collection of letters, dated three years before Queen Victoria came to the throne, which throw new light on one of the saddest incidents in the agricultural history of the past century, the transportation for seven years of six Wessex farmworkers for what the 'Annual Register' for 1834 termed 'swearing agricultural labourers and binding them to the observance of an illegal oath by ceremonies partaking of mingled folly, superstition and ferocity'.

THE story begins in these MSS. with a letter from a Mr. Frampton, a justice of the peace, who at the end of January tells Lord Digby that 'within this last fortnight I have had private information that nightly meetings have been for some time held by agricultural labourers in the parishes of Tolpuddle and Bere Regis, where Societies, or, as I believe they are called Unions, are formed, where they Bind themselves by an oath to certain articles. I am told they are conveyed blindfolded to the place and do not see the person who administers the oath. I am informed that they are to strike work whenever ordered by their superiors, and that they are to demand an increase of wages.'

Lord Melbourne is communicated with concerning these 'combinations of a dangerous and alarming kind'. The difficulty is 'how to proceed to bring the persons concerned under the cognizance of the Law'. Lord Melbourne is careful, but suggests that 'in cases of this description statutable provisions relative to the administration of secret oaths have been frequently resorted to with advantage'. On March 1 Mr. Frampton is advising Lord Melbourne that he has committed six men for administering unlawful oaths. Nevertheless 'it is the opinion of many respectable Inhabitants that we shall not be able to suppress these meetings, but that they will continue to increase to an extent that will be truly alarming unless your Lordship should think proper to recommend the issuing of some Proclamation against such a Society or offering some reward for the discovery of the offenders.'

Lord Melbourne has doubts of the prudence of this course.

But his correspondent is persistent, and Mr. Frampton has a long and characteristic 'private and confidential' letter from Lord Melbourne in autograph. The Secretary of State says that he had 'not ventured to express himself fully in a public letter, the substance of which might find itself into the Newspaper'. He goes on: Is it possible for the Government to advise the magistrates or for the magistrates to advise the farmers to discharge these men for doing that which may not only be legal but just and reasonable. Would not the respectable Parties so acting take upon themselves a great responsibility, incur much odium and subject themselves to observations which it would be difficult to reply to? It has always been found difficult to obtain co-operation among the Master Manufacturers, and the Farmers are still more timid, more disunited, more attentive to their particular situation and individual interests and at the same time less intelligent and apprehensive. My impression is that if the recommendation of the magistrates became very unpopular, or in any way seemed in danger of failure, you would be abandoned by many of them. You will naturally ask me, Are we to wait, with our arms folded whilst this combination spreads itself through the peasantry and prepares undisturbed the most dangerous results. I am compelled to answer that in the present state of the law and of the public feeling I see no safe or effective method of prevention.'

After the Assizes and the transportations the magistrates are much concerned about a mysterious man who came down from London into the district 'for the purpose of conveying money to the wives and families of the convicts'. He is discovered to have been employed in 'making the cases for the Time Pieces of the Guards of the Mail Coaches'. There is a correspondence with Lord Melbourne on this and also on the subject of relief having been refused to these poor people. Mr. Frampton admits that the magistrates did direct the overseer to allow no relief to families of persons who had taken the illegal oath 'as none of these persons has ever in any way acknowledged his error or expressed any sorrow'.

So far the British Museum documents. The facts about the Tolpuddle martyrs are these. The Tolpuddle labourers, led by one of their class, George Loveless, had requested a rise in wages, and an agreement was made between the farmers and the men, in the presence of the village parson, that the wages should be those paid in the neighbouring districts. This involved a rise from 9s. to 10s. a week. The farmers refused to keep their word. They reduced wages to 8s. a week. An appeal was made to the chairman of the local bench, who decided that men must work for whatever their masters chose to pay them. The parson, who had at first promised his help, now turned against them, and the masters promptly reduced the wages to 7s. a week. Loveless, a Wesleyan lay preacher and a man of great intelligence, has given an account of what followed. 'The labouring men consulted together what had better be done, as they knew it was impossible to live honestly on such scanty means. I had seen at different times accounts of Trade Societies; I told them of this, and they willingly consented to form a friendly society. Nothing particular occurred from this time until February 21st, 1834, when placards were posted up from the magistrates threatening to punish with seven years' transportation any man who should join the Union.' Early in 1834 George Loveless and five of his companions were arrested. The prisoners were approached separately with inducements to give evidence one against the other. Such attempts did not succeed. Endeavours to find something in their character or conduct that would stand against them also proved unavailing. Their masters had to admit that they were faithful and trustworthy servants. But in the existing state of the country it was considered dangerous for such societies to be permitted. In the words of the judge, 'if such societies were allowed to exist it would ruin the masters, cause stagnation of trade, and destroy property'. The Combination Laws had been repealed ten years before, and the Union was perfectly legal.

But the judge directed that the men should be tried for mutiny under an Act of George III passed to deal with the mutiny at the Nore. Loveless made a manly and intelligent defence in which he said, 'My Lord, if we have violated any law it was not done intentionally; we have injured no man's reputation, character, person or property. We were united together to preserve ourselves, our wives, and children from utter starvation'. But a true bill had been brought in by a grand jury of landowners, and a petty jury of farmers found them guilty. Although one of the counsel for the defence protested that not one of the charges brought against the prisoners had been proved, the judge addressed them in the following terms: 'Not for anything you have done, or as I can prove you intended to do, but as an example to others I consider it my duty to pass the sentence of seven years' penal transportation across His Majesty's high seas upon each and every one of you'. On reaching Salisbury prison, the clerk of the prison had some qualms when the prisoners appeared in irons. He offered to have them taken off, but Loveless said that being conscious of his innocence he was not ashamed to be seen in irons. But the men were greatly depressed when they came to Portsmouth and saw the hulks. However, they found a good friend in the captain, who had been apprised of the whole circumstances of the case, and treated them on the voyage with humane consideration.

The prosecution of these Dorset labourers shocked the conscience of the best men of the time. At first Lord Melbourne's Government was adamant. In the opinion of the 'Times', combinations of workmen were to be put down like the pestilence. Eventually public opinion forced the Government to give way and Lord John Russell announced that the men would be brought home 'with every necessary comfort'. Four of them went to Canada and one came to England. The fifth, George Loveless, after unconscionable ill-treatment, did not get home till 1837. The following lines, which were tossed to the crowd by George Loveless on his way back to prison after the trial, reveal the greatness of the minds and spirits of these injured men, as well as the ability of their leader:

> God is our guide! No swords we draw,
> We kindle not war's battle fires ;
> By reason, union, justice, law,
> We claim the birthright of our sires.
> We raise the watchword liberty,
> We will, we will, we will be free.

How I Made a Mixed Border
by Mark Fenwick

NEARLY all borders have—in addition to herbaceous plants—bulbs, annuals, biennials, half-hardy plants and often flowering shrubs and roses. I think it will be found that a border containing a judicious selection of all of them will give a much longer period of bloom than one which is planted with herbaceous plants only. No doubt a mixed border requires rather more labour, but it certainly gives a better return.

It is not really easy to make a three-season border gay from, say, early April to the end of October, and if space and money are available I would have three borders, one for spring and summer and autumn. If three borders are too many it might still be possible to have two.

The first consideration is the site, which should face south if possible. The next most important thing is the background. There is no doubt that an old stone or brick wall 9 or 10 feet high makes the best background. Failing this, a criss-cross rough oak fence is quite suitable, as roses, clematis, etc., are easily tied to it. If it is thought that a yew fence would eventually make a better background, young plants about 2 feet 6 inches tall might be planted behind the oak fence where they would not be seen. In a few years time these would make a respectable fence.

The width of the border is an important matter. I think it should be made at least 12 feet wide, especially if shrubs and roses are to be included. Early autumn is probably the best time to start making a border. It should first of all be double-dug, cleaned and manured. If made in new ground it will probably require a dressing of lime. It is most important that every scrap of noxious weed like couch grass, bindweed and ground elder should be eradicated or there will never be any peace.

I will assume that all this has been done and that the border is ready to plant by the first week in November. It must not be

---

The author was a neighbour who lived at Abbotswood, Stow-on-the-Wold, where, among other achievements, he effected a pleasant junction between his garden and a wood.

expected that the new border will be at its best the first year. Herbaceous plants, shrubs and roses will certainly take a couple of years to make a good show. On the other hand, hardy annuals such as Shirley and Umbrosum poppies, half-hardy annuals like Nemesias, Stocks and Asters, biennials like Sweet Williams, Canterbury Bells (all of which should be sown between March and early June), and hardy perennials like Pentstemons will give of their best the first season.

The width, 12 feet, will allow of about five rows of plants from back to front. The plants will not necessarily be in straight rows. There ought to be about four plants in each group. Sometimes choice plants up to say 3 feet to 4 feet high might be planted in the first row, preferably slender growers such as Aquilegias, Pentstemon barbatus Torreyi, Eryn-ginum planum and Œnothera Youngii.

I have said nothing about the length of the border. It must depend on the size of the garden. There would be no diffi-culty in filling a border of almost any length, especially if shrubs and roses are to be planted. The difficulty is to restrict the number, but I will name only the best things, especially 'rent-payers', that is those plants which bloom for a long period.

I think shrubs and roses are most important, as once planted they will remain and contribute to the beauty of the border for many years, whereas herbaceous plants must be lifted and replanted fairly often. I think it is hardly worth while having flowers in the border before April. Crocus, Chionodoxas, Scillas, Hepaticas, early Daffodils, etc., which bloom in March, belong rather to the rock garden. April has Daffodils, early Tulips, Anemones (appenina). May is the month of Tulips, Forget-me-nots, Aubretias, and Narcissus. In June there are Iris, Paeonies, Oriental Poppies, Lupins and Columbines; in July, Roses, Delphiniums and Lilies; in August, Phloxes, Hollyhocks and Dahlias; in September, Kniphofias, Phloxes, Sunflowers and Lobelias; and in October, by the end of which month the mixed border will be about over, Michaelmas Daisies and Chrysanthemums.

And now as to planting. Beginners never leave sufficient space between their plants. I would leave at least 3 feet or more between each clump of plants. The spaces can always be filled up with bulbs or annuals. Beginners are also apt to plant weedy things at first in order to fill their borders quickly. In this way French Willow, Senecio Tanguticus, Polygonum and Helianthus Miss Mellish may find their way into the garden.

It is advisable to commence planting from the back. On the wall or fence I should plant Wistaria, Roses, Clematis, and Honeysuckle. Probably everyone will like to choose his own roses, but six good ones which I can recommend are Paul's Scarlet Climber. Paul's Carmine Pillar, Lady Waterlow, Mermaid, Francois Juranville, Chaplin Climber, and, if another is wanted, Debutante. The following six Clematis are all first class and almost indispensible: Nellie Moser, Lazurstern, President, Comtesse de Bouchard, Lady Northcliffe and Henryi I. If there is room for one of the Viticella varieties, Kermesina is charming.

I might mention here a few shrubs which would be suitable for any border. Tamarix hispida aestivalis, the purple-leaved Rhus Cotinus and Ceanothus Gloire de Versailles planted fairly near but not touching each other make a striking trio. For about the centre of the border Philadelphus Sybile is one of the best of the Syringas, and only grows about 4 feet high. Philadelphus microphyllus is much dwarfer and should be planted nearer the front and cut back nearly to the ground each year. Viburnum tomentosum Mariesii, about 4 feet 6 inches, one of the very best of all shrubs, might go about the centre of the border. Spiraea arguta, one of the best of this family, grows about 4 feet. Cytisus Cornish Cream, Potentilla Farreri, Diervilla rosea purpurea, the dwarf Almond and Cydonia Simoni can go nearer the front, and Caryoptris Tangutica, about 3 feet high, blooms from August to October.

I would not suggest planting H.T. roses, which are more for the show-table than a Mixed Border; but a few species and old-fashioned roses are quite suitable, though it must be remembered that these only bloom once. I think R. Hugonis, R. Willmottiae and R. Rubrifolia would not be too big for the back row, while for the middle rows the old Moss, White Provence, Mme Pierre Oger, Dometil Becard, Pax, Salmon

Spray, York and Lancaster, Mme Isaac Periere and Tricolor de Flandre are all delightful old-fashioned roses of long ago. One plant of each would be sufficient, but the Paulsen roses—Kersten and Elsie—should be planted in groups of three each in the second row. Plant Rose de Meaux in the front row, also Eblouissant, which is a good crimson-coloured dwarf Polyantha and Chatillon.

A few of the Delphiniums I consider the best are Mrs. Nelke (the most admired of all), Blue Bird, Doris (a pure mauve), Lord Derby (a deeper shade), Capri (Eton blue), Norah Ferguson and two Belladonna kinds—Muse sacrum, light blue, and Madame Boeckel, dark blue. The last two grow about 5 feet to 5 feet 6 ins., have pretty loose spikes of flowers which do not seed, and therefore remain in bloom a very long time.

Lilies require good cultivation, but a few easy ones suitable for a border are Croceum, Henryi, Martagon album, Pardalinum, Regale, Szovitzianum, Testaceum and Umbellatum. Among bulbs May Tulips, Spanish and English Iris, Montbretias, Gladiolus and Galtonias are all suitable for the second and third rows.

Now for annuals. Opium and Shirley Poppies may be sown broadcast over the border, and then thinned out to one or two plants together, which can be pulled up when they have finished blooming. This is better than having them in clumps, which would leave bare places when over. Lavatera, Nemesias, Dimophothecas, Clarkias, Viscaria, Alonsoa, Anagallis, Phlox Drummondii and Love in a Mist are all good. A clump of Yucca Recurva, Fuchsia Riccartoni or Kniphofia caulescens are suitable for the ends of the border.

I have left herbaceous plants to the last and I am appalled by the number of good plants which should be in every good mixed border. I can only give a few of the best: For the back (5th): Hollyhocks, Dahlias, Eremuri, Delphiniums, Artemisia lactiflora, Lilium Pardalinum, Tall Asters, Aconitum Napellus, and A. Wilsoni, Lathyrus albus, Helianthus Monarch, Rudbeckias, Campanula lactiflora, Lavatera Olbae, Helenium Moorhiem Beauty. Fourth Row: Anchusa Opale, Achillea Eupatorium, Sidalceas Alstromerias, Echinops, Erynginum, Salvia virgata, Lilium Testaceum and Henryi, Verbascum Cotswold Gem and Verbascum Olympicum, Asters. Second and Third Rows: Aster Frikarti, Orange Lily, Asters, Lil. Regale, Oriental Poppies, Erynginum planum, Delphinium Muse Sacrum, Helenium Mme. Catinet, Erigon Quakeress, Paeonies, Baptisia australis, Anemone Japonica, Aster acris, Thalictrum purpureum, Dictamnus fraxinella, Gypsophila, Geranium Ibericum, Anthemis tinctoria, Dielyis spectabilis, Monarda didyma, Pentstemons, Columbines, Antirrhinums, Linum Narbonense, Iris in variety, Pyrethrums, Pentstemon barbatus Torreyi, Œnothera Youngi, Salvia pratense, Aster Thompsonii, Kniphofias, Phloxes, Campanula Telham Beauty and C. Grandis, Tradescantias. First Row: Linum arboreum, L. Narbonense, Pinks in variety, Gentiana Lagodeckiana, Anthericum liliastrum major and A. graminifolium, Statice incana, Aquilegias (long-spurred vars., better dotted than in groups), Campanula carpatica, Violas Lady Crisp, Thuringiana and Jersey Blue Gem, Nepeta Mussini, Agapanthus Moorei, Aquilegia pyrenaica, Helianthemums, Artemisia incana, Veronica incana, Campanula muralis.

The plants I have named should be enough for a start.

✿

Yew ha' tew winter 'em and summer 'em 'fore yew git tew know 'em.

Elder (to young local preacher who has been over-long in his discourse), 'I tell thee, tent no good pumping on a full bucket.'

Dalesman of eighty-five, to summer holiday-maker who has asked him how he spends his time in the winter evenings: 'We makes up a good fire i' t' kitchen, an' all sits round, an' talks about t' queer folk as 'ave bin 'ere in t'summer.'

A visitor to the Cheviots thought it was silly for sheep to go up the hillside at night. 'If I were a sheep,' he said, 'I'd be inclined to come down to the shelter of the farm at night.' 'If ye were a sheep,' replied the farmer, 'ye'd hae mair sense.'

The lad from a fishing village in Aberdeenshire was 'fee'd hame' to a farm to 'sort the nowte' (attend to the cows). His first job was to 'muck the byre.' Back he came to the farmhouse to say, 'Fat wey can I muck yer kye, an' them a' sittin'?' ('How can I clean your cows and them sitting?')

Cobbett Calls on Arthur Young

An Imaginary Conversation

A mild spring day in 1792. Two men have just seated themselves in the library of Bradfield Hall, Suffolk. This workaday room is walled by bookshelves, their contents chiefly concerned with agriculture, though observable besides are a complete edition of Rousseau, and 'Cecilia' in five volumes, for Fanny Burney is step-niece by marriage of Arthur Young, F.R.S., the owner of the library. Latticed windows look over grass, a fish-pond, a Chinese bridge and cabbages. Through an open door is seen a small laboratory, filled with seeds in glass jars, retorts, plans of barns, models of ploughs. The older of the men is middle-aged, in face lively, in manner easy and unaffected. He wears buckskins and top-boots below a drab coat, and his unpowdered brown hair is tied behind. The other man, the visitor, twenty years his junior, tall and sturdy, carries himself with drilled stiffness. He is in nondescript dark attire of cheap quality, but, though obviously inferior in rank, William Cobbett yields nothing in self-respect and blunt sincerity of demeanour. The two are talking eagerly.

COBBETT. For a moment I watched little Miss, wishful to add some early violets to her bunch of flowers. In the sunny wall where she was about to lean her hand I suddenly espied a movement of sliding gristle. I pulled her back and hit the viper dead with my stick.

YOUNG, Only your promptness saved my cherished daughter from snake-bite. I was riding home from our turn-pike meeting when I came up with you. Little did I guess. . . . Are you staying in the neighbourhood?

The late Mrs. Clement Parsons, to whose skill we owe this imaginary scene, lived at Broadway. She had a considerable knowledge of the eighteenth century and was a most attractive personality.

The years of Arthur Young's life were between 1741 and 1820. William Cobbett lived between 1762 and 1835. In the spring of 1792, the time that Mrs. Parsons has fixed for her colloquy, Cobbett was thirty and undeveloped and Young was in his prime. Mrs. Parsons no doubt chose her date for the practical reason that she could find no other on which it is likely that the two could have met. In my reading I have found no note of their having actually met. Did they meet? Late in 1791, Cobbett came back to England from his six to seven years of soldiering in Nova Scotia and New Brunswick, and in the late spring of 1792 he left England as an exile under fear of arrest and lived, first in France for a few months, then in America till 1800. In 1797 Young's darling daughter, 'Bobbin', died, and happiness for him died with her. After her death he saw little avoidable company, though from 1793 he had been settled in London as Secretary to the newly formed Board of Agriculture. His melancholy gradually deepened into religious fanaticism. In June, 1810, Cobbett began two years in Newgate Prison. In 1817 he went back to America for two years. Young was totally blind from 1812 to his death in 1820. In March, 1792, Young was writing the last portion of his 'Travels in France,' that is the supplement he called 'on the Revolution in France'. Of this his thoughts would naturally have been full at the period Mrs. Parsons has selected for Cobbett's call on him.

232

COBBETT. I walked over from Bury, where my wife has relations, with the actual purpose of waiting on you, Mr. Young. I know your 'Annals' almost by heart, and, emboldened by this letter of recommendation from Dr. Priestley, was hoping for information you, above all men, could impart.

YOUNG [*glancing through the letter*]. After the signal service you have rendered me no such recommendation—save for its own interest—is needed. I shall willingly serve you if within my power. What are these hard circumstances of which my good friend speaks?

COBBETT. At the end of six years with the army in New Brunswick, and discharged with honourable mention, I find myself in danger of arrest and imprisonment because I, a non-commissioned officer denounced the embezzlements of certain commissioned officers in my regiment and, what was worse, joined in an appeal to increase foot soldiers' pay. I am advised to quit England immediately. My inclination wavered between America and France when three days ago in London I met with your phenomenal contribution to international knowledge—I refer, sir, to 'Travels in France'.

YOUNG. Disturbed though France still is, and with war on Austria just declared, you could do worse than reside there for six months. English gardeners and agriculturalists are still in demand. An emigration to America might follow.

COBBETT. In France I should hope to better my French and teach English. My wife and I have saved two hundred pounds. I thought of Caudebec as a small place and one of the prettiest situated. I abhor great towns with their stenches and noise. My mind is wrapped up in everything belonging to fields and woods.

YOUNG. I judged you no cock-neigh. Plenty come prating here who scarce know wheat from barley, whereas, in farming, science is respectable only when the outcome of practice. As an agricultural maxim, the more a man works experimentally and the less he writes the better.

COBBETT. I have reason to believe that taste for a thing begets understanding. I was born on a Surrey farm and having got my rudiments in a smock-frock at the plough tail, I have never lost one particle of my passion for those heart-cheering pursuits in which every day presents something new. Though humble efforts of mine must ever remain at a vast distance beneath your own exertions, my ambition is to study the husbandry of other countries in order to introduce reforms in the still rude and pitiable cultivation of much British land.

YOUNG [*whose attention has wandered*]. Glance through that window, Mr. Cobbett. The old fellow mowing is eighty.

COBBETT [*readily responsive to a practical observation, hastens to the window*]. And I thought scything, even when I was young, the hardest thing I had to do! To look on, it seems nothing; but it tries every sinew if you go upright and do your work well. A man must be of surprising strength to mow short grass at eighty. [*After a pause.*] Do you consider, sir, he uses the scythe correctly? But perhaps his stooping action is necessary; lawn shaving is a thing I never did.

YOUNG. Your comment is just, however. The swing of his body goes ever before the scythe instead of following it as it should.

COBBETT. With all that, it is good so old a man can still earn, even though his pursuit be a waste of time.

YOUNG. Nay I differ from you. It is good husbandry to keep the homestead neat. A farmer who takes pride in his garden's tidiness will take the more thought for the orderliness of his land. His ricks must be well shaped, manure neatly stacked, hedges and ditches trimmed and cleaned, and, bent on seeing his farm shipshape in every detail, he will not brook ragged grass round his house.

COBBETT. I accept your rebuke. A labourer—such as I have been—looks only to bodily wants in rural doings, and, living, as labourers must, in damp dens fitter for the dead than the quick, we get the habit of thinking a garden a luxury for the rich.

YOUNG [*offering Cobbett his snuff-box*]. France is a country to learn in, not, as I was half tempted, to farm in. House rent is low. What one profits by is the cheap mode of living; invariably bed-chambers are people's parlours. I recommend Picardy as more eligible than Normandy; more country is enclosed, also there are more new houses—that sure sign of prosperity.

COBBETT. What are the noticeable objects on highroads?

YOUNG. The superb causeways themselves. Yet circulation remains meagre in the extreme. Not a chaise, not a voiture of any description for miles. Great cities in France have not the hundredth part of intercommunication that much inferior places enjoy with us. As for newspapers, outside Paris I found none.

COBBETT. Is the present ferment more directly due to Rousseau and Voltaire or to the example set by America's revolution?

YOUNG. Hunger has been the immediate cause. The remoter causes were privilege, exemptions and absenteeism. When the Bishop of Llandaff spoke to me of the frothy revolutionary Frenchman with Voltaire in his head and the devil in his heart I replied this was a being I nowhere met.

COBBETT. Trust a fat prelate to take the wrong side in whatever concerns the welfare of the people.

YOUNG. Your contempt for episcopacy is scathing.

COBBETT. I include bishops, priests and beadles. Big and little, they enrage me. Not excepting your namesake who wrote that bombastical stuff called 'Night Thoughts'.

YOUNG [laughing]. No relation, I assure you.

At this moment a tray is brought in with sherry, whey and cake. COBBETT *drinks—in whey alone—to* Miss Bobbin—did I hear your daughter's name aright, sir?—may she live to be the toast of the county!

To which YOUNG, *smiling acknowledgements, responds by pledging* The Maximum Output from British Land.

YOUNG. I have sent turnip seed and seed potatoes all over France where good sorts are still disastrously wanting. To look for a course of crops is vain. They sow white corn twice, thrice, even four times in succession. When I recommended turnips or cabbages for breaking their rotations of grain everyone laughed. The waste of land is scandalous. I itched to see the great park of Chambord laid to turnips. Yet in some forms of cultivation the French are ahead of us. I am growing chicory advantageously here from seed I brought from Lyons. Mr. Cobbett, I burn to own a score of farms

235

from Land's End to the Cheviots and visit and direct their tillage by turns!

COBBETT. A Government worth its salt would create you Knight Premier of the Plough.

YOUNG. Now let us take a turn out of doors. I beg you to stay dinner which should be ready in twenty minutes though I regret Mrs. Young is too indifferent to quit her room.

COBBETT. I gladly accept of your hospitality.

YOUNG [*as they cross the kitchen garden*]. I will reserve the livestock till after dinner when I will show you the merino ram of which His Majesty made me a present.

COBBETT. I enjoyed its portrait in the 'Annals'.

YOUNG. Let us look forward to patriotism that shall pay more homage to the prince who gives a ram to a farmer than for flourishing a dubious sceptre over Bengal as till lately over Massachusetts. Yet I doubt whether the merino breed will count for as much as my lamented friend Lord Orford's importation of Southdowns into Norfolk.

COBBETT [*with a sigh of admiration as they enter a field*]. What a beautiful sight! Not a weed.

YOUNG. You flatter. I would God Almighty had left couch and crabgrass out of his creation.

COBBETT [*lovingly, as he walks, crumbling earth between his fingers, looks about him.*] Give me a farm with fields like yours, all rectangular, no crooked pastures, no open ditches, but the plough running right up to the roots of the fence. The land I love is deep tillage land where the only grass fields are rotation seeds and clover.

YOUNG. And all drilled. By drilling, a farm keeps as clean with a summer fallow once in six years as in broadcast husbandry fallowed every fourth year. Remarkable experiments are being carried out in our neighbouring county by Mr. Coke of Holkham. For five years he has grown wheat—wheat in West Norfolk?

COBBETT. Is he a wizard?

YOUNG. His wand is marl. But what think you of yon row of ash trees? Timber being rare hereabouts, I planted twelve years back rather for ornament than profit. However, the second year I cut 'em down within an inch of the ground, and, now, the annual prunings give a reasonable return in fences, broomsticks and fuel. My cook even pickles the ash-keys in salt and vinegar. Luckily, no one yet asked me to sever and hold open one of my ash in order to push a sick child through the aperture in hopes of a cure.

COBBETT. It was a common operation in Sussex. My father firmly believed that if the cleft would rejoin the poor babe would get well.

YOUNG. A universal pollarding disfigures East Anglia.

COBBETT. I love lofty trees. I sometimes think life's dearest satisfaction must be to watch a crow build in an elm oneself has planted. The interest of woods lies in their thousandfold sights, sounds and incidents. Even in winter a coppice is pleasant to the eye while conforting the mind with the idea of shelter.

YOUNG. People think of birds as having a hard time in winter and forget the warmth of woods which exceeds anything to be found in farmyards.

COBBETT. A tree is the second most wonderful thing in nature.

YOUNG. What exceeds it?

COBBETT. Birds and their flight. Birds in their frail way are as profound as trees.

YOUNG. Talk not of the flight of birds. Last November a gaggle of honking geese alighted on a field of mine and gobbled up all my winter greens.

COBBETT. And so, sir, the spirited and sensible people of France have ridded themselves of tithes and salt tax. When shall we do the like?

YOUNG. Our insolent game laws must go first.

COBBETT. The sooner the better. A poacher is a man habitually half starved to whom a pheasant is not a thing of delicate flavour but something to still his aching belly. Seven years if he kills a pheasant; hanging if he lifts his hand to a keeper. Savage, is it not?

YOUNG. We must distinguish. The man who 'lifts his hand' is, or may be a murderer. How much, in your opinion, does a labourer require to eat?

COBBETT. Require? Say one fiftieth of the food his labour

produces. Say a pound of bread and half a pound of meat. What he gets compared with this reduces many a hardy and would-be honest man to a dejected assemblage of skin and bone.

YOUNG [*looking at his watch*]. Time we turned homewards. A hot griskin of pork awaits us.

COBBETT. Then I thank God and your politeness that the ration just stated as the meed of labourers will not to-day be imposed on myself.

YOUNG. And now, Mr. Cobbett, we are by the pump. My maid has placed for us a napkin and a piece of soap by which I know dinner is ready to be served.

Old Fellows' Testimony

SIR HERBERT MAXWELL, whose books have given so much pleasure, wrote to *The Countryman* at 89: 'If I were asked to specify the chief source of the enjoyment which has fallen to my lot in the course of a long life, I should have no hesitation in declaring it to have been the cultivation of trees, shrubs and herbs. I have had in the past a full share of fox-hunting, salmon and trout fishing, deer-stalking and shooting game; but the love of woodland and garden has outlived them all, and I am well able to endorse Andrew Lang's description of horticulture as "a device of Providence for the pottering peace of virtuous eld." I own gratefully that I have been specially favoured in the matter of environment, for my lot having been cast on the west coast, where the climate is mild and moist and the soil a generous loam, we have been able to enjoy a full share of the countless treasures which enterprising collectors have brought in vast variety from distant lands.' And at 95 WILLIAM ROBINSON, author of 'The English Flower Garden' and other works, said, 'My message to gardeners is, *Laborare est orare*'.

More than once, Sussex women have been heard to refer to the birth of a first child as 'my first obedience'. The connection between this and the 'love, honour, and obey' is sufficiently striking.

My Diving and Surface Ducks
by the Earl Buxton, G.C.M.G.

My moat at Newtimber in Sussex, in which my ducks live and prosper, covers a considerable area of water, is entirely fed by springs coming up through the chalk and the water is very clear. Trout—Brown and Rainbow—live and thrive; and the Golden Orfe attain a good age and a considerable size. There are, at present, some fifteen to twenty pinioned ducks on the moat. I used to have a considerable variety, but now practically confine myself to comparatively common or inexpensive ducks, as, unfortunately, the moat cannot be made into a 'sanctuary', and a big wood adjoins in which depredating foxes abound. By experience I have found that it was useless to turn out ducks of bright plumage, as they only attracted the foxes; and that it was better to have diving ducks, which seldom leave the moat or keep close to the edge of the bank, rather than surface ducks, which are inclined to sleep farther from the water and wander afield to nest. I have from time to time had Wigeon, Pintail, Shoveller, Golden Eye, Teal, etc., but now have practically only the Tufted Duck, the Common Pochard and the Red-Crested Pochard.

It is easy enough to induce the ducks, with the exception of the Teal to come to be fed, But, though I have more than once turned out Teal, I have never been able to tame them in the slightest degree. They swim about in the distance, and after a short time go off to the stew ponds, and are there, no doubt, promptly picked up by the foxes. The ducks are a source of perpetual pleasure, interest and amusement, especially the diving ducks. The water being very limpid, all their movements when diving can be clearly seen. The trout and the diving ducks are good friends and do not interfere with one another. At feeding time they both dive and swim about together, without taking the slightest notice of one another though sometimes a fish, rushing to seize a chunk of

Among much good public work done by the writer as Sydney Buxton, was making postage to the United States uniform with home postage. His *Handbook to Public Questions* ran through many editions. In 1914 he was raised to the peerage and became Governor General of South Africa.

bread at which a duck is nibbling, chucks the latter violently under the chin, which is not appreciated. The Golden Eye, however, has light coloured feet, and the trout, presumably thinking that these were alive and eatable, used, at feeding time, greatly to annoy the Golden Eye by nibbling at its toes. The food consists of scrap bread and maize. When the maize is thrown in, the Tufted Ducks and the Pochards instantly dive after it; while, as the grains sink, the fish constantly dart at them, suck them in and immediately eject them. The ducks in order to obtain the necessary impetus, make a slight forward and upward jump and break the surface with scarcely any splash. The legs are stuck out at right angles to the body, while the feet are paddled at a great rate as the duck twists and turns in pursuit of the corn. To retrieve the grains which sink to the bottom the ducks stand on their heads in the familiar manner, with nothing visible in the water but two quick paddling webbed feet and the top of a tail. Presently, the task accomplished, the duck claps its legs to its side and rapidly shoots up to the surface, gleaming with drops of water, which to prove the truth of the proverb, at once roll off, leaving the plumage absolutely dry. Meanwhile, the surface ducks, which cannot dive, are left on short commons, for apart from the bread they are only able to secure a few grains of the sinking corn while it is yet within neck-stretching distance. This disability leads to envy, hatred and malice on their part; and the temper of one particular Widgeon was thereby permanently soured. The divers, when feeding in the ordinary way, stay down about twenty seconds at the most. When being fed they naturally come up much more quickly, cock an eye and ask for more.

The ducks breed fairly freely, like with like. A Pochard and a Tufted Duck occasionally pair, but these hybrids have neither the effective colouring not the smart appearance of their respective parents. It is indeed not an uncommon thing for diving ducks of one species to intermix with a diving duck of a different species and the same occurs with surface ducks. But is is very rare, I believe, for a diving drake to mate with a surface duck. In 1925 a Red-Crested Pochard drake, a diving duck, paired with a widowed duck Widgeon, a surface duck—

a combination which I believe to be unique. For three years in succession they paired. Three of the hybrids were reared in the first year but one was killed by a dog. The next year five more were reared. In 1927 the Widgeon laid again. In this case the eggs were not taken nor the ducklings pinioned, as I hoped they might possibly stay about. However, about the end of September they flew away and have never come back. I have surviving a duck and a drake belonging to the first brood. They are greatly attached to one another and are inseparable but have never nested. I gave Messrs. Maclean and Wormald a pair of the second brood, hoping that they might induce the two to mate, but they never nested. The drake bird, handsome, dignified and well groomed, does not take after either its father or the drake Widgeon. In writing about these birds to Lord Grey, my typist invented an appropriate euphemism by designating them as 'highbred' instead of 'hybrid'. Their diving habits are peculiar. They practically never dive when the other ducks are diving for corn, but I have seen them when alone and feeding, dive, clumsily and with effort, and remain under the surface for some time.

The various broods of tiny ducklings of different sorts are very attractive, especially the young divers, which dive and feed the day on which they are born. It is delightful to see the mother and six or seven chicks, balls of brown fluff, diving and feeding together with thorough enjoyment. I have of late given up pinioning the young ones. Born about June, they disappear in September. In earlier days a moat-born Widgeon occasionally returned on a visit, and a Pochard on rare occasions; but, as far as I know, no Tufted Duck has ever come back. The duck is a careless mother; constantly on the move she over-exercises her chicks. She is moreover unable apparently to count beyond two or even one, and if she can keep one or two chicks in sight, she is content, the others are left to fend for themselves, and get scattered about, being picked up or not, as the case may be, on her next circumnavigation of the moat. Sometimes an unfortunate temporary orphan spies another brood in the offing, makes for it, only to be savaged and driven away by the alien mother. The result of this neglect is usually that of a brood of seven or nine, only a limited number, as a rule, survive their drastic treatment. Last year I had two broods of Tufted Duck which hatched almost simultaneously—one of nine and one of seven. When the little ducklings were only three days old, a tremendous hailstorm took place, which killed all of them except one. The mothers had not sufficient sense to take the young ones into shelter. Some young moorhen chicks of about the same age all survived, the mother having sheltered them in the reeds.

There are plenty of moorhens and the young ones, till they are about three-quarters grown, come and feed with the ducks. But though we have been here some thirty years, the old ones still remain as shy as ever and will not come within feeding distance, and if a piece of bread is thrown out to them, they hurriedly retire with it into the reeds. From time to time coots attempt to take up their abode on the moat, but they are quarrelsome, and interfere with the ducks especially at breeding time. So they have to be effectively shown that their room is preferable to their company. We are seldom without an elusive dabchick or two, and they occasionally nest.

ᴓ

'I'm as happy as a lamb with two mothers,' said old Mary.

Ancient and modern (Oxfordshire): "'Ow are ye to-day, Betty?' 'Why can't ye say, "'Ow be y'?" Y'aven't bin to college, 'ave ye?'

From an advertisement: 'Dogs as a paying business taught by post. Also Farming, Poultry, Pigs, Land Agency.' As a kind of extra, no doubt.

Bank manager, visiting a farm to see if the overdraft is safe, 'That's a fine crop of mustard for the sheep.' It was charlock, but the farmer agreed with him.

The old farmer and his wife had just returned from what was to them a far off land, Scotland. 'An' when we comed to that Forth Bridge and looked down,' he said, 'the missus she says to me, "My Gawd, Ambrose, hode tight".'

The London chauffeur, driving in Norfolk, came to a stop in the rear of a large herd of cattle. The man in charge seemed to be in no hurry to make way and after a time the chauffeur mildly enquired when he proposed to let him get past his cows. The man turned his head and drawled, 'They ain't cows, they're bullocks.'

How I Turned Inn-keeper

by S. B. Russell of the Lygon Arms, Broadway

FROM banking in London to inn-keeping in the Cotswolds is a far cry, and yet it seemed to come about by a natural evolution, for I remember first reading about the Lygon Arms in one of those chatty books on road travel written by J. J. Hissey, 'Across England in a Dog Cart', which I got from the Bank library about 1896, and, later on, being thrilled by a large sale bill, with full description, which was hanging in the chambers of the Bank's solicitors, in New Square, Lincolns Inn, where I had gone on Bank business. In 1901 I was offered the post at Burton-on-Trent under Sir Charles Stewart (afterwards Public Trustee), as head of a department which managed the properties of Samuel Allsopp & Dons, and found that the Lygon Arms was one of them.

It was in 1903 that I was able to see it for the first time. There was no railway to Broadway in those days, and I well remember the drive from Evesham by dog-cart and the impression made on me by the weathered stone frontage of the old inn, with its well-proportioned gables, and the distant hills in the background. But, steeped as I was in Mr. Hissey's description, the inside was disappointing. There was much of interest in premises that had been an inn since 1530, but very much had been hidden and wrongly treated. Beautiful sixteenth century stone doorways had been painted, open fireplaces bricked up and fitted with cheap register grates. The plaster work in many rooms was held together by the many wallpapers, pasted one on the other and going back to the little rosebud patterns of early Victorian times. In the only sitting-room on the ground floor the ingle-nook had been enclosed by cupboards and the beam had been papered over. Some tattered coco-matting, a few armchairs in American

Besides being the perfect hotel keeper, as anyone who watched him receiving guests, making a salad, or caring for the contents of his old inn could see, the writer of this article was a skilful collector, an accomplished letterer and a kind and wise Sunday visitor of the prisoners in Gloucester gaol. These pages have been kindly read through by his son Gordon Russell, M.C., C.B.E., the assiduous and skilful Director of the Council of Industrial Design, of the firm of Gordon Russell, Ltd., furniture manufacturers, in the premises adjoining the inn. The first five hundred furniture designs produced by the firm were his work. A memorial slab of his own cutting in a wall at Idbury was his generous gift.

243

cloth, without castors, and the groggy gas chandelier with one weight missing, created depression, the more so, as part of the room had been allocated as a passage-way to others beyond, by placing deal store cupboards back to back. In the front rooms at the west end there was an untidy smoke room and bar. At the east end an assembly room had been erected about 1860 without any regard to preserving light and air for several rooms. This assembly room seemed to have originated in the purchase by the owner of four large windows and two large double doors at a sale in Cheltenham. In the yard at the back was stabling for thirty or forty horses.

Notwithstanding the unsuitable furniture everywhere, and the sordid atmosphere of the place, I could not fail to be impressed by the original staircase, the panelling in the Oak parlour, and the beautiful plaster work and Elizabethan fireplace in the Cromwell Room, and could not help feeling that much of equal interest was hidden.

Notwithstanding the one and only bathroom, a particularly unpleasing apartment, and the many evidences of unsympathetic furnishing, equipment, and management, the visitors' book showed that many well-known people had come to the inn. I noted the names of Arthur J. Balfour, Lord and Lady Elcho, Phil May, J. M. Barrie, the Duke of Norfolk, Forbes-Robertson, Owen Seaman, Alma Tadema, Canon Ainger, Ellen Terry and Conan Doyle. It was on my way home that the idea came to me that this inn offered great possibilities if properly developed. It was going to be a big job, but it would be worth while, and finding that Allsopp's were willing to sell what could never be regarded as a brewers' property, I made another visit, and in January, 1904, I was in possession.

Experience had shown me that many inns of similar age and character failed in attempting too much. One found a smoke room and bar frequented by village tradespeople, with the farmers' noisy bustle on market days, commercial and stock rooms for travellers, catering for large parties, and lastly, the tourist, who often received but scant attention from a staff tired by the labours of the day. My plan was to look after the tourist entirely, to do away with the public bars, and to make the inn as much like a large private house at it was

What can I get up to next?

Oldsters watching village cricket

RECREATION

THE SPIDER'S CLAWS

possible for it to be. One of the first things I did was to have a careful survey made by an architect, and the wisdom of this step was manifest afterwards, for when we came to make restorations we knew exactly what was above and below.

While so much of the inside of the inn had been kept intact, the fashion for sash windows in the eighteenth century had led to the removal of many of the mullions from the ground and first floors. These were gradually replaced, and casements with leaded glass substituted.

Furniture was a pressing problem. I had brought with me from Repton my own small collection of old pieces, and it was at this point that my study of seventeenth century furniture became valuable. I was unable to afford the purchase of fine examples for all the rooms, but those were days when original pieces requiring repair could be bought at reasonable prices. Many of them had been stored for years in barns and lofts, since the fashion for oak had given place to mahogany. There was in the hotel buildings a carpenter's shop, and I looked round for an intelligent carpenter who could do these repairs under my supervision, and found in James Turner an excellent local man, who had been an estate carpenter. It is a pleasant reflection that after twenty-seven years, he is still in our employment in the workshops of Gordon Russell, Ltd., and that three of his sons have been apprenticed to us as they left schoool.

My youngest son was only a month old when we came to the Lygon, but I had wonderful co-operation from my wife in all the work and re-organization. Everything wanted attention, bedrooms, kitchens, lighting, heating, and equipment. Work was going on, dirty, dusty work, continuously in some part of the house, and this had to be schemed so as not to make it an annoyance or inconvenience to visitors. It was at this time that I devoutly wished that everything could have been closed down for a year, so that I could get on more rapidly with this necessary work. But my capital would not permit of this course, and I now see how fortunate it was, for so much would have been done, without the light of experience, which would have had to be done over again.

During the progress of this work on the old part of the Inn, by which a number of the rooms were restored to their original condition, many objects were discovered that shed new light on its antiquity, and I often look back on my part in retrieving them. For, clad in my oldest clothes, holding a wet towel to my nose, I have been in rooms so thick with dust and falling plaster that I could not see a yard ahead. But I kept a keen ear for the clink of a falling coin or other object dislodged after centuries of hiding. Many such finds are now gathered together in a cabinet on the ground floor and comprise coins of Edward I, Elizabeth, James I, Charles I, and copper coins of all the Georges, many tobacco pipes going back to the early part of the seventeenth century, old black wine bottles, one still retaining its worm-eaten cork, and evidently hidden by a thirsty workman long years ago. There were also tokens of one Michael Russell, who lived in Broadway in 1670, records of candles made in the inn in the eighteenth century, and a carefully fashioned apple scoop in wood, carved with the name of AN TREAVIS, who was the third daughter of John Treavis, the landlord of the inn from 1604 to 1641, to whom there is an interesting brass on the floor of the chancel in Broadway old Church. Nor shall I forget the thrill when on removing whitewash nearly a quarter of an inch thick, from the mullions in one room, we came across a number of initials and dates, the earliest being Richard Jervis 1586, who was born in Broadway in 1548, with dates 1623, 1624, and 1626 several times repeated. Among the many initials were T.T. and R.S., the former probably Thomas Trevis, who died in 1649, and the latter Richard Savage, at whose house in Broadway, King Charles I slept, on Sunday, June the 2nd, 1644.

Visitors came in increasing numbers, so that hardly a day passed without my coming into contact with some well-known and interesting personality, keen on everything that was being done to reinstate the hospitality of former days, and appreciative of staying under the roof of an historic inn which provided the comforts of a country house. When, in these latter years, I have been congratulated on what has been achieved, my reply has always been that my own part has been a singularly modest one, for I owe so much of the success to suggestions volunteered by distinguished visitors, very often architects and engineers at the top of their profession. Great help always comes to those who are good listeners and cultivate retentive memories. May I give an instance? The building of the great hall, on the site of the old assembly room, required much thought in planning, and many schemes were got out which were not happy in their arrangement or quite suitable for the purpose the hall had to fill. Just at the time when I could not see daylight, a well-known architect came to spend Easter. He asked me to take him round and show him the house, and in conversation I mentioned our next move and its difficulties. He said, 'You will readily understand that I cannot advise you professionally on the plans you have prepared, but if you like to show them to me as a friend, something may occur to me which may help.' I shall not easily forget the flash of genius when, on looking at the plans for a few minutes he said, 'Why not put it the other way?' I saw at once how wonderfully this would fit in, and it resulted in a building which is universally admired as being in harmony with the old structure, both outside and inside.

Looking back on those days, I cannot now realize how it was possible to put in so much work, for not only were repairs going on inside, but there was the re-organization of the kitchens, the collection of an efficient staff of English servants, the ramifications of a decaying posting business— which, one could see so plainly, was to make way for mechanical transport in the near future, requiring efficient garage accommodation—the purchase of an orchard of two acres immediately behind the building, and making the garden sufficiently large to grow our own produce. Above and beyond all these activities, I was managing director of the largest hotel in Newquay, besides being on the board of hotels in Bournemouth and Swanage, and acting as manager of a large estate which included a well-known London tavern. But it was the additional income this brought in which helped me to realize my ideals for the inn which was soon to become one of the show places of England.

In 1908 my eldest son, Gordon, left school, and, after a voyage to the Argentine, came to my help. With an interest in design and traditional methods in Cotswold building, he superintended the repair work going on, including the carpenters' shop, where we now had additional men repairing furniture. Visitors were always asking if they could purchase certain pieces of old furniture and decorative objects but I made a firm decision from the first, that I could not combine the sale of furniture with innkeeping, except as a separate business. Old pieces which had been selected for various positions in the inn as being in keeping with some particular room, and other things which filled the qualities of being decorative and fit for their purpose would be looked for by returning visitors. An opportunity occurred of acquiring a fine old house on the east side, part of the bargain being that I should plan and build a house for the owner on another site he possessed in the village. Upon getting possession we started a separate business in geniune old pieces, which grew very rapidly and led to the designing and making by skilled craftsmen of modern furniture. In the Paris Exhibition a cabinet designed by Gordon Russell was awarded the only gold medal given for English furniture and to-day my son controls, as managing director, this important offshoot. In the following year, 1909, my second son, Donald, left school, and after a few months of business training, came to take his share in a rapidly expanding business. He seems to have a natural gift for all that goes to good inn-keeping, and for many years now, he has, with the help of his able wife, been in charge of the Lygon.

A few words must be said about my inn-keeping during the War. Both my sons and all our men joined up. This left Mrs. Russell and myself unaided. When food was rationed, but before the issue of food coupons, urgent regulations were issued to inns and hotels, limiting meat, bread and sugar to each person for every meal. I did not weigh out these articles as directed, but wrote a notice for the dining-room stating that since 1540 the Lygon had sheltered guests, and that I felt sure that its guests in these days might be trusted to keep to the amount allowed, and with regard to meat if they would ask for it either fat or lean, as they preferred, nothing would be wasted. Bread and sugar were put on the tables. It is good to think that for twelve months we were considerably on the right side of the allowances. During the War I always got down to my office at 5 a.m. It was the two hours thus secured that enabled me to plan for the day, overtake correspondence and do public work.

As to stories I remember one afternoon, during a busy tea-time, a casual visitor sauntered around the tables with a bowler hat on his head and his hands in his trouser pockets. When I asked him his requirements, he said 'Am an' eggs', to which I could only say quietly, 'Here is a table; I will send a waitress; she will take your order and your hat.'

Charming friends from America come again and again, and appreciate the associations of Broadway and its neighbourhood with the early history of their own country. The greater part of my private correspondence is with American friends. On each occasion of my visits to America, I have been overwhelmed with friendliness and hospitality.

The late Lord Montague of Beaulieu was one of our earliest visitors and never ceased to take an interest in the inn, and his tribute to my efforts which he published in 1910 gave me much encouragement. I have many tokens of his friendship. The late Dr. A. C. Benson, Master of Magdalene, was a frequent visitor. I treasure a copy of the 'Upton Letters' which he gave to me inscribed with the statement that a large part of it was written under my roof. Interesting people have reached the Lygon in coach-and-four, Cape-cart, and tandem dog-cart. Early one Sunday morning I was called by the night porter to see a gentleman who could not speak English. I went down to find Monsieur Aumont Theville who explained that he had left Paris in the Gordon Bennett Balloon Race the previous afternoon and not having seen terra firma for fog when over the Thames valley, had come down on Broadway Hill. After having breakfast, he took me to the spot and I was amazed to find the balloon carefully folded and stored in the basket car, and hidden as far as possible by bushes. Colonel the Master of Sempill was the first guest to arrive by aeroplane.

To those who, like myself, have an urge to keep an inn, I may say that no occupation can offer such an opportunity of meeting people of all classes and varied interests, and give a man such a chance of spreading good-fellowship. But an inn-keeper must be prepared to work early and late, must have a sense of humour and remember that his guests, although sometimes unreasonable are probably right. He must be able to meet the tired and peevish guest with a smile and an endeavour to dispel the cares of travelling by serving a good dinner in cheery surroundings. I would like particularly to stress the need for cheerful decoration and furnishings. We all remember the plush curtains, horse-hair covers, Crimea engravings, and large dingy mirrors of the end of the last century. Better inns mean more people touring England.

The Old Farm

A poem by Yi Kyoobo (1168-1241) the king's right hand when Kublai Khan's hordes threatened Korea. The Japanese statesman, Prince Ito, in ordering a reprint of Korean literature, made Kyoobo's writings the first two volumes. The translation, sent by the translator, the Korean scholar, Dr. James S. Gale, is as literal as possible, line for line.

THE morning's late, and yet I lie abed,
   While swallow on the eaves make sport of me.
The servant lads, bound for the fields, pull by the cart.
'Come! Come!' they shout, 'it's late!'
Up quick I get, unwashed, my head uncombed,
Whistling my thoughts, out through the pinewood gate.
Beneath the shade I cannot see the sun,
While all the grass hangs wet with morning dew.
Slowly I wend, down to the sparkling brook,
Across whose stones spin spouting streams of rain.
The women, dressed in creeper-coats, weed o'er the field;
While men, outdecked in hempen blue, work by and sing.
The hand-hoes move like waving clouds.*
The season of the iris and the apricot,
The time to plough, the time of seed is here.

---

*Hand-hoes in the original is 'over the shoulder' and in the simile they are described as 'waving' or 'curling.' They require a good swing.

These Young Farmers' Clubs

by the Duke of Norfolk

IT is a pleasure to me to write about Young Farmers' Clubs because, as President of their National Federation, I take a very live interest in them, and because, in *The Countryman*, I am in touch with men and women who, like myself, have at heart the interests and welfare of the countryside. In the very difficult times through which we are passing most of us at one time or another are led to disagree with even the best of our friends. When Young Farmers' Clubs are mentioned, I have yet to discover the person who does not share my conviction that they are of the utmost value to the country in general and to young people in rural areas in particular. The welfare of youth is a policy on which everyone, irrespective of creed or party, is on common ground.

You may say, 'Why then discourse on a subject on which all minds think alike?' The reason is that there are about 14,000 villages in England and Wales, and there are at the present time no more than 1,300 of our Young Farmers' Clubs. I do not say that we wish to put a club into every village, but we do aim to develop the movement to the extent that every area which can turn a Club to good account shall have one, and every boy and girl who wants to join a Club shall have the opportunity of membership.

Now what is a Young Farmers' Club? It is a group of boys and girls between the ages of 10 and 21, banded together to care for some living thing—a calf, a pig, poultry, bees, rabbits, or plants in a garden plot. Each member undertakes himself or herself not only to care for the stock or plants allotted but to keep accurate records of feeding and costs, to attend Club meetings, and to take part in all organized activities. May I say that membership is not confined to the sons and daughters of farmers, but is open to all young people

---

The Duke—Earl Marshal and Chief Butler of England and Premier Duke and Earl, A.D. 1139—was Joint Parliamentary Secretary of the Ministry of Agriculture during the War, and, travelling about the country, did much, among the young people on the farms and their parents, to sustain agricultural effort.

The clubs have about 58,000 members.

251

between the ages I have mentioned?

Each Club has an adult leader and an advisory committee of adults, but the Club is essentially democratic in its organization. Chairman, secretary and treasurer must be elected annually by the members from among themselves. A Club, in its early beginnings, naturally relies largely upon the guidance and advice of its leader and adviser of committee, but our object is to train members to manage their own affairs.

During Mr. MacDonald's Prime Ministership I had the pleasure of attending an 'At Home' in Downing Street, given by the Prime Minister and Miss MacDonald on behalf of our National Federation. In the course of her address, Miss MacDonald said that she could never agree with the view so commonly held that the best boys and girls of the family should desert the country and come to the towns. Assuredly, if we intend to lessen the migration from the country and to build up a sound and prosperous agricultural industry, we have got to do two things: (1) ensure to the rising generation in rural areas a better and more attractive life, and (2) see that the young people are properly equipped to follow the calling to which they were born.

Our movement has spread to every quarter of the globe. In the United States it has a membership of over a million. In Australia, Canada, New Zealand the Clubs are a powerful factor in the national life.

In this country the movement has the support of the Ministry of Agriculture and the Carnegie United Kingdom Trust, and has received much help from agricultural education authorities and the backing of the National Farmers' Union and many societies; but it is essentially a movement dependent on the voluntary work of people of good-will who have at heart the welfare of the younger generation in the countryside. The possibilities are great, and it is noteworthy that the lines of development are all such as fulfil present-day needs: (1) interest in the conduct of agricultural operations on a basis which is scientifically and economically sound, (2) encouragement of co-operative effort, (3) training for public work and public responsibilities, (4) bridging of the gap between town and country, since Clubs may also be formed in urban and suburban areas, (5) discovery and development of the talent of young people.

The Clubs naturally vary enormously. We have the small stock Clubs in which the activities require only a small initial outlay of capital, and, again, as in my own county—West Sussex—three Clubs the value of whose stock is approximately £2,000. They have become serious business enterprises. In every county in which the movement has obtained a firm footing, there is a yearly increase in the number of Clubs. In every village in which there is an active Club a new spirit of keenness and enthusiasm had been introduced. There are many boys and girls who in after years will look back to the day they enrolled as Young Farmers, as the first milestone on their road to success. Would you not like to help the movement? You have only to write to 55 Gower Street, W.C.1, in order to get the fullest particulars.

*

Her Way of Life, by E. Roberts Ellis

'THIS sup o' tea u'll help me along t' road nicely', she said, as she set the mug on the table with a clatter, 'but tea's nowt by itself, it needs summat to help it down.' She took another large bite of the ham and bread and munched it heartily and noisily. I looked at my visitor as she sat on a kitchen chair by the open door. There was nothing pleasing about her. A rough, coarsened old woman, wearing cast-off clothes. Her overcoat, with two big patch pockets, must have been made for an outsize man. It was held in position by two large safety pins and an old leather belt, and reached to her ankles. Her grey hair straggled from under an old hat, her face was lined, her hands dirty and knobbly. She finished the meal, then rubbed the back of her hand across her mouth and nose, took a broken clay pipe from her pocket and began to fill it with bits of twist.

'Happen you'll spare me a match, missis.' I passed the match box to her, and after lighting the pipe, she slipped the matches into her pocket, and puffed away. 'Aye, I'm a believer in fruit miself,' she continued. 'I allus think an orange is a good finish to a meal, don't you, missis? Of course if you haven't one, you can't give one.' On the dresser there was a dish of fruit which I knew she had seen. I gave the largest Jaffa to her. It was slipped into the same pocket as the matches.

'Well, I mun get to Clithon Union toneet, and it's a fairish stretch.' She took the pipe from her mouth and wrapped it in an old red handkerchief. 'Why', I said, 'it's twenty-two miles to Clithon.' She stood up and guffawed. 'Nay, don't worry, missis, I shall get there reet enough. There'll be a lot o' lorries and vans on t' main road and they gen'lly take pity on an owd un.' 'Yes, but supposing you can't get a lift?' She made a grimace, then put her foot up on the chair to tighten her bootlace. 'I shall tramp as far as Gaston, to where t' road chaps are working. There's a watchman there an' he'll hev a hut an' a fire, so I shall spend t' night wi him. Them chaps are allus glad of a bit o' company. Then there's sure to be plenty o' motors passing in t' morning.'

I prepared to bid her farewell. She was not to be hurried. 'Eh, by gum! these socks are about done for.' She examined her legs carefully. 'Happen yer owd man has a pair o' socks he's not wearing, missis? They'll hev to be woollen for tramping in this sort o' weather.' I found a pair of man's woollen socks. She took them and thrust her hand inside one of them. 'Um, they's darned a lot, but they'll manage till I get another pair somewhere. My job's rough on socks; one pair is nowt.' However she pushed them into her pocket alongside the orange and the matches.

'Surely', I said, 'at your age, you would prefer to settle down and rest, rather than tramp the country in all weathers. You don't even know where the next meal is coming from.' She looked at me with scorn, then sat down. 'No, missis, I wouldn't. Not after forty-two years on t'road. I should choke if I was to live in a poky little house, an' as for t' Union— Ugh! Never! Fancy me stopping wi a lot o' cackling owd women, dressed in a print frock, an' a little shawl on mi head, scrubbing tables an' peeling taters.' She rubbed her mouth vigorously with her hand, then spat. 'No, I've managed so long an' if mi rheumatics don't beat me, I'll hev mi freedom to th' end.'

Again she stood up 'I'm nobbut going to Clithon to meet a pal ut's bin in hospital. He'll wait for me till he sees me. Him an' me u'll be going south together. It's a bit warmer, an' farmers are a bit softer down there, but we shall come back in summer.'

I went to the door to watch her down the path. Half-way she stopped and turned. 'Eh, I'd nearly forgotten, will yer give me a screw o' tea an' sugar, then yon night-watchman 'ull make a sup o' tea in mi billy can?' Once more satisfied she said 'Good day,' and again ambled down the path. Near the gate, a sack of potatoes had been emptied on the grass to dry. With an astonishing liveliness she stooped and quickly filled her empty pocket with potatoes. Then, without a turn of the head or a backward glance, she passed outside the gate and trudged down the inviting road.

Woodlark's Song at Midnight

by E. W. Hendy

ARE all the waking hours of April days
    Too short to ease your ecstasy, that you
    Beneath the Moon's irradiancy bestrew
Even the midnight silences with song
As silver-dewy as her shimmering rays,
    In early aubade or late serenade;
    Spill triolets in trill and shake, along
Each glimmering meadow and umbrageous glade?

Ah, small wise singer, do you know too well
    How short is the rich revel of the spring,
    How brief her blissful days of burgeoning?
Sing, spendthrift, day and night; dull senses seal
Beauty's full vision from us; you reveal
    In part; the whole nor you nor we can tell.

A farmer who had taken a few minutes' trip in an aeroplane remarked on his return, "Ah joost paid 5s. to leeak at mi beeats!" (Too nervous to look over, looked at his boots.)

Experiences with Bats

by Michael Blackmore

I HAD reached a deep ravine cut in the great limestone rocks of Somerset. There are dozens of caverns and most of them afford a shelter for bats of six or seven different species. Horseshoe bats, both Greater and Lesser, are abundant. Like the huge chrysalids of some prehistoric butterfly, they hang from the roof and walls of the caverns, still, silent and torpid. But shine an electric torch on their dusky bodies or breathe ever so lightly on them and they flex their legs and draw themselves up tightly to the rock. They are profoundly asleep; you have watched merely a reflex movement of the muscles. In these caverns lives the handsome Natterer's bat, a pretty creature, with long, almost transparent ears. Its underside is a soft white, very noticeable when the bat is on the wing. In fact among some country-folk this species has been dubbed the 'White-waistcoat bat'. Another species, a near relation to the last, known as the Whiskered bat, also inhabits the same caves. It has goblin-like expression and its fur is grizzled chestnut above and dusky beneath. Both these bats are difficult to capture, for they wedge themselves deep in the crevices. With luck a Long-eared bat may be found here. Its enormous ears are as long as its body. When the bat sleeps it folds its ears alongside its body. Its piteous eyes stand out like beads, also large for the size of the body compared with the eyes of other bats. Why has this species got such large ears? Perhaps, because it hunts so late at night when insects are scarce. The rarest of the bats inhabiting these caves is the Barbastelle. One April I could plainly see one with its curiously-formed ears, its evil-looking face and black shining eyes, as my electric torch revealed it in the depths of a narrow crevice. For a few minutes it defied me from its fastness, squeaking in a querulous manner. Finally it crept out of sight, though for quite a while I heard it crying its protest until its voice faded away into a deep, metallic buzz. Another cave-haunting bat was Daubenton's bat. I found a pair in March hibernating in a crevice in a North Devon

The writer's book on bats should be read.

manganese mine. Their backs were a warm reddish-brown in colour and the fur was slightly grizzled on its surface. Below, the underside was a silver-grey, extremely soft and fine. The eyes of these bats are sad and melancholy, their faces piteous and miserable. But the habits of Daubenton's bat are interesting. It hovers for its food over water, flying just above the surface of lakes, pools, and ponds. The flight somewhat resembles that of a sand-martin when engaged in the same occupation. Hence its second name, the water bat. I took my two captives home, relieved them of their fleas, and put them on a table. I then introduced them to Toby, my pet noctule, whereupon the bats commenced a sad, wailing cry, alternated with harsh, grating sounds of defiance. Toby, evidently understanding the nature of bats' language, pattered away on her sprawling feet and sought shelter between the leaves of Hugh Walpoles' 'Hans Frost'.

You would like to hear of a strange adventure which is hard to credit, but each fact can be vouched for by witnesses. In mid-July, owing to my having left a window slightly open while the bats were being exercised, they both escaped. (I had them a year and nine months; they had travelled 1,850 miles by train, boat and car.) When they did not return for a week I thought our acquaintance of many months was at an end. Imagine my surprise when, a fortnight later, a maid employed at a school some distance away, told me how a bat had 'attacked' her by flying round her head very persistently as she was attempting to fetch some coal from the coal-house. Fortunately, the bat had followed her into the coal-house and she had locked it in. When I entered the coal-house I found my lost female bat. On taking her home she evidently recognized her old haunts and flew to my hand for food. On August 30 I walked to Watermouth Castle, a distance of over four miles from my house. This old castle had been the home of my male bat, Brannock. As I was walking round by some old chambers built under the Castle I explored, and at the far end of a small passage was not surprised to see a Greater Horseshoe hanging. But imagine my astonishment when the creature flew towards me and settled on my hand, licking it in evident recognition of an old friend. It would be absolutely

257

impossible for me to describe my feelings at this happy moment. I took the truant home and opened his cage. He flew straight in and immediately made for his mate. That they recognized each other instantly, I am sure, for they licked each other's faces, which is a sign of friendship among Horseshoe bats! After this happy re-union (in which Toby, my noctule bat took a great interest) the bats both flew to my hand. All the three pets are very well at the present time.

Mrs. Culver, by Eleanor Boniface

WHEN Mrs. Culver was 'queen' of the hopping she collected women to serve in the hop-fields. Early in October she would shepherd them home again, having been responsible for their work and behaviour. Though rather crippled, she enjoys life, and has a forehead like Beethoven's! While watching her bending over a small gramophone, I was struck by the likeness. 'Yaas,' she said, looking at the gramophone, 'this is a bit o' lighten our darkness, and no mistake! But Oh, 'tis Bands that is my admiration, Bands! Bands marching by here, marching! and shining! and they trumpets blaasting out "tra ra" and the drum agwine "rap, raap, row, row." Oh! it does seem to lift ye up like. That's where I misses the hopping. There was the Salvation Army, and we often did a turn to their waltz tunes, and every night we had the concertinas; they used to make 'em just rip out, they did. My old man was a wonder on the penny whistle. Oh! a gurt per-former. Of course 'twas in the hopes of music that I was over-persuaded to goo to that garn party at the rectory. Only a tinny, lil harmonicum. Oh I did feel re-jected, and the rector's lady she played it, but she seemed somehows skeered of the instrument, and went tip-tapping at it like a hen on a bucket. The tea was a kind thing to do. Enjoy ourselves? Oh, we bored about! The rector and his lady meant well, but he's an old blunderbuss! I expects 'twas the want of the music that made it dull. Now when we used to goo hopping, such a lil thing would please us and set us all hollering and singing and laughing! I always seemed to get an ad-mirer too! There was old Benny Parrett, he was a reglar beau of mine for the dancing. He's old now and wore out, he's got lopadated in his dress, but I won't have him laughed at, no! There was Olive, my grand-daughter, a giggling at him only last week, so "Olive!" I says, "adone now! adone-do!" That gal, she queers me! She comes here with her dog, and he un-rolled a hedgehog out o' the bank, so I hits the hedgehog on the nose with my stick. You've only to tap 'em just enough to draw a bubble of blood, and they dies quick. Olive she pouches her face at me and she says: "Oh Gran! you're crool, you've killed the hedgehog," and busts out a'crying! I says, "Yaas, I've killed a hedgehog, and not the first time my lady!" Why! we used to kill and cook 'em at the hopping, and roll 'em up in greasy brown paper and bake 'em, and they'd come out of their spikes as tender as a chicken, a'most. Pinch a few taters from the farmer, and there! you'd have a banquet. We used to get turnips too and one night some of the young lads they pinched a gurt turnip, hollowed it out, and set it on a stick with a lighted dip inside it, and then come wavering along in the di-rection of my dwelling. "Let's skeer ole Mother Culver," they says. I hears 'un, so I waits till they comes up close and then I pops out and I empt' a pail of soapy water over 'em, empt' it clean I did, and barks like a dog at 'em, and they did just re-tire in a hurry!

'Waal, my old man, he's gone now, and I expects he's enjoying the music. I feels happy about him, for up to the last he would always say his prayer. "God bless me an' make me a good boy for Christ's sake, Amen." And when I says to him, "Oh, don't say that, and you over seventy!" he says, " 'Tis a simple prayer, and Harriet, my gal, you can't be too simple when you're afore the Throne of Grace." And I thinks, "You poor poverty-struck creature you! and yet so nice, so nice in your thoughts.' "

✍

Old Elijah (proud of his fine head of hair), looking at old Ambrose's bald pate, 'My! My! Ambrose, you be got bald!' 'Aye, Lige,' you be a practical sort o' man, and you knows you can't grow two good crops on the same bit o' land; you can't grow 'air and brains.' 'No, Ambrose, very likely you can't, but an empty barn don't require no thatch.'

Are Farmers Fools?

IN one county we may find the farmer engrossed in hops and chicken-raising, for the higglers of the district are men of substance and will buy birds at good prices. In another corner of England the farmer is a sheep breeder and has never seen hops or a Dorking. Elsewhere he may have no sheep and may be a dairy farmer; most of his land is grass, like the sheep farmer's, but it is milk, butter or cheese, that he labours to produce. In a different part of the country, the farmer proves to be largely a grower of fruit. Journeying some few counties farther on, one may come across an agriculturist who makes much of his money by growing cabbage seed, nasturtium seed or turnip seed for nurserymen. There are farmers who keep scores of pigs, and farmers who have none. Others are producers of fat beasts. Some turn their attention to pedigree stock; they have a reputation in the horsey world of their county, or they possess a herd with a name. There are farmers who are corn growers, and farmers who never devote an acre more to cereals than is necessary to produce the straw and grain they need for their stock. One farmer may have seven hundred acres, and his neighbour only seventy. One may pass his day almost wholly on horseback and 'never soil his hands', confining his work, properly and profitably, to the directing of others. Another, perhaps with less land to manage, may drive his own sowing, mowing and reaping machines. One may possess several engines and the latest in threshing machines and grist mills. Another may not own a self-binder. One may have every implement and all the power he needs from one year's end to another. Another may find it more profitable to get his threshing and not a little other work done for him by neighbours. One man may keep as large a number of hands as the land will carry. Another may employ so little labour that if the weather is the least 'awkward' he runs great risk of endangering his crops. One man may make out of his farm every penny he gets. Another, in addition to

These intentionally elementary papers were written to help townsmen and townswomen with whose misunderstandings I had become acquainted in correspondence or in conversation. They were reprinted (with some condensation and alterations), from a book of mine called 'The Townsman's Farm', long since out of print.

260

his farming, may be a dealer, or derive profits from machine letting. One man may never go into the fields without a spud. Another man may have a foreman, or a bailiff, and may give tennis parties, and even a hunt breakfast. One man may be in a position to put into practice the latest lessons of agricultural science, may have notions as to the steaming of cattle food and the application of liquid manure, and may send his lads, whom he expects to follow him in the possession of the farm, to finish their education at an agricultural college. Another may 'take no stock in this 'ere science', have no prejudices against using super-phosphate and kainit instead of nitrate 'if it comes cheaper', and believe in 'the exploded fetish of the fallow' and the sanitary advantage of keeping a billy goat with sheep or horses. One man may be under the thumb of the corn merchant. Another, by the fortune of marriage or by the luck of being an only son or by good farming, may own his farm. One man may hunt and course and take no interest in politics. Another may be an orator at local meetings or a preacher. One man's house may be but a shelter for the rearing, feeding and sleeping of a family. Another farmhouse may be the scene of as keen and intellectual a life as was ever led in a London flat. How, again, compare one of the toilers on the stiff clays of Essex or Warwickshire with the dalesmen of Cumberland, the farmers of the sandy soil of Hampshire with the cultivators of the ground above granite in the Highlands? Their day's work is as different as the earth they till. Mr. Poyser from the the Midlands would be as much at a loss on Drumsheugh's land at Drumtochty as a Wessex agriculturist would be in the Eastern Counties parish of 'Juicy Joe'. Their technologies would be as strange to one another as their tools. They make their hay differently, they cock their corn differently, and they build it into stacks of a different pattern. What is the north-countryman likely to imagine a 'linhay' or a 'barton' to be, and what will the south-countryman make of 'byre' or 'braird', or 'police manure'? And think of the differences in 'the custom of the county'—in other words, in the unwritten agricultural law which so often involves the newcomer to a district in difficulties!

The man who sets out to learn farming by apprenticing himself to a farmer had need, indeed, to know his exact requirements, and to choose his instructor with care. Undoubtedly the popular impression of the work of the farmer is still that it does not need brains. Does the cartoonist's farmer seem to have brains? But try to realise what a series of obstacles the farmer has to encounter. To start with, he is often sorely hampered for want of capital. To farm to the best advantage you want good implements and plenty of labour. Now both are costly. The land must also be done well. This means a considerable bill for artificial manures and feeding stuffs—that is, linseed and cotton cakes, barley meal, middlings, bran, and so on, with which to stimulate the crops at second hand. Without a sufficiency of capital a man is tempted to cut his expenditure under these heads very fine indeed, and the land, which mostly treats the farmer as he treats it, uses him accordingly. Then there is the matter of rent. Though there may be cheap (and dirty) land in some places, the rents in not a few parts of England are admittedly high.

But the three most important factors of which the farmer has to take account have yet to be mentioned.

The first is the weather. The best farmer that was ever bred cannot do well in bad weather. If the sun bakes his fields so that his roots are dried up, so that there is no grass for his flocks or herds, or to such a degree that he cannot break up the clods on his roughly ploughed land; if rain keeps the earth too sticky for working or cleaning, or hinders the stacking of hay crop till the grass has dropped its seed or (if it has been cut) till much of the goodness is washed out of it, or prevents the corn harvest being gathered till the grain is knocked out or sprouting; if, instead of these visitations, there is not rain enough or heat enough when needed—of what avail is the most skilful agriculture?

A second factor in the commercial success of a farm is bird, animal, and insect pests. Whether it be corn, beans, or potatoes, the rooks may dig them out. If the corn reaches maturity its heads may be pulled. There may be the depredations of game. As to rats, I have known eighty to be killed out of one stack. Think what they spoiled as well as ate. Then there are mice, and 'the rat of the air', the sparrow, against which the farmer organizes sparrow clubs in vain. Foxes also prey on his poultry. Finally, there are insect and fungus pests, so numerous that it has taken dozens of Board of Agriculture leaflets to describe them.

The third difficulty is that, in spite of the great strides made of late years, farming is not an exact science. A certain course of action in the fields will not infallibly produce a certain result. Although much is known as to the conditions of success in agriculture, much is still to know. There are wide gaps in our knowledge. There are many working hypotheses,

'The worst of the country is that the lanes are so much alike!'
The drawing is by E. G. Barlow

but we have little more. Things may turn out as reckoned on, or they may not. For example, there is no one perfect way of manuring. A course of treatment which may answer in the next county, or the next parish, or the next field, is not necessarily the best to follow on other ground. In the early, self-satisfied days of artificial manuring the chemists gave themselves great airs as the farmers' friends. It was all so perfectly simple. You took a pound of soil, found out what it was made of, and you had simply to provide, by way of manure, the constituents it lacked. What could be easier? But we know now that there is a bacterial as well as a physical side to the soil, that what it contains of good must be not inert but effective, and that the soil must be able to assimilate what is given to it. The thing that makes farming so difficult, and also prevents the townsman from realising its difficulties, is that it is first and foremost a matter of experience, of practice, of industry, business aptitude, and common sense. These are not showy things. They are not things that you can get out of books, not things that are likely to be impressed on the mind of the townsman visitor to the fields during harvest. His impressions of the difficulties of farming are about as far-reaching as the average man's notion of the work of the baker, derived from the contemplation of the toast on the breakfast table.

Who is the average person who presumes to sit in hasty judgment, which is worth so little, on the followers of an art older than any other practised on earth? A man from a town, the conditions of life in which—if you come to consider the matter—are as different from the conditions of life in the country as Iceland is different from Italy. Within the period of a year he is in a rural district perhaps a whole month, possibly only a fortnight, very little of which, after all, is given to the study of agriculture.

Does he know enough of the business in hand to be able to tell whether the crop in the field he is passing is kohl rabi, swedes, mangel, or turnips? Does he know that meadows have to be manured; that, by manuring, one sort of plant therein may be increased and another exterminated—that, in fact, a hay crop has to be grown? Does he know that when the

264

corn is cut there is, as like as not, already another crop in the ground—clover, perhaps—getting ready for next year; and that the lucerne over there, which is being cut as green food for cattle, may give four crops a year for seven years, and may be sending its roots down into the soil the depth of a room? Does either 'valuation' or 'drainage' convey any practical idea to him? Do turnips present themselves to his mind as merely a means to an end? Are the rotation of crops, the signs of the ripening of grass and grain, the manner of their drying in stook and stack, and the bacterial action of clover in the ground, which makes it unnecessary to manure the wheat which succeeds it, a mystery?

The holiday-making critic not only talks of a subject of which he knows little or nothing, but a panacea of his for all farming ills, which he produces without apology, does not strike the farmer as altogether according to knowledge. He says what the farmer wants is education and modern methods. As we should most of us probably be the better for more education and more scientific methods in our work, the advice is not profound. No doubt the farmer would be the better for more education and more up-to-date methods. But the farmer wonders whether these things will alter the weather or the cost of labour. Will they make his farm buildings more convenient or provide him with capital?

The farmer from whom you may be inclined to generalize may be given to sitting by the fire in his socks. He may be doubtful as to the number of l's in 'always', and his blotting paper may be inferior. He may see no newspaper but the local weekly and a farming paper, and read little of them. He may be slow of speech and in talking to him it may be easy to use words he does not understand, and to speak of problems of which he has never heard. What is more natural than that he should meet with distrust the ignorance of townsfolk of his methods of work, and the real conditions in which he labours? He may be called conservative, behind the times, and content to get his living in a way involving (as the townsman believes) no great expenditure of brains. But he has the comfort of feeling, if he thinks of these matters, that he follows the calling which is perhaps the most honourable and the most rational of all; that, when the whole sum of things is reckoned, he may perhaps earn merit as one who, in feverish times, is content with a vocation which often yields those devoted to it little more than a livelihood, and in which independence, a life in the open air, and a position of a certain dignity, may be counted as a part of riches. No man in Britain keeps healthier hours than the farmer; his children are as a class, the most robust that are born; and it is in the strength of the loins of such as he that the towns, which deride him, live and move and have their being. The average farmer is probably twice as good a man as the average town critic imagines him to be.

❧

The Thatcher

THERE ain't nothing can beat a dumplin'. When my son and me was down in Wilt Shire last summer, thatchin' we missed 'em terrible. Our landlady, she say, if I'll tell her how to make 'em she'll have a try. So I kind o' 'splained to her as best I could, and one Sunday she made some. Man alive, you never see such things! Could 'a played football with 'em, and little totty things an' all, no bigger than the palm of your hand. Eat 'em? 'Tain't likely. Couldn't get 'em down! There was a man staying with us two Bank Holidays ago, hadn't seen a dumplin' for twenty-five year. He ate four on 'em right away. There was another on the dish, and I axed him if he wouldn't have that one. 'No', he say, 'I've done my share an' all; but I hadn't eaten a dumplin' for twenty-five year, and I wanted to make sure'.—*B.N.*

❧

A minister bought a car for pastoral visitations. Meeting a parishioner one day, he explained to him—only to be told, 'Your Master had a bigger parish, but He did it a' on His ain twa feet, an' whiles the back o' a cuddy.'

The boy at the Scottish village school would sniff. Every day the teacher asked him if he had a handkerchief and he never had. At last she said, 'Hasn't your father a handkerchief?' 'Aye,' he said, 'he's got two—yin for his neck and yin for his piece (lunch).'

Survivals of Pre-Enclosure England
by C. D. Linnell

ALTHOUGH, as far as I can ascertain, there is no perfect specimen of a village such as existed almost everywhere in our Midland counties for at least a thousand years before the enclosure movement of 1750–1840, it is possible to reconstruct one from several partial survivals, each having several of the following characteristics: (1) The three-field system, with the rotation of wheat, spring corn, and fallow; (2) the division of each 'field' into furlongs; (3) the division of each furlong into acre and half-acre strips; (4) grass baulks between the furlongs; (5) ridge-and-furrow cultivation; (6) common pasture; (7) common meadow, often subject to annual re-allotment of its strips; (8) waste; (9) rights of common attached to 'ancient tenements'; (10) a court to settle disputes.

Following more or less in the steps of Dr. Slater, who twenty-five years ago set out on a tour of exploration before writing his 'English Peasantry and the Enclosure of Common Fields', I visited in the course of 1931 the representative villages of Laxton in Notts, Yarnton in Oxfordshire, and Soham in Cambridgeshire; now I propose to describe in some detail what I saw there. At Laxton I had the privilege of being conducted round the parish by Mr. Cartledge, the clerk of the field-jury. I found three large open fields of some 350 acres each, with the ancient rotation of wheat, spring corn (or roots, clover, and peas), and fallow. These fields are divided into ridged-up strips, which are separated by furrows, with short stakes at intervals to mark the boundaries between the various holdings. Here, however, the old system has been somewhat modernized; for, whereas formerly a middling farmer had 40 or 50 scattered strips averaging half-an-acre each, these are now larger and more regular, and the same man has now only five or six strips of four or five acres each, distributed fairly equally between the three fields. This is due to the action of Earl Manvers, the lord of the manor, who, having bought up all the open-field land, consolidated and redistributed the ancient strips about twenty years ago, in order to make matters more convenient all round.

The system is administered by a field-jury, which consists of twelve men and a foreman. The jurymen are pricked off in turn by the bailiff of the manor from the suit roll, which contains the names of all the owners of common rights. Any man pricked for the jury who refuses to serve is fined half-a-crown. The decisions of the jury are confirmed by the manor court, or court-leet, which meets every November after the jury has perambulated the fields. In the course of this itinerary it inspects ditches and baulks and, later, reports delinquents to the Court. On occasion the lord himself has been fined for non-observance of the regulations. The jury also announces the 'breaking of the field' after harvest, and the annual sales of the grass on the lanes and 'sykes'.

As regards common rights, these were formerly attached to the possession of a toft, or 'ancient tenement', and the possession of land in the open arable fields conferred no additional advantage. Again, a man could buy up several tofts, but could exercise only one right. There are now sixteen common rights attached to cottages without open-field land, some of these being owned by freeholders, the rest by Lord Manvers. In accordance with the revision of the rules in 1908 these rights can only be exercised on the common, or moor, while the Earl's open-field tenants alone are allowed to 'graze' the open fields. Each right is limited to ten sheep, three beasts, or two horses, and no one may sub-let. Moreover there are other rights divided unequally between the tofts—now more often called common right houses—and known as gait-rights. Apparently the common meadow was enclosed in the eighteenth century, so that many 'small' farmers largely depend for their hay on patches of grass—about twenty-eight in number—which lie scattered over the open fields. These are called sykes (pronounced 'sicks'), and those situated near by the two fields under crops are sold, for mowing, by auction. The proceeds are divided among the commoners in proportion to the number of gait-rights they possess. On the wheat and the bean-and-clover field unlimited stock can be turned out for a few weeks after the 'breaking of the field'. On the fallow field, from November 23 to October 8, twenty sheep—but no cattle or horses—are allowed to each holder. The system enables 'small' commoners who are industrious to become open-field farmers; indeed it is stated that most of the farmers were once labourers or sons of such. They are all, I was told, more than ready to help one another with horses and labour, and, as a rule, they cheerfully pay the fines levied on them by the jury. If this is so, Laxton is a genuine survival of the ancient village community, not only in outward appearance, but in spirit.

The old and once widely spread custom of annually reallotting the common meadow, which, in spite of the yearly sale of the sykes, can hardly be said to survive at Laxton, I found in full force at Yarnton. The striking resemblance of the local method to that of certain Indian villages, described by Gomme in his "Village Community", cannot be accidental and indicates that it dates back to a remote antiquity. Even the language of the sale catalogue is archaic, for various lots are respectively described as Three-quarters of William of Bladon; the Tidals; Dun; Half of Rothe; Walter Geoffrey, etc. At the sale, which takes place early in July, it is not so much the meadow strips which are auctioned as thirteen wooden balls, each of which has its special name, e.g., 'Harry', 'Parry', 'Watery Molly', 'Bolton', 'Green', these names being identical with names of the strips. Two annually elected officials, known as 'meadsmen', are responsible for the custody of the balls, which are carefully stored in a bag. On the Monday after the sale the buyers assemble at the middle of the nearest meadow, called Oxey or Oxhay, where they are met by the two meadsmen with the bag. Oxey, to which I paid a visit, is divided into three 'draughts', each of which contains thirteen strips, or 'lots', set out by wooden posts. There are also four acres of rectorial glebe called tydals. As soon as everyone is ready, some independent person—a woman by preference—is deputed to extract the balls. Perhaps she begins by pulling out the ball known as 'Harry'. One of the meadsmen calls out the name, and the buyer of 'Harry' comes forward and claims the first strip 'drawn'. This receives the name 'Harry' for the ensuing year.

He is followed by a mower, who swishes off the grass round him in a circle, whereupon another man with a knife cuts the initials of the purchaser in the cleared space. The company now moves on to the second strip, where the same ceremony takes place; and so across all the first thirteen strips. The other two 'draughts' are dealt with in exactly the same way, one meadsman carrying the bag, the other recording in a note-book the names of the buyers and the location of the strips. West Mead is 'drawn' on the following Thursday; Pixey, on the following Monday. The final phase of the ceremony is known as 'running the treads', certain men being appointed to tread out narrow stripes between the 'lots' in order to prevent confusion and unpleasantness later. The lots are put up for auction by farmers who for any reason do not wish to mow theirs, the lord of the manor, and the rector. How-ever, not all the lots in the three meadows are auctioned, as many strips are let with the local farms. At the sale the 'commons' are also sold—ten 'commons' usually going to one lot. Each 'common' entitles one horse and one cow to share in the 'after-field' from August 24 onwards. The boundaries between the lots are then no longer respected. I have obtained my knowledge from various kindly local informants, especially Miss Walton (a 'meadsman'), the vicar, and Mrs. Hounsell, the schoolmistress; also from an interesting narrative, written before the War, by Miss Agnes Evans. A full account of the procedure, with its history and, incidentally a description of the disorder and fighting that used to go on up to 1817, is given in 'Three Oxfordshire Parishes' by Mrs. Bryan Stapleton (Oxford Historical Society's publications).

Like almost every open-field village, Soham has its special peculiarities. Most of the land is, or rather was, copyhold and, as such, was administered by a manorial court. There are no furlongs, but the strips still lie intermixed. Only they are much larger and fewer than formerly, since, whenever a strip is sold, it is almost invariably bought by the owner of one of the contiguous strips and thrown into his holding. The even course of such consolidation is however hindered by the fact that isolated strips of church and charity land lie irregularly all over the parish. There are four large commons and two horse-fens. The latter can only be used by holders of open-field land, each of whom has the right to turn out one horse or one bullock for every twelve acres of arable. Mr. Fisk, my guide and informant, holds the office of 'fen-reeve'. The system pertinent to the commons properly so-called is quite different: every cottager who pays a rent of less than £6 a year has a common right. This is unusual, as in most villages possessing commons these rights belong only to owners of 'ancient tenements' and are very jealously guarded.

The only important feature of the old English village-community which I have not yet seen is the sub-division of a field known as a furlong or 'shot'. Such areas may still exist and some reader may be able to tell me about them.

The Skimmity Ride

ONE evening, sixty years ago, just as dusk was falling, my sisters and I and our nurse, at our nursery window, heard the noise of kettles and pans, and, I think, a drum being beaten in the distance, to the quick march of a large body of men and some women. As the crowd passed we, with our little snub noses (I know mine was) flattened against the panes, were frightened by the apparition of two ghostly figures, hung high on 12-foot poles. Our old nurse said, 'It's the "skimmity" for Jack Evans and Meg Haspey. I knowed it would come to this'. There were big dolls dressed in white night clothes, with the grotesque head of a man and a woman, one crowning each pole. The bearers of the poles jigged about and the 'ghosts' followed these movements, sometimes with their faces turned towards each other and again turning away as though they would be apart. These were taken to a field in the village at night time and the people of the neighbour-hood danced round them to the light of flares.—*M*.

Riddles. When it's up it's down, and when it's down it's up; what is it? (Peewit and it's crest.) Two lookers, two crookers, four stiff-standers, four diddle-danders, and a wig-wag. (A cow).

Water, by *Thomas Rayson, F.R.I.B.A.*

THERE are countrified places in which a main supply is possible. Apart from such a company water supply, the village you have hit on may have some sort of a piped supply from a little resevoir filled by a ram or a windmill. If the source or system is already fully taxed, you might offer to increase catchment areas or extend retaining tanks to increase it. The local sanitary inspector will explain the situation. Perhaps you must be independent. Your land may have a watercourse emerging at a level thirty feet or so higher than the level of the position selected for your house. You should find the running water course, drive back into the earth till you get it clear and uncontaminated, and build in bricks in cement, a well at least six feet deep and 2 ft. 6 ins. diameter, covered down with concrete. From this well run a half-inch galvanized iron or jointed earthenware pipe to a storage tank, of say 1,000 gallons, from which you will take your supply. Thus you will be served by gravity without machine pumping (which, by the way, may be by one sort of ram or another, by windmill or by a motor with a cable from your electric light outfit or the company's line.)

Normally you will sink a well. Don't be prejudiced; geology and water divining appear to be opposed, but be wise and employ a diviner.* Take implicitly his guidance with regard to the presence of water. Take notice of his estimate of its strength and take with a pinch of salt his guess at the probable depth at which you will reach water. Water will percolate all permeable material such as sand until it reaches the retaining stratum of rock or clay. This is certain to have an irregular surface, so there is an underground system of watercourses. Your diviner will indicate a point over one or more of these lines. In an area of green sand at a considerable depth you may get a sort of lake or a subjugated Thames; then you will get water 'anywhere'. Make your well large enough to give you a good storage and build it in open brickwork sufficiently to allow for the flow of water. Above that

---

*Two books are *The Modern Dowser   A practical Guide* by Vicomte Henry de France, and *Water Diviners and their Methods*, by Henri Mager.

build in bricks in cement or concrete tubes well puddled at the back with clay. If you use bricks, well bricks of $4\frac{1}{2}$ in. thickness are stronger than ordinary bricks of 9 in. thickness. Do not try to use ordinary bricks laid $4\frac{1}{2}$ in. thick. It is not only courting further trouble, but is dangerous to the well-sinker if he builds on a drum.

The best position for the well may be in a part of the garden where an erection for the engine or dynamo would be an obstruction. Then construct a chamber below ground which will accommodate the plant. A manhole cover on top and step irons will make it accessible. A hole must be left in the top just over the line of the ram for the extraction of the rod in case of repairs. To ventilate this chamber, flues should be formed in the thickness of the walls and on opposite sides, one going to the floor, the other just under the ceiling. In times of frost these should be stopped, especially if there is a water-cooled engine. The pump must be placed within a distance of 25 feet of the water. It is usually fixed on two baulks of oak, built into the walls of the well and operated by a rod from the machine above. If you do not provide some permanent means of descending into the well (and very seldom is this done) place your manhole cover so that a ladder can be put down.

As to the tank in the roof space for storage of water pumped from the well, beware of frost. Case and pack the tanks and thoroughly wrap the pipes exposed to any unheated atmosphere. A novel way of protecting the main tank, if it is in the roof space, is to case it and seal it above and to construct a lattice or other open panel in the ceiling just under. The hot air from the house will rise and keep the water from freezing.

*

A newcomer to our village favoured hand-woven material for her window-curtains. 'Hey, mister,' said an old inhabitant one day to the lady's husband, 'when's thy missus gwain ter taake down they sack bags an' put up summat proper?'

A farmer came to an estate office to get some drain pipes. The agent's lad who was of the age when he thought himself extremely clever, said, 'We'll have to raise your rent.' The reply was, 'Yes, my lad, I wish you would, for it takes me all *my* time to raise it.'

The Truth About the Dunmow Flitch

THE first mention of the Dunmow Flitch—Dunmow (with the accent on the first syllable) is in Essex—is in Chaucer and in 'The Vision of William concerning Piers the Plowman'. As the modern ceremony is but an August Bank Holiday diversion, without historical justification, it is of interest to turn to the Chartulary of Dunmow Priory (at the British Museum) and see exactly what happened, in the words of Dugdale's *Monasticon*, when a man 'that repents him not of his marriage in a year and a day lawfully went to Dunmow' for the bacon. The entry of 1445 runs: 'Memorandum: that one Richard Wright, of Badbourge, near the City of Norwich, in the County of Norfolk, Yeoman, came and required the bacon of Dunmow on the 27th day of April, in the 23rd year of the reign of King Henry VI, and according to the form of the charter, was sworn before John Cannon, Prior to this place and the Convent, and many other neighbours, and there was delivered to him, the said Richard, one Flitch of Bacon'. An entry of 1510 (temp. Henry VIII) records the success of Thomas le Fuller before Prior Tils, 'as also before a multitude of neighbours'.

After the dissolution of the monasteries, the bacon-giving seems to have passed to the lords of the manor of Little Dunmow. They held their courts—as they have been held within living memory—at Priory Place, formerly a farmhouse and now four cottages. In a parchment book belonging to a former lord an account of the ceremonies of 1701 is as follows: 'A Court Baron of the worshipful Sir Thomas May, Knight, there holden of Fryday, the 27th day of June in the Thirteenth year of King William ye Third and in ye year 1701 before Thomas Wheeler, Gent., steward of the said Court. Be it remembered that att the Said Court it is found and presented by the Homage aforesaid that John Reynolds of Hatffeld Regis, alias Hatfield Broadoak, in the County of Essex, gent., and Ann his wife have been married for the space of ten years last, part and upwards, and it is likewise found, presented by the Homage aforesaid that the said John

---

This was condensed from a little book I once wrote, *The Story of the Dunmow Flitch*.

Reynolds and Ann his wife by means of their Quiet, Peaceable, Tender and Loving Cohabitation for the said space of time, came and claimed the Bacon. Whereupon the said Steward, with the Jury, suitors and other officers of the Court, proceded with the usual solemnity to the ancient and accustomed place for the Administration of the Oath (and receiving the the Bacon aforesaid), that is to say to the two great stones lying near the church door (the stones still lie there) within the said Manor. Whereupon the said John Reynolds and Ann kneeling down on the said two stones the said Steward did administer unto them the Oaths (that they in a twelve month and a day repented not in thought any way), and immediately thereupon ye said John Reynolds and Ann, claiming the said Bacon, the Court pronounced sentence for the same, and accordingly a Gammon of Bacon with the usual solemnity was delivered unto John Reynolds and Ann his wife'.

With the gift of the bacon, in 1751, to Thomas Shakeshaft, weaver, and his wife Ann—the proceedings are reported in the *Gentlemen's Magazine* of the time and a painting was made by a local artist, David Ogbourne—we have 'the last legitimate instance' of the ceremony. The certificate of the worthy Thomas survives. Both his wife and he signed with a cross.

*

'Well ye know, mum, James be main bad, be he; 'e lost conscientiousness.'

'If ye want to know where he lives, he lives by the church; but if ye want to know where he bides, he bides at the public.'

'These 'ere ditches wants cleanin' out,' said the roadman; 'bungful o' sentiment.'

Teacher in a northern infant school, 'How old are you?' Sandy: 'Aw dinna ken.' Teacher: 'Ask your mother then, Sandy, and let me know.' Sandy: 'A' richt, teacher, aw'll speir, bit aw dinna think ma mither wad ken. Aw wis born doon at ma granny's.'

The vicar thought of buying a horse from him, and, after the farmer got the Reverend into the trap with him it ran away. The vicar said, 'I'd give a pound to be out of this cart, Brown.' The old chap replied, 'If ye divvent hold tight, hinney, ye'll be out for nowt.'

Why do Chimneys Smoke?

FIRSTLY a chimney needs height, because the 'draw' or upward movement of air and smoke through it depends upon the fact that the hot air in the flue is expanded—and therefore lighter in weight than an equal volume of the colder air, outside the flue. Secondly, there must be an ample supply of cold air to support combustion of the fuel, and to displace the heated air and smoke, thus forcing them up the flue. If all the doors and windows in a room are tightly sealed, and there is a fire in the grate, the cool air that cannot get in by any other means will actually pass down the same flue, although in doing so it will certainly bring a great deal of the smoke with it. If you find that the flue draws when the door is open, but not when it is shut, cut a small hole in the hearth and lay a pipe from it to the open air outside the house. If you have wood floors in the lower storey of the house it is usually sufficient to knock a hole through the hearth into the space under the floor. The air then comes through the ventilators that are always provided to prevent the woodwork rotting. In regard to the flue itself, it should be of an even size throughout its length, so that the rising current of hot air and smoke is not caused to eddy and whirl. A frequent defect is the existence of a cavernous space just above the fire due to the fireplace opening having been built too high, The cold air that collects in this space chills the rising gases; as they become heavy when cold they descend into the room. If you find that rain drops hiss and splutter in the fire, the flue runs straight up to the chimney pot. A careful builder makes the flue travel, first to one side, and then to the other, so that when the bricklayer looks up it, from the fireplace, before the grate is fixed, he cannot see daylight. This cranking of the flue is of great help in breaking up the down draughts. 'Down draughts may be caused by the wind striking the side of a higher building, or trees, thus setting up swirling air currents. Sometimes a strong wind will blow so fiercely across the top of a flue that it will not let the smoke come out, and this may be suspected when the wind in a certain quarter always causes smoking. A revolving 'lobster back' cowl is usually a cure for this trouble. An old-fashioned remedy is to bed a half-round ridge tile over the top of the flue, with its side facing the direction from which the troublesome winds flow.

When rain soaks that part of a chimney above the roof it makes it cold and causes sluggish draught. Many chimneys have only 4½ inches of brickwork around the flues. Nine inches, that is, a whole brick thickness, is not too much, and in a new house, where the external walls are built hollow, the chimneys would gain in appearance and efficiency if this hollow walling were extended to encase and protect the flues in the stacks. If there is no aesthetic objection, existing chimney-stacks that are rain-soaked may be plastered on their exposed surfaces with waterproofed cement mortar. All new chimney stacks might with advantage be built with waterproofed cement mortar from below where they emerge from the roof. Every bed joint is then a horizontal damp-proof course, and prevents the rain which drives into the bricks from soaking down, and showing in the rooms.—*L.E.W.*

❦

'I wants a garment for the missus, Miss, but I don't know what you calls it, but if it were for I, it ud be a vest and a pair of pants.'

From a market town teashop: 'Let's go to the pictures.' 'What's the film?' ' "Rhodes of Africa".' 'Oh, I suppose they do have roads there now.'

'Keeping boys and girls to school till they be fifteen, will they? Next they'll be having them there maternical centres.'

Country builder on being consulted about getting the greatest possible amount of sunshine into the proposed bungalow: 'Why not build it like a hell?' (An 'L'.)

Farmer to man crossing field: 'Nar then, neäbor, thar beant nar road 'cross thar.' 'No, an' ah beant gawn ter starp 'en make narn, but t'were a ner cut ter wer ah had ter get.'

'Have had 56 years in the fish trade,' the Grimsby fishmonger wrote to his country customer, 'and never had such a week as this. Fog, snow, inability to get supplies, rumours of war, and everything rotten, then this King business and a big fire in our street and no herrings and no kips, anyway I have done my best, and it won't matter in 2036.'

Jane Wenham, a Witch
by Raymond Walker

IT is only 220 years since the prosecution in this country of a woman as a witch. The trial took place at the Hertford Assizes, the accused being Jane Wenham of Walkern, a village near Stevenage, about thirty miles out of London along the Great North Road.

The case provoked a series of pamphlets—those virulent attacks and counter-attacks which were a feature of life in the seventeenth and eighteenth centuries. The first pamphlet was written by the Rev. Francis Bragge, the grandson of the magistrate who committed Jane to gaol. This forty-page production, entitled 'A Full and Impartial Account of the Discovery of Sorcery and Witchcraft, Practis'd by Jane Wenham upon the Bodies of Anne Thorn, Anne Street, &c.', sold for sixpence a copy and ran into five editions (four in a month). There were two replies. One is 'A Full Confutation of Witchcraft: In a Letter from a Physician in Hertfordshire'. The other sets out to prove 'The Impossibility of Witchcraft'. The Rev. Francis Bragge duly replied in 'Witchcraft Farther Display'd', and was answered by other pamphlets. The best and longest is 'The Case of the Hertfordshire Witch-craft Considered', in which the author shrewdly remarks that 'Age, Poverty, and a Perverse Temper of Mind, are the three principal Ingredients which enter into the Composition of a Modern Witch'.

The story opens with John Chapman, a farmer at Walkern, who, in the Rev. Francis Bragge's words, 'long entertain's a Suspicion, that the strange Deaths of many of his and the Neighbours Horses and Cattle were occasion'd by the Witch-crafts of this Woman, and thought that he himself had suffer'd by them to the value of 200*l.* in a short Time; but not being able to prove any Thing upon her, he waited till Time should present a favourable Opportunity of Convicting her.' Then: 'Matthew Gilston, Servant to the abovesaid John Chapman, before Sir Henry Chauncy, says upon Oath, That on New-Year's-Day past, he, carrying Straw upon a Fork from Mr.

Gardiner's Barn, met Jane Wenham, who asked him for some Straw, which he refused to give her. That when this Informant was threshing in the Barn of his Master, an old Woman in a Riding hood or Cloak, he knows not which, came to the Barn Door, and asked him for a Pennyworth of Straw; he told her he could give her none, and she went away muttering. And this Informant saith, That after the Woman was gone he was not able to work, but ran out of the Barn as far as a Place called Munder's Hill (which is about Three Miles from Walkerne) and asked at a House there for a Pennyworth of Straw, and they refusing to give him any, he went farther to some Dung-heaps, and took some Straw from thence, and pull'd off his Shirt, and brought it Home in his Shirt; he knows not what moved him to this, but says he was forc'd to it, he knows not how. This odd Story made John Chapman suspect that Jane Wenham had play'd this trick upon his Servant; and soon after he meeting her, told her, of it, and in Heat of Anger call'd her a Witch and Bitch.'

Naturally, Jane resented this, and went to Sir Henry Chauncy to obtain redress for the slander. Sir Henry referred the parties to the rector, the Rev. Godfrey Gardiner, who gave both the farmer and the witch pastoral advice and ordered the man to pay Jane one shilling. Enraged by this paltry award Jane went away, ominously remarking that if she could not obtain justice there she would get it elsewhere.

Now the rector had a maid named Anne Thorn, aged sixteen, whose knee had just been set after dislocation. A few minutes after Jane Wenham had left the rectory, a shrieking from the kitchen made the rector and Mrs. Gardiner rush there. They found Anne Thorn stripped to her shift, screaming and pointing to a bundle of twigs wrapped in her clothes. When she calmed down she related a story not unlike that told by Matthew Gilston, of a goose-chase to gather twigs, with the additional details that she had leaped a five-barred gate and run for over a mile (at a rate exceeding eight miles per hour!) despite her recently dislocated knee; and that an old woman met her when she was gathering the twigs and gave her a crooked pin to fasten the bundle. To take a pin from a witch, it was well known, made the recipient an easy victim for future witchcraft.

Mrs. Gardiner, remembering the country superstition that a witch would appear immediately if anything belonging to her were burnt, threw the pin and sticks on the fire—and in walked Jane Wenham. Her excuse about having forgotten a message for Anne's mother did nothing to counteract the sensation of her untimely arrival.

Anne Thorn continued for several days to have these impulses to run and leap, and at first the whole village, including Arthur Chauncy, the Magistrate's son, followed her to see what would happen and to restrain the suicidal tendencies that also developed. Further, some kind of convulsions accompanied the impulses, so that now she felt as if she were being pinched, now she was in terrible pain, and now she 'was in great Misery and Torture, Speechless, but all the Time very sensible'.

It was considered only proper to make Jane Wenham visit Ann Thorn to try and calm the girl by taking off the spell; but despite all entreaties and offers of money the old woman absolutely refused to emerge from her cottage, and double-locked the door. The village constable, armed with a warrant for her apprehension on a charge of felony and witchcraft broke in, arrested her and took her to the rectory. Immediately Anne Thorn saw Jane she flew at her and scratched her forehead so hard that 'the noise of her Nails seem'd as it were scratching against a Wainscot'. Jane merely held her head still and said 'Scratch harder, Nan, and fetch Blood of me if you can'—but no blood came: a sure proof that Jane was indeed a witch! Not quite satisfied about this test Arthur Chauncy later took one of the many pins that had been magically and invisibly conveyed into Anne's hand and stuck it a great many times right up to its head in Jane's arm. But again no blood flowed, only a little thin, watery serum.

As another test, Mr. Strutt, vicar of Ardeley, tried in vain to make Jane repeat the Lord's Prayer correctly, but, like all witches, she invariably stumbled at the clause 'Lead us not into temptation'. A day or two later Jane was searched for marks of witchcraft, i.e. teats that the Devil could suck.

'But no Mole or Wart, or any Excrescency, passing current for the Stamp of the Devil', was found. Shortly after her arrest, under a cross-examination by Mr. Strutt and Mr. Gardiner, the two parsons, Jane Wenham confessed that she had been a witch for sixteen years and had bewitched Anne Thorn. But by that time the old woman was herself in a bewitched condition, and would have answered 'Yes' to almost any questions suggested to her.

Meanwhile the episode of the Cats began. 'About 7 or 8 at Night she (Anne Thorn) said she saw Things like Cats appear to her' and 'A dismal Noise of Cats was heard . . . about the House, sometimes their cry resembling that of Young Children at other times they made a Hellish Noise to which nothing can be resembled; this was accompany'd by Scratchings heard by all that were in the House, under the Windows, and Doors'. Later Arthur Chauncy bravely killed a prowling tom-cat and the noises ceased. But from then till after the trial, Anne Thorn, and a later victim of the witch, a girl named Anne Street, continued to be visited by an 'Apparition either of Jane Wenham in her own Shape, or that of a Cat, which speaks to her, and tempts her to destroy her self with a Knife'. The grand jury found a True Bill. At the trial the Lord's Prayer and other tests, the dislocated knee, the cats, and Anne Thorn's fits—Anne conveniently had one in Court —were offered in evidence, and the common jury were convinced. Not so the judge, and though Jane was found guilty and condemned, he reprieved her until further orders.

The judge, the Honourable Sir John Powell, Kt., 'was an old fellow with grey hairs, the merriest old gentleman ever seen, who spoke pleasant things until he chuckled and cried again'—that, at least, is how Swift described him to Stella. After the trial was over he obtained a free pardon for Jane from the Queen.

Jane lived for nearly twenty years after her trial, though she was then over seventy, dying on January 11th, 1730, and was buried in Hertingfordbury churchyard.

✍

'Just a line hoping this finds you as it leaves me,' wrote the cottager's wife to her old mistress, 'in very low spirits and expecting again soon.'

Things I should Now Do Differently

by an ex-Londoner

I F I were once more making my trek from London into the country, the first thing I should do differently would be to have a smaller house. In going to live in the country, where so many things seem to be cheaper than in London, it is easier than in town to slip into taking a house that is bigger than one's needs. But every additional room counts in the cost and strain of living.

I am clear that I should have done well to have had a better view. Whether from the garden on a fine day or from the house on a wet or very cold day, satisfying, I should almost say, bracing prospects, and a wide view of the stars at night play no small part in the happy life.

I do not regret buying my house. But, if I were to start all over again, I should hold even a firmer control over myself than I thought I was doing and wait until I had been a year or even two in the house before spending quite so much on the property. One may think one is spending prudently, but only after one has been some time in a place is it possible to know what expenditure is really desirable and defensible. I should certainly not get for my place, if I sold it, as much as I have spent on it.

I am sure that I did right in having an architect. I wish I had spent more on him.

The only thing that I ought to have spent more freely on at the beginning was trees. I continually regret that some of my trees have missed the year's growth they would have had if I had planted more confidently when I first arrived.

In making a garden I am sure that one has to check one's tendency to make extensions. There is no use in having more than enough. One must continually view the garden—and the lawns—in the light of being one person's or two persons' or as-many-more-persons-as-you-like's work. Are these persons available?

I ought certainly to have satisfied myself more completely about the water supply. And I ought to have dug underground

282

tanks and arranged for the electric light engine to do the pumping. Electric light, central heating, an Aga and a good laundry I have not regretted. This is an anxious matter. I think my central heating (a thing in which there are constant advances) could have been better planned. I ought to have spent more.

In the matter of domestic and even outdoor labour I am more and more disposed to believe that the more educated it is the more economical it is. If I were beginning again I should have every reasonable labour-saving device (provided that it could be easily repaired when necessary). But there is little profit in placing labour-saving devices in the hands of people who cannot understand or appreciate them.

We have not regretted any of the local public work we have done. But if the village is small it is a mistake to allow organisations to lean on one. Set them going and (after resolutely cross-examining yourself as to their real value) contrive to help them to keep going; but as soon as ever possible, let them move under their own steam. In a village it is only too easy to take oneself too seriously. On the other hand, there is a great deal in most rural districts which wants taking very seriously indeed. And a constant danger is, if not idleness, at least having an easier and more complacent life of it than one would be likely to have if one were still in London under the observation of people of equal or wider information and experience. One must not be a refugee from life. It is imperative to possess facilities, by being on a good train service, for getting frequently a kind of mental wash and brush up.

I have said nothing of livestock. I have never regretted having too little. I have often found I had too much.

❧

Aged sexton to equally aged colonel in the churchyard, 'I don't want to hurry you, sir, but you'd best pick your bit or all the best places will be took.'

Irishwoman on her husband: 'Himself's that durty, the durt's just ditched intil 'im. One day I cu'd stand the look ov him no longer, so I got a good bucket ov hot wather an' a scrubbing brush, an' I riz a foam on his face ye'd a' thought 'twas the Atlantic ocean.'

A Countryman on Holiday in 1758

IT is Mr. Albert Harland, who was for six years one of the M.P.'s for Sheffield, to whom indebtedness must be expressed for this record of a rural Yorkshireman's record of a holiday in 1758. The writer was Richard Sawdon, of Brompton,which is ten miles from Scarborough. Sawdon's daughter married Captain Pierson, who was the father of Mr. Harland's grandmother. The Brompton farm came to Mr. Harland's grandfather, Dr. Harland of Scarborough—see Smiles' Invention and Industry—and is now owned by Mr. Harland's youngest brother. The diary passed to Mr. Harland from his uncle, Henry Seaton Harland, who obtained it from the widow of Henry Gowan Hudson of Leeds, Mr. Harland's first cousin.

The degree to which the document is concerned with eating is extraordinary. This profound interest in meals is characteristic, however, of other personal memoranda of the period. Sawdon seems to have been a dullish fellow, but the records of his sight-seeing and his dining are of some historical value; and he does make us understand how restricted was the point of view of thousands of reasonably well-to-do people a hundred and seventy years ago. There is a monument to him in Brompton church. His diary is reproduced without alteration, except for the insertion of a few full stops to make the meaning clear.

July 10, 1758.—At 11 a Clock set out for Malton. Dined there on a couple of boiled Rabbits & rosted Fowls & at five the same Day set out for York.

York.—Arived at half past eight. Suped on boiled salmon & a Couple of rosted Fowls & Breakfasted and Dined next Day at Mr. Ogels with Brother and Miss Farnip. On Thursday Morning set of in the post Chase

Ferrybridge, July 12.—Arived at four a Clock. Dined on a Couple of boiled Rabbits & beef Stakes with Tarts; Jellies &c as usual

Doncaster, July 12.—Arived at eight in the Evening, suped on rosted Fowls, ham & green Pease: next Morning called upon Mr. Haugh: returned to our Inn & Dined upon Mutton Chops and rost Ducks & drank Tea at Mr Haughs. Dined

& drank Tea the next Day at his House. On Sunday the 15th went to Church. Herd a sermon by the Revd. Mr. Rudd, text Ecclesiastees, Chap. 11th, vers 15th. Dined at the Inn on beef stakes, rosted Rabbits, a rice Pudding, Tarts &c., Drank Tea & supped at Mr. Haugh's. Took Chase on Monday at twelve a Clock

Retford, July 16.—at four a Clock Dined on Sammon & Lam stakes: walked out to see the Stocking Weaver at Work. Bought Goosberys of him at a penney pr pound: in the morning some of the Inhabitants was taken into Custodey for Exciteing the Soldgers quarter'd there to Mutany & afterwards striking the Collonel

Grantham.—Suped at half past nine on veal Beef stakes & Tarts. Found Iron upon the road which the Driver observed was tending to good Furton to us all. Breakfasted at nine and then perseeded on our Jurney at ten a Clock

Stamford, July 17.—Arived at half past two at the Georg Inn. Walked thence to Burleigh Castle. Spent three ours in seeing the Paintings, one pice which was Buteful vallied at sixteen thousand pound which was our Savour Blessing the Elements: the Whole Painting is extreemley Buteful & esteem the first Collection in England. After seeing the House was treated by a Lady with Peaches. Returned to the Inn at five a Clock & Dined on veal Cutlets & rost Beef and tarts &c. On passing Milton saw the barriks for Soldiers & ten Thousand Prisners. They was made of Wood & Coverd with tile & appeard like a little village. Chainged & perseeded.

Bugden, July 18.—arived at half past 11. Drank Tea for which they Charged two shillings each. Took Chase at six in the morning

Stevenage.—Breakfasted at nine, walked in the Garden, saw some Courous Shroubs, one pirticlur calld the Sider Bladder

Barnet, July 19.—Dined at four a Clock on beef & a fillet of veal with Tarts, charged 2s 6d each

London.—Arived at Snow Hill and in the Evening walked to see St. Palls

July 20.—Went to see the Bank of England which was Crouded with People & large Heaps of Gould, surprising to see & not usal to be seen in Yorkshire with Shovels to take it up. Then went to see the Royal Exchange which is a very Noble Bulding. Then perseeded to Mr. Seatons. He went a long with us to Mrs Comas who soon recolected us & was glad to see us. Drank Tea with us at our Lodgen.

July 21.—In the Morning went to see Blackfriers Bridge & the River. Perseeded to Summerset House. Went in to difrant apartments of it, from thense to Drury Lane Theatre to see it. From thence to Charing cross & up pall Mall. Saw Carlton House the resedence of the Prince of Wales. Went through St James and after that to the Kings Pallace. Went to see the Armour. From thence to St James park a long the bird Cage Walk to near Buckingham House. Then went round the Perade & to the Horse guards past by the Duke of Yorks House & white Hall. Bought severel artickels at Shops in the Strand, Fleet Street &c. After that returned to our Lodgens and spent the Evening very agreeable

Sunday, July 22.—In the morning went to St Pauls. Herd a Sermon perticklar Addressed to the Fleet Street Vollanteers who marched in form with musick from the Church Where there was Thouseands of People. We went & Dined with Mrs. Combs in Kings Street Holborn. Went in the Evening to the Foundling Chappel. Returned to Mrs. Comes and Supped.

Monday, 23.—In the Morning at 8 went to Smith Field Market where we saw a surprising number of fat Cattle. From thence to Bartholomew Hospital. Dined at Home in the Evening. Went to Sadlers Wells & was Highley entertained with three Dancers And the Invashon of England by the Danes. King Alfred Exertions to drive them out of the Country was Astonishing Great, all the Kings & Queens from Alfred to his present Madgesty George the Third past in Succrssion across the Stage.

Tuesday, 24.—Being a wet Day was confined in the House till Evening. Calld a Coach & went to the royal Circus where we saw Estradnery performance by Horses and there Riders with a veriety of performance upon the Stage similar to a Play one part of it was calld Blue Bird with Harlquin & Columbine. The House was very full suposed maney Thousands of people was there & is a Butifull place

Wedsonday, 25.—Morning being wet pervented us going out till towards Evening. Drank Tea with Mrs Comes. Went to see the Vollanteers Exersise in the Duke of Bedford park. Returned to ur Lodgins & supped

Thursday, 26.—In the morning walked out to difrant Shops in Fleet Street & Holburn. Purchased sevral artickels of silver Plate. Afternoon being raney was confined to the House.

Friday, 27.—In the morning went into Cheapside to purchas some Cheaney & difrant articles. In the Evening walked in to Holborn & Linconsin Fields & calld upon Mrs Comes

Saturday, 28.—In the Morning went in to Cheapside aShoping. Bought some silver Buckels. From thence to Guild Hall. Saw Gog & Magog Earl of Chatham Monument and other Courisoteys there and from thence to see the Monument which was Built in Commemoration of the Great fire inding there at that Place. From thence to London Bridge where we saw the Water wheels at Work which suplied the greatest part of London with water. On our return went to the Bank & through the Royal Exchainge, then returned Home to Dine at three a Clock

Sunday, *July* 29.—In the morning went to Bermondsey Church. Herd a sermon by the Revd. Mr Cox Masons. Dined near the Oblilisk. Charged 1s. 3d for one rost Duck, one shilling for two slices of Beef, a shilling for a small Tart, bread & sheese six pence. Went from thence to Lambeth Church wich is joining the Bishop of Cantebery Pallace who it is said is oblidged to Entertain Travlers with rost Beef & Porter. Having but latley Dined deferd calling upon him. From thence went to the Magdalen at six a Clock where we had prayers & a sermon. Girls sang delightfuley. In the Evening returned to our Lodgins

Monday, *July* 30.—Walked out in the morning in to Cheapside. Had Companey in the Afternon to Tea. In the Evening went through the fleet Market up to Temple Bare. Then returned Home

Tuesday, *July* 31.—In the morning went to see the Bank Where there was a great resort a bout Reciving there Dividen. They was Shuvling up there Gould as usual. From there to the stock Exchange where theae was very thr'ong work. Went from thence to a Cheany Shop near the Monument. Returned by Corn Hill & saw Mr. Wilkinson print Shop. Saw the Carractar of Mr Pitt in a Duel with a Mr Ducrney. In the Evening walked four times round Smith Fiels being pleasant and Arey after a very hot Day.

August 1.—At aleaven a Clock went to the Leavey. Saw the King light from his Carrage. After wards we went up stays in the Pallice & saw the Nobility as They went to the Levy Room. Stayd too hours. Then went & dined in Pick a Dily. After returned Home in a Coach.

August 2.—In the Morning went to St James. Was shoud to an apartment up stays where we saw the Ladys & Gentlemen pop through to the Drowing Room which was over a bout four a Clock. We dined in Pic a Diley after went to the Haymarket Theatre where we was Hiley entertaind with the porformence. Took a Choach from there & got Home at twelve a Clock

August 3.—Dined at Home in the Evening. Calld upon Mr Fox in fleet Street, went with him from thence to the Founling where the Bloomsbery Vollanteers was Exersising Composed prinsable of Lawyers & Men of Fortune. There number consisted of upwards of eight Hundred. They Clothed & armed themselves with every other Requsit at there own Expence to defray which they subscribed eight Hundred Pound

August 4.—The Morning being a little raney was Confined in the House but in the Afternoon went to drink Tea with a Bachlor

Sunday 5.—Went in a Coach to Battersea which was five miles from Town. Stoped at the Church and went to here a sermon. Spent the Day very agreeable with Mr Horncastle. Was treated with grapes & difrant sorts of fruit. Walk from thince to see Chelsea Hospital. Took a Coach there to Buckingham Gate. Walked through St Jamese Park where there was a very great Conguest of People, According to Yorkshire phrase was as thick as midges; took a Coach at Spring Gardens and returned Home

Monday 6.—In the Morning went in to Holborn a Shoping from thence went to near the Moniment & purchesed a set of China. Returned home at three a Clock to Dinner. Purcased a Milon for one shilling & toopence which wied near three pound

Tuesday, 7.—In the Morning went over black fryers Bridge to St Ashton Liver Museum which abounded With surprising Coureoseys such as Birds of all sorts from foran Countreys, one of which was eight foot high, others of difrant sises & Butifull Coullars all kind of fishes & wild Beasts from foran Countreys, an Elephant, sords & all sorts of armer made by the Indin and was persented by them to Capton Cook on his voyges round the World, sevarel vestment & robes which was given to him by the Chiefs of difrant Ilands, also difrant sorts of fishing takle dextrous made of hard Wood & pointed with the tooth of an Annimal, not having eath Iron or Steel to make them of, of cose no edge tool to form them, but cut them with the edge of a shell or a pice of hard stone. Also it is Courous to see the largest & smallest birds in the World close by each other, the one a Ostrech ten foot high the other the Huming Bird a bout the sise of a Bumble bee. There Collection of Shels was surprising Brileant and difrant sorts of Metal

Wedsonday, 8.—In the morning went a Shoping bought a Tea Bord and water. Paid for things that was Bought & had them sent a Bord a ship in the After noon. Went into Newgate street. Bought some Musling Hankercheefs & a Shall. Bought a dowson oringes for sixpence

Thursday, 7.—At five a Clock set of for Liverpool. Stoped to sup & Chainged Horses. Supped at one a Clock. Breakfasted at the next Stage. Arived at Bringam at thre. Dined there on a Fowl & beef stackes. Walked out to see the Town which has very good Building & a pleasant place. A great Trade carred on there. Drank Tea & then set of half past eight. Traveld all the night and next Day arived at Liverpool at five in the Afternoon. Drunk Tea at the Inn & then went in a Coach to our Privite Lodgins. Mrs. Robinsons. The next Day Sunday being rany was Confined in the House. On Tuesday went on Bord of the John & Mary. Then walked to the Mount where there is very nice Serpantine walks. Returned to ur Lodgins & had Companey to Tea

Liverpoole, Wedsonday, 15.—Capton Franch, one of the Borders that was arived from the West Indies had a small ventur of his own which Consested of Brandey Wine Coffey Tamrans Castor Oil &c Valued at a Hundred pound, was seased by the Officers. The 23 at Seven in the Morning the John & Mary set Sail from Liverpool

Wedsonday, 30.—went to see the Baths which is Comfortable little roms for each Lady, with one Chair & a Glass. There is another barth which is very Compleat & room to walk in & drink the Water. Went to see the Frensh Prison which is a very large Bulding & too Thousand Prisners with soldgers To guard them. There is difrant artickels of wood made by them which is cut out with a nife such as shoase & Boxes &c

Thursday.—In the morning walked out to the Mount where there is a very nice Garden with Sirpentine Walks which is surported by the Corperation & free for aney strangers to walk in. Met some Forreners with there Black servant Mades to attend the Childer

September 3.—in the morning went to the Funral of an officer who was found Dead in his Bed with Excess of Licker. All the Lodgers attended & a very great Concourse People, though to be Sis or seven Thousand

Wedsonday.—Went to a play

Thursday.—Went to see the Pottery which we saw in all its difrant states, first the working of the Clay, the making up of the pott, the backing of them, scalloping of the edges, the Glasing & then pensiling of them after dried in oven

Friday.—in the morning went to take a Walk as fare as the Baths & the prison & bought a Glass which was made by the Prisonr

September 8, *Saturday Morning.*—Set of from Liverpool in a Shase which went a Stage of twenty miles & then dined at the Inn & went the same distance down the Carnell & arived at Manchester at seven in the Evening. Stayd there all night. Set of in the morning at sis a Clock in there Chase for which we was charged fiften pence pr mile. Breakfasted at nine a Clock at Rochdale. Riding a few miles got to the remarkable Emenance called Blackston edge from which one had a most extenceve & Butifull prospect over Rochdale towards Mancester. From the top of this high Hill we disend in to the vale of Ripenden which is a most butifull place, the rising ground on each side being butifuley ornimented with Plantations, At the Bortam of which is a Riverlet which runs a many miles & on which a maney manifacturs are Built & turned by the stream, Gentlemen Houses on the sides of the Hills which has a most pleasing & Extencive prospect. Stoped at Halifax & Cainged Horses. Saw the Cloth Hall where the Clothers Exibits there wares, & is the onley place in the Nighbourhood where it is sold by Wholesale. There seems some Hundreds of apartments & is said to cover five Ackers of Ground. The Countrey There is very prittey & Romantack, Woods Hills & vales at the Bottam of which purling Riverlets. The next place was Bradford where we Dined & Chainged Horses there, which took us to Tadcaster. The night was stormey & dark but pereseverd and arived at York at nine a Clock. Nex Morning went to Mrs Ogles where we stayd till Friday & then set of for Branpton where we arived the fourteent. Stayd there a Mounth and came to Falsgrove The ninth of October on Tusday morning to Dine where an Eligent Dinner which was propore upon the accation.

❧

The farmer is said to have grumbled that his potatoes were so good this year that there were no little ones for the pigs.

One of his parishioners said tolerantly, 'Well *he* antics a bit, and *us* antics a bit, but, there, we don't mind; we likes him.'

When the kitchen parrot was brought upstairs to be shown to a visitor, and the bell rang, the bird startled the hostess by crying, 'Let them ring!'

Heard in a Somerset ironmonger's shop: Woman customer. 'What are those dear little guns?' Assistant. 'Those are air-guns, madam. You shoot slugs with them.' Woman Customer. 'Well! Fancy special guns for that. Gardeners are always getting something new, aren't they?'

The Rural District Councillor
by his Daughter

A GREAT man, the District Councillor, my father, was for planting. 'Any fool can saw a tree down,' he would say,' but it takes a wise man to plant one!' And sometimes in my stiff-necked thirtyness I wouldn't say it. The day we got in that apple-tree was one of the times we got fractious with each other. It was one busy Saturday morning and he said to me, 'Just come and get that Blenheim Orange in—you aren't going out?' (This last menacingly. I was.) 'Well —' I said, 'Oh, all right, then—when do you want me?' 'Ha, dear', says he, with a sigh. Of all his five what had he done to be left with Jane who had thwarted and defied him ever since she was christened? The others had got married, of course; no wonder this one hadn't. 'No, no wonder this one hadn't', thought she, as she followed him down to the stables, and lifted out the spade and fork. 'Now then, fetch some more out of that side and see she stands upright. Be careful now. You've got your foot just—humph—give me the fork— Now *that*'s the way. There now, I'm glad that's done, though *I* shan't ever live to see the fruit. It's all for you.' 'It's all for me.' 'Humph—what a habit you've got into of repeating every word I say. It isn't very kind. Will now you hear how it sounds to me.'

And then I was glad to run back up the path in answer to a ferocious knocking on the door of the house. A bicycle and a panting man. 'Is yer father in, miss, and will he sign me this paper?' ('Good heavens!' thought I, 'and he like he is.') 'Well, he's rather busy in his garden at the moment. Could you call back?' Man (angrily), 'No, I can't, and the blinking paper has to be posted to-day and I've slipped in while the boss went to bank, and the missus, she's bad.' 'All right then, I'll see,' I said, but it was in fright that I approached that vigorous old figure. 'Can you come and sign a—' 'No, I can't.' 'But he's cycled over from Bowfield and the paper must be in to-day.' 'Tell him, No.' 'But his missus she,'s bad.' 'Yes, you

---

This sketch was written by one of the best village schoolmistresses I have known, the late Miss J. K. Jones of Idbury.

would take the man's part. All right then.' And up the garden path he stumped, shoes full of mould, right through the house and on to the freshly swept carpet, me after him with the brush and dustpan, saying to mother, who had died a year ago, 'Oh, my love, come to me.' And mother said, 'All right, my dear,' and came instantly in an exquisite chuckle, for behind the sitting-room door we heard, 'Do you consider vaccination prejudical to the health of this child?' Shuffles, mumbles signifying that he DO. And mother made life heaven in the next room by showing through the door crack an old white head and a young tousled head, with its very white forehead and sunburned face, doing their utmost in the midst of the day's toil to save a little baby and its weary mother from what they believed would do it harm.

And I waylaid the man at the door, with a smile and a pot of black-currant jam, for that was all I could lay hands on in the urgency of the moment. 'I'm glad you thought of that jam,' said father, happy at once. 'Those trees will come on well next year.' He spoke of six new black currants, And mother's own peace came back with us into the garden. . . .

The Schoolmistress's Day

Once I had to cane eight young hopefuls. Next day they turned up with gifts: (1) Glass jar with small quantity of treacle (for some small experiment hinted at in the previous day's lesson). (2) A bow and arrow, the bow wound with red flannel 'for where you puts your hand'. (3) Arrow of Neolithic pattern, 'like you said'. (4) Daffodil. (5) Hyacinth. (6) Moss with snail shells adhering. (7) A new indiarubber. (8) A page of voluntary homework—two sums right, one wrong. Absolutely no malice in a single heart. Time was somehow found to make them a gaudy target, and they are now busy killing one another in trying to hit the bull's eye. *Later*—I've just wrenched Goulding and Attridge apart. Clasped in deadly combat because Goulding had 100 up when it was Attridge's turn to shoot. Replay, with referee, gave 10 versus 10.

The Day of a Gentleman Farmer

HALF woke as usual about 5. Heard the cows mooing and the rattle of pails in the dairy, and, as usual, proceeded to doze again.

6.15, thick mist, tree tops all wet.

6.45, tea, letters and a message—says 'Ted says Polly has a calf, Sir; it's a bull.' I'd rather have had a heifer. Ted is great with the two servants. The chat and repartee that go on between kitchen window and dairy door used to scandalize my aunt when she stayed here but I look upon it as a useful by-product of the farm; it makes for smooth running of the domestic machine.

7.30, I get up and, from the bathroom window, which opens on the farmyard, call to Brown my 'working bailiff' who does everything from driving the tractor to keeping the house supplied with wood. To 'Good morning, how is everything?' he replies 'Can't hoe roots this morning, Sir, rained heavy last night.' I reply, 'Well, let the carter clean out Strawberry's box. (One of my maternity wards, which is only mucked out when opportunity offers, fresh straw being thrown on top of the dirty between times.) Put the dung on the heap in the Pheasant field. Tell him to pile it high; it's getting spread all over the place. What are you going to do?' 'Well, Sir, it's time those potatoes was hoed up; the wet won't matter for them' ('those potatoes' being about a rood I grow for the house, the only ones I have, except a few 'new potatoes' in the garden). 'All right; tell Ted to go with you when he has washed up. Remember to kill the cockerels.' I dress, enter up my diary for yesterday, write a letter and fill in the time till breakfast. After breakfast the papers.

9.30, I go out, have a chat with Ted the cowman, have a look at the new calf and a general look round. Then off to town with seven cockerels. Every year I sell a few dozen, from 3 to 4 lbs., being those superfluous to house needs. I usually get 1s. 4d. per lb. This year I am getting 1s. 6d., and the poulterer is buying American frozen Spring chickens at 1s. 4d., which shows something wrong somewhere. 1s. 4d. is a

The scene is Hampshire.

294

jolly good price, especially now with cheap corn, and it is rather ridiculous that we should let the Americans in on those terms. Of course it is not business for me to run the car ten miles each way to sell seven cockerels for 35s., but I do some shopping for my wife including the buying of some fresh salmon which comes out of the river on which the town is situated. Most people buying a 2 or 3 lb. piece of salmon go for the middle cut, which is a great mistake, as in boiling the two open sides let out all the flavour. A tail piece presents only one open side. I enjoy my run in the car. The roads are charming in the early sunshine now the mist has cleared away. My shopping amuses me too. I look over the poultry in the shop where I sell mine, gently depreciating the boiling fowls. 'Yes,' says the shopkeeper, 'they are not so good as usual, but I got them cheap'. I talk about some I want to sell, 'about 7 to 8 lbs.' 'A bit big for my trade', he says but "So-and-so", (mentioning a man about ten miles the other way from me) will probably take them.' At another shop I buy some good English cheese, 'a new lot from Mr. Dash'.

Home about 11, and take a walk round the farm. All satisfactory considering the pouring wet weather we're having. There is a tremendous lot of grass in the hay fields but all beaten down with the rain. It will probably lift up again if we get some dry weather. If? I don't worry very much; I have been at this sort of thing all my life, and, after all, things somehow come right in the end. Anyhow I have enough hay left over from last year to see me through the winter even if I can make no hay at all. Having no hay this year would leave me no emergency ration to sell if I wanted a bit of extra cash, and no safeguard against a bad season next year; but if one were of the temperament to worry about next year's possible troubles one would probably never have become a farmer. I pass on and find the oats slow; the cold wet season I suppose. The grass ley I have sown with them is coming along fine. The rain is doing that good anyway. I get into the field where the cows are; lashings of grass, and the cows certainly do look well. I sit a few minutes on my shooting stick looking them over, move about among them, sitting on the stick between times. I notice Dewdrop wants her horn cutting or it will grow into her head. The more I look at the cows the more I feel pleased with them. Rain or no rain the lot of them are growing into money. It is a better herd than it was last year or ever has been. I continue my round through the mangels. I did manage to run the horse hoe through them on a dryish day. A few have been cut out but now the ground is too wet to do anything to them. The weeds are growing badly and I see no prospect of better weather. I go on again, not unduly worrying. I come to a field where my young stock are. Again lots of grass and the stock looking as well as they could look. On again passing 12 acres of wheat, I see it looks splendid. It is in a naturally drained field which stands up to wet weather. If the harvest weather is right the wheat ought to thresh out well. Another 'If'. 'Farmers live on hope and die of despair.' I always feel that farmers are really optimists: you should know that farmers' pessimism is a sort of propitiatory offering to Nemesis. I go on home past some other fields of which I do not take much notice to-day. I have mouched about and it is nearly 1 p.m. I wash and tidy up and sit down with a paper waiting dinner. The bell goes at 1.20. I always tell my wife to impress on the cook that at dinner time I set more store by having everything cooked right than by punctuality. The salmon I brought back is excellent. A farm chicken follows with a salad crisp from the garden. The King could not eat better. After stewed gooseberries and cheese we go in to the sitting-room and talk over a cup of coffee in front of a window looking over the garden, which now has a fair show of flowers backed by a typically English field surrounded by large hedgerow trees. I feel that life cannot offer much better than a farmer's life, bad times and bad seasons all thrown in. It comes to my mind that I ought not to forget my 'other sources of income' which shelter me from the storm which is distressing and destroying many others.

To sit in an easy chair till 3 p.m. strikes on the hall clock is my usual practice. I read through the daily and weekly papers and any pamphlets, etc., that come along. I rarely read a book at this hour of the day. To-day I have to attend a local show committee at 2.30 so I go off. If milk prices are bad next Michaelmas I fear one man on the committee will be done for, but as his father-in-law is a fairly prosperous shopkeeper I suppose he will be kept afloat somehow. He won't starve anyhow. Most of the others have had a good War and are not uneasy about living on capital for a few years. Others are men doing a retail trade direct from their farms, and, if not doing well, are holding their own. The chairman is a substantial landowner farming his home farm. As I watch the men present I feel that as a sample of the countryside they are a creditable lot.

I get home just before 5. My wife is out so I have tea alone and read 'Waverley'. Though I am not a Scotsman I know all Scott by heart nearly. After tea I stroll round the farmyard, kitchen garden, etc., see all is well, muse over various things to do, come in and 'just sit' till

6.15 when I listen to the Wireless. More rain, I change out of breeches and tweed and continue 'Waverley', as I am in that mood, till supper at

7. This is a light meal. Afterwards we sit in front of a small fire of our own wood. Although it is summer a fire is welcome. My wife has some needlework to do to-night so we talk. She has been busy all day, so there is plenty to talk about till

9.30. And so to bed. But first I cross the yard and look in the dairy to see all is well or perhaps look out of the windows as I shut them. The drowsy charm of the farm at night always fascinates me. As I tear myself away from the last window I feel that my lines have indeed been cast in pleasant places, and envy nobody in the world. But I must go to bed. I have the Bench in the morning and after that a Committee—or is it two?

*

'Oh, look at the horses in the field,' cried a town four-year old, catching sight of ploughing for the first time, 'A man's pushing them.'

Little girl: 'I think when I go to Heaven I'd like to take a cow.' Mother: 'But cows are not allowed in Heaven.' Little girl: 'Who has to go down to Hell for the milk?'

Aged villager indignantly to doctor, who has told him the pains he complains of in one of his legs may be due to old age: 'Old age be danged! T'other leg, he's the same age and he's all right!'

'Them must a' been very high up learned folks, weren't they?' asked the labourer when the distinguished visitors had gone. 'Yes, a thought so; they didn't seem to know nowt.'

Rural Recipes, *by an Innkeeper's Daughter*

IN the spring the countrywoman can put her hand on an abundance of wild plants with which she can vary her cooking. In the first place the shoots of hops, or hop-tops as they are called, are in perfection. Wild ones are found in some districts in hedges and woods. The shoots of cultivated hops can be had for the asking in May and June when the hops are trimmed. They should be placed in cold water for about an hour, well washed, tied in small bunches, thrown into boiling, slightly salted water and cooked like asparagus. When hot they can be served with hot butter and a dash of lemon juice, or with a cream sauce, and should be accompanied by poached eggs. The flowering stems of turnips and the tender shoots of elders may be cooked and served in the same manner. And, when cold, any of these cooked shoots make delicious salads with a dressing of oil, vinegar, or lemon, pepper and salt. Hop-tops also make a good spring soup. Prepare the hops as above by laying in water for an hour. Then cut into inch lengths. Have ready three quarts of boiling hot thin pea soup, made of water in which bacon or ham has been boiled, with the fat removed. Throw in the hop-tops, and four kitchen spoonfuls of onion juice, pepper and salt. Boil up again, and when the hop-tops are cooked, soak some crusts of bread in the broth and serve. As the hops have tonic properties, this soup is an excellent appetizer. But as with all these good things, it must be prepared with intelligence. It may be good to make this soup creamy by adding yolks of egg, or by adding butter and flour cooked together in a separate saucepan and diluted with some of the broth.

The young tops of the true stinging nettle—it has a round hairy stalk—are more delicious than spinach if cooked in the same way; they also make excellent soup, and an excellent nettle haggis, as it is called in Westmorland. Pepys calls it nettle porridge, and pronounces it 'very good'.

Oatmeal is a fine thickener for all soups made with herbs,

The writer was Florence White, a remarkable woman, who really cared about good cookery and was the author of *Good Things in England*, and the founder of the National Folk Cookery Association—of which she persuaded me to be president.

it goes well with them, suits their character.

In the way of salads we have young dandelion leaves, the leaves of cowslips, and the flowers of both cowslips and primroses, as well as violets.

This month also sees the advent of morels and of the St. George's mushroom, the earliest of the year. We should have mushrooms of one sort or another from now on to December, but must be careful which we eat. Many are poisonous, but not perhaps so many as we imagine.

TO MAKE A COWSLIP PUDDING PIE. Nip the white base off a quantity of cowslip pips and cook them till tender in a little cream; cool this; beat up some dry curd (of cheese) with a little butter and sugar; add the cowslip cream; beat all well together with a little ground mace. Whisk the white of egg stiffly and fold that in. Line some deep tins with puff pastry and fill with the mixture. Scatter a few currants on top and bake in a good oven.

PRIMROSE, GOOSEBERRY AND RHUBARB VINEGARS: Many of us grumble because the vinegar we buy to-day is frequently not good. Why don't we make our own? A friend writes that when she was a girl in Worcestershire, forty-five to fifty years ago, they always made their own vinegar from primroses and gooseberries, and on looking up the manuscript recipes I have inherited I find recipes for these and one also for rhubarb vinegar. My friend adds, 'We considered primrose vinegar the most delicate but gooseberry was very good.' And, now I come to think of it, the housewives of Wakefield formerly prided themselves on this particular kind, but I never made it although I have made many different flavoured vinegars with the bought stuff by simply steeping various leaves in it. It is too late in the year to give directions for making vinegar from primroses, but here are two well-tested ones for making it from gooseberries and rhubarb. They are inexpensive.

GOOSEBERRY VINEGAR—Take gooseberries when fully ripe. Crush them well, then measure them. To every quart of pulp put three of water, boiled and quite cold before the pulp is put in. Let it stand twenty-seven hours, then strain through a sieve. To every gallon of liquor put one and a half-pounds of brown sugar, stirring it well before it is put in the barrel. *Not* to be worked with barm.

RHUBARB VINEGAR—To one gallon of cold water put 1 lb. sugar and 2 lb. rhubarb cut in pieces, put them all in a tub together, and let them remain covered up for fourteen days, then boil them and strain the liquid through a sieve. Put the liquor in a barrel with some yeast and let it work well. It must be made quite air-tight and kept near the fire for twelve months, then bottled, and in twelve months more it will be ready for use.

CONSERVES is an old English term derived from the French *conserver* to preserve, which has been and is variously used for fruit, etc., preserved with sugar. The name is frequently used to-day in America to indicate a stiff jam-jelly (a mixture of fruit cooked and put through a sieve and then boiled up with sugar) resembling the damson cheese of our great-great-grandmothers. On the other hand the name is given to fresh flowers, fruits, and roots preserved by beating with powdered sugar to the consistency of stiff paste, the object being to retain as much as possible of the natural properties of the raw fruit.

*

Discussing dog intelligence: 'I say to my dog, "Will you come to me or not?" and he comes—or not!'

'Warn't 'arf a lot!' said the cowman describing the meet; 'we'll never had a crowd here again like this afore.'

Small boy to mother on being told that they are going to visit her birthplace, 'Shall we see your manger, mother?'

'Well, if he do ride that there bike agin,' said the farm-worker, 'it can't be the same un, cos it's three parts new.'

To a missioner who had expressed concern at an old woman's sad-looking face, 'Oh, sir, it's just a year sin' our old billy goat died, and wen you was in the pulpit you looked so like him I could ha' thought you was our old billy on end, a-talkin' to us.'

'Not a very nice day for Spanish Waters,' said the cottager's wife on Palm Sunday as the east wind howled round the house. 'For what?' 'Liquorice Sunday—every year they all go into the forest with bottles of liquorice water to drink.' 'Why do they—is it good for you?' 'They don't seem to know, but it's the custom—ever so many goes.'

Sam, by J. C. Moore

SAM is a thief, a liar and a poacher. He has been in gaol not once, but many times. Nevertheless I like Sam. I made his acquaintance one Sunday. I had taken a stroll round the outskirts of my farm and was returning through a small covert when I came face-to-face with a shabby person carrying a gun.

'What are you doing here?' I asked.

'Walkin', sir', was the undoubtedly accurate answer.

'Who are you that you should come walking through my woods?' I said.

'Sam 'Odges.'

'Indeed', I asked, becoming nettled, 'and does Mr. Sam Hodges think he owns the Long Covert?'

'Don't do no 'arm by walkin',' he answered sullenly.

'And the gun? Is that a substitute for a walking stick?'

'Allus carries a gun, wherever I goes,' said Sam with conviction. Now the clear evidence of his guilt in the shape of the tail-feathers of two pheasants that had overflowed his coat-pockets had been before my eyes for the last five minutes; yet he had shown no sign of confusion, and began to wax eloquent on the question of the gun.

'This 'ere fowlin' piece is my Gawd,' he announced. 'Almos' as my Gawd, I should say. Where I goes I takes it with me. Should no more leave it be'ind than I should leave my trousies at 'ome'.

I tackled Mr. Hodges about the tail-feathers. He was not in the least nonplussed. He 'put it to me'.

'If you was a-walkin' through the woods (the woods not belongin' to you), an' you was carryin' a gun quite by accident, an' not with intent to shoot, an' sudden-like, up gets two birds rocketin' over your head, wouldn't you put up your gun an' let fly at them? Corse you would. It comes nat'ral. It's instick, that's wot it is. You'd put up your gun to your shoulder and pull the triggers quite without thinkin', that's wot you'd do. And', he added roguishly, 'if you *wus* a good shot you'd 'ave one bird with one barrel and one with the t'other.'

301

It was late July and I had a strong suspicion that, far from rocketing up in the air, the two young cocks had been strutting on terra firma.

'Corse', continued Sam, 'when I *'ad* shot 'em, I was overcome with remorse like, pertickly when I realised that they belonged to such a nice gentleman as yourself, beggin' your pardin', sir'.

So Sam won. It was the triumph of oratory over justice. I said good-bye to Sam and he went off with my birds. As I opened the drive-gate at my farm I thought I heard the sound of a shot from the direction of the Long Covert, but I may have been mistaken.

After that day I met Sam frequently in the village. He would touch his cap obsequiously and pass a pleasantry on the subject of the weather. Once I stopped to ask him if he had enjoyed the pheasants.

'Me an' my old 'oman,' he said, 'we 'ad a reg'lar beanfeast, we did. My old 'oman, in fack, was so genuine grateful that she took the liberty of mentionin' you in 'er prayers.'

That same afternoon I noticed Sam in the poulterer's. He did not see me and seemed engrossed in a business conversation of importance. The suspicion that then formed in my mind grew to a certainty in later years. I could never rid myself of a sense of injustice when I passed that poulterer's shop. Pheasants were much alike, of course, but there was something in the expression of the birds that hung there that seemed to suggest kinship with my own.

❧

In the baptismal record of Speen parish church, Berks, there is the name of a boy baptized 'Plain Bill.'

'He's all right,' said the villager, 'but he doesn't do nawthin' for the place: sort o' rich man without any money.'

Small girl, 'Mummy, could I eat grass?' Mother, 'Yes, dear; I don't think it would hurt you.' Small girl, 'If I did, would my body be filled with milk?'

The newly-married labourer went to a great deal of trouble over the whitewashing of his cottage. Chaffed about his thoroughness, he replied, 'Well, the last two families that lived here had twins, and I'm making sure there's no infection!'

The Passing of the Years

1815. 'They tell me, miller, you're going to have one of those newfangled windmills'. 'Aye, parson', said Sam Eldridge; 'it's no good going on wi' me old contraption. I can't manage all the grist they brings me. A windmill it's got to be, and there bain't no place to put 'im except up on the Down where there's some wind. I'm sorry, sir, if it's going to jigger up your view of the Downs, but—'

1932. 'Yes', said Charlie Eldridge, the miller, Sam's grandson, 'I were for scrapping the old mill, it's no use to me; but here's this Society come along, and they say 'twould be a sin to do away with a fine old landmark. It don't seem like sense, but they're going to put 'im in order, and they're going to pay me—well, they're doin' the thing 'andsome'. 'What's all this about these 'ere pylons, Bill?' asked the blacksmith. 'Why, Tom, they wants to give us 'lectric light, and it means they've got to put up big tower things to carry the wires, and some of these London folks say it's goin' to spoil the Downs'. At that moment there came along a little man in knickerbockers, with a rucksack, a straggling beard and glasses. 'I have been looking at your lovely Downs for my Society,' he began; 'we are putting up a very strong protest about carrying a line of pylons right across, and I hope—'

2034. In the inn the television set was presenting an impassioned appeal by the President of the Society for the Protection of the Countryside. 'And now I come to the latest proposal made in the name of progress by our modern vandals, who wish to take down the line of graceful early twentieth-century pylons on the Downs. My Society is going to fight this sacrilege with all its power. Although the structures do not serve any practical purpose in these days of radio distribution of power, these fine old creeper-grown monuments of the past stand against the sky as one of a fast diminishing number of relics of an England that is gone. Let us buy the ground each pylon stands upon.'—*A.L.J.H.*

✍

A Devon crescendo: 'Aw, my dear sawl! Aw, my dear life!! Aw, my dear days!!!'

My Carrion Crow

by Hamish Nicol, F.R.C.S., F.Z.S.

I GOT her before she could walk. I found her easy to feed with raw meat, bread and occasionally a spot or two of cod-liver oil. I gave her water from a piece of wet cotton wool. She appeared happy and contented, grew rapidly, and in a few days could walk well and strongly.

Having known no other parent but me she has no fear of me or my family though she is shy with strangers. She is very clean and loves to take a bath, which she often has with me. Every morning she is brought up to the bath-room, where she plays with sundry toys and sits on the side of the bath. She will often jump down on top of me and, after having a good drink of the water, will have a bath. I splash the water over her which she much enjoys.

The instinct of self-preservation was there from the first. She has always been ready to defend herself with her formidable beak and she can now use it very cleverly. It is quite impossible to touch her against her will. Her beak is everywhere and she can peck very hard!

She will notice at once anything she has not seen before. Though always ready for instant flight or defence, her curiosity will induce her to hold her ground at a distance. She will walk round and examine the object from every point of view, gradually getting closer until she is near enough to peck it. This she will do and jump back. She will do this several times till she has made up her mind that it is safe. Then she will examine the object closely and try to pull it to pieces. Once she has examined a thing she will remember it on other occasions and is never afraid again.

It was amusing to see her trying to hide her food at first. She would place a small leaf or stone on the top of quite a large piece of meat and walk away, apparently quite satisfied that it was hidden. On coming back she would see the meat and take it up again and hide it in a fresh place with no better success. Very soon, however, she got more clever, and now she will hide a thing so quickly and cleverly that, if one is not watching closely, it is very difficult to find. This hiding habit was a little trying sometimes since she selected clothes as good hiding-places. My wife and daughters were not pleased to find pieces of meat carefully tucked away in their slippers and stockings. On one occasion she selected my wife's bath sponge and studded it with pieces of not very fresh meat, like currants in a bun!

For toys, anything bright will do or better still something she can pull to pieces. Seedsmen's catalogues are popular, especially if they have plenty of bright pictures. In the garden she will pick off all the bright flowers.

She is fond of a game she invented herself. It is quite simple. She has to peck my foot and I have to dodge; she is quicker than I am and my feet and socks suffer, so I have had to discourage this game. It is very tiring, too, because she never seems to get tired. That there is no malice in it is shown by the fact that when we are resting she will come up to be caressed.

She is wonderful at catching things. She is as clever as a sea lion. She will catch a small ball of paper time after time when thrown to her and from a long distance. She will even catch a match.

She shows distinct signs of affection. When I am in the garden she will come and sit on my knee or the back of the chair and if I go away will cry out till I come back. She loves being fondled by me and will run to me for protection when frightened. She will walk round the garden with me just like a dog.

I often try to estimate her thinking powers. One method has been to place some bright object in a little tin box, allowing her to see me putting it in and then place the top on. She will stand over me while I am doing it and try to stop me. When given the box she will try to open it. After a very short time she learnt the way to do it. She would hold the box steady with one foot and hammer away with her beak at the junction of the lid with the box. After two or three hard pecks delivered with considerable force and wonderful precision the lid would come away and she would take out the hidden object. Now when given the box she will have the lid off in less than a minute.

Her main article of diet is meat which is given to her in one large piece. She stands on it and pulls off pieces with her beak just like a hawk. The pieces she pulls off are very small but when she has reduced the bulk she will swallow the remainder, often a piece one would imagine impossible to swallow. She appears to be able to digest anything. One morning she ate a large piece of sheet indiarubber, quite a lot of paper, the best part of two matches and a lot of my sponge besides meat and bread. She did not seem any the worse. She had a good drink of hot soapy water to wash it all down.

She will often carry things about in her beak, like a pelican, while she looks for a hiding place. If she cannot find a suitable place she will lay out her treasures in a row and swallow one after the other.

She likes bread soaked in water. I am trying to teach her to soak the bread for herself. I think she will soon learn. She will often sit on the side of the bath and drop things into the water. I am quite sure she does this so that I shall pick them out for her. She will wait for them to be handed back and sometimes she will do this over and over again.

I suppose that most people would laugh if told that a crow can sing. But the crow has a large vocabulary and quite a good song. The well known 'craw craw' of the crow, I take to be a call to its mate; there is another 'craw' much louder and with a distinct note of alarm in it. This is uttered as a warning, and my bird will utter this cry when she sees anything she is frightened of. She will cry out like this if she sees a cat in the garden or something strange in the house. There is no doubt as to the meaning of this cry. Then there is a soft crooning sound she will utter when she is being caressed. She will walk round and round in front of one, with beak to the ground, rather like a ruff, uttering this sound and continue to do it when on the hand being stroked. Then there is a chattering sound, a mixture of all sorts of cries which she will make when by herself playing in her run. It sounds like a conversation, which it probably is. There are other notes she utters which I have not yet been able to separate. Lastly her 'song'. This is quite distinctive. She will extend her neck, raise her head and her tail and utter a series of Ha! ha! ha's!

306

in quick succession, ending in a kind of quick caw caw caw. I have counted as many as twenty Ha's. Sometimes she will do this over and over again.

A Deed without a Name
by Eleanor Steuart

I HEARD such a barking of dogs, shouting men, and general commotion that I went to the door to see what was happening. My nearest neighbour, with a gun under his arm, was walking excitedly to and fro along the river side. He was urging the activities of three sheep dogs who were plunging into the water and out of it again in a rapid succession of rollicking leaps and bounds, accompanied by their own vocal efforts and his. On the opposite bank were several more of my neighbours and friends. They were heavily engaged in beating the water with big sticks. 'What is it?' I called, 'an otter?' 'A salmon, Miss, a real beauty. Ga away, Sweep, lig doon theer, Mop—he' Bright—he' Bright—he' Bright.' Never having seen a salmon pursued by dogs and a gun before, I moved nearer. The salmon itself I could not see; it was somewhere in the middle of the stream. The men's object appeared to be to induce the dogs to drive the salmon within range of the gun. The dogs' object was undoubtedly to enjoy themselves as much as possible. Suddenly the gun was fired. The next thing was an attempt on the part of the men to make the dogs retrieve the salmon. This was an out-and-out-failure. The dogs were ready enough to plunge into the water over and over again, but not to fetch out the salmon. Their only experiences of water hitherto had been connected with sheep-washing, and they were entirely ignorant of the duties of a water spaniel. Finally one of the men waded in and fetched the salmon out. 'Twelve pund!' he called triumphantly. But at once there fell a silence. Two men had come into view on a distant bridge. Water watchers! They were looking for the salmon.

Had they come a little farther they would have *found* the salmon. But they didn't. They gave it up as lost and turned back. It was an *excellent* salmon.

307

Those Good Old Days
by W. J. Titcomb

WALKING one evening in 1880 in the village of Swafield, which adjoins North Walsham in Norfolk, my attention was attracted by a somewhat barrack-like three-storey building in the shape of a capital E, minus the middle. The building was divided into cottages, and I spoke with the occupant of one of them. In the early days, he said, the building had been a workhouse. To it resorted every autumn, at the close of the harvest, the labourers with their wives and families from miles around. His own father and mother were among the number, and every year he accompanied them. There would be there all the winter as many as 400 persons—men, women, and children. If accommodation allowed, there was a room for each family, but generally two or more families occupied each room for eating and sleeping, and every other domestic need. In fact, a great many had to sleep on the landings, staircases and passages.

The children did very well, as they could play about, but the grown-ups were bored to death. The women had very little to do in the way of washing, cooking or cleaning, and spent their time gossiping. The men were entirely without occupation. The garden was then a flagged yard, and the men in order to relieve the monotony of standing and sitting about, used to get up sham fights. Sometimes they would take up all the flags, and build them into walls and huts, or perhaps into a fortress, and have a mock siege. After a few days of playing in this way, the men would relay the flags as they found them. After a short interval, they would take them up again and repeat the process.

The women were always scandal-mongering. These things led to quarrels and fights. Very often these fights were not merely between two women, but between seven or eight.

When the farming season opened in Spring everybody went out of the house and by the end of March the place was empty and nearly a ruin. Everything burnable and removable had been cut up and burnt—doors, bannisters, stairs and so on.

308